Bog
Standard

Bog Standard

Daniel Ken

PORTICO

First published in the United Kingdom in 2008 by
Portico Books
10 Southcombe Street
London
W14 0RA

An imprint of Anova Books Company Ltd

ISBN 9781906032180

A CIP catalogue record for this book is available from the British Library.

10 9 8 7 6 5 4 3 2 1

Typeset by SX Composing DTP, Rayleigh, Essex
Printed and bound by CPI Mackays, Chatham, ME5 8TD

This book can be ordered direct from the publisher.
Contact the marketing department, but try your bookshop first.

www.anovabooks.com

For J

I have never let my schooling interfere with my education.
– Mark Twain

Bog Standard is based on the blog *Blog Standard* that I have been writing, on and off, for a few years for the *Times Educational Supplement* website. I have written both under the pseudonym Daniel Ken – even though, as you'll see, my 'real' name in the book is Daniel Keane. As the pupils rechristened their teacher Daniel Ken, so have most people who have read the blog, and the name has stuck.

While the book is a factual representation of events, the names, dates and locations of all characters, and places, within the book have been changed. This is for two reasons: firstly, to protect the anonymity of both myself and everyone involved; and secondly, to emphasise the point that my story could have been told by any teacher in any school. West Bognor Technology College doesn't exist, and yet at the same time it does everywhere.

Prologue

I hated school and school hated me.

At the age of sixteen I walked out through the gates of my secondary school, holding in my hand a sheet that listed my dismal failure as an academic, vowing never to return. I'd learned only three things at school; how to fight, how to run away, and that I was never, ever going to set foot inside a secondary school again.

And it had started so well. I'd entered the Big School at eleven, a bookish, enthusiastic and happy little boy. I wanted to learn, to do well. I wanted to succeed. But after the first six months of boredom, while I waited for other students in my 'mixed ability' class to catch up to the point where the lesson would begin to engage me, I began to get fidgety. I wasn't naughty, but I was fast becoming disengaged.

Then one morning I got beaten up by a boy who was a couple of years older than me. It wasn't pleasant, but at least it got my attention. So I went home, did some reading and research on how to have a fight and, shortly after, I embarked on a career of passive resistance in class and active resistance outside of it; I'd submerged, become just another dissatisfied, under-achieving secondary student, obsessed with girls and cheap cider and having a laugh.

So what have my own unsuccessful schooldays got to do with a book about life as a schoolteacher?

I'm not sure, really. Perhaps I'll discover the answer as I write this book. All I know is that after leaving school I spent my days working in a succession of dead-end jobs and I spent my evenings and Saturday mornings in the library, reading all the stuff I should have read when I was at school.

Unguided, I read whatever took my fancy. Whatever looked or sounded interesting. Every novel was a gift, and every author hugely generous. Jane Austen, the Brontes, Oscar Wilde, Ernest Hemingway, Fitzgerald, Blake, Poe.

Here I was, an unqualified seventeen-year-old from a council estate, I should have been quaffing cheap cider, smoking spliffs and shoplifting, and instead I was devouring books down at my local library.

Like Thomas Hardy, I fell in love with Tess Durbeyfield, and like Vita, I recognised Woolf's novel *Orlando* for the extended love letter it was. And I understood why Mercutio had to die. Things fell into place. I read everything and anything I could lay hold of; novels, newspapers, comics. I did them all; I was a most promiscuous reader. And after a while a conviction grew, slowly at first, but inexorably – it would be a good thing to finish my education.

So one evening I went to a friend's house (her father was a lecturer), and I asked him how I went about studying literature. Kindly, and in retrospect generously, considering my track record, he explained the route I'd have to take. And I did. I did well. I was motivated. And eventually I had a degree in English.

But still, I never wanted to be a schoolteacher.

West Bognor Technology College

Motto: Try Your Best

1

Monday, 8.31am – West Bognor Technology College

'Daniel!'

Judy greeted me at the front office. She held out her hand and shook mine firmly: 'Good to see you again.'

I mustered my most winning smile and replied, 'You too.'

She turned to glare over her spectacles at a small child who had arrived at the school and had the audacity to make a noise in her presence. This child, obviously a new starter like me, no more than four foot tall, and wearing something that was at best only distantly related to the official school uniform, looked at me with some interest before scuttling off.

'Ankle biters,' Judy announced. 'Hate 'em.' Then she smiled sweetly at me, 'Don't you?'

I was about to fudge some sort of reply when she giggled and said, 'But of course, you have one. You're a *single* parent, I seem to recall.'

'Yes, Joe. He's...'

Glancing briskly at her watch, Judy interrupted me, 'I'll show to your room and you can get started. OK?'

'Uh, OK,' I said, following her along a corridor. Foolishly I'd expected some sort of induction programme; this looked like it was going to be the deep-end approach to workplace re-entry.

She walked quickly, with the posture of a ballet dancer, the authority of a Sergeant-Major and the dress code of Miss Jean Brodie. 'The school serves a community that is described in various official documents as disadvantaged,' she told me, 'though you could substitute the words deprived, disillusioned, disenfranchised or any other one of about thirty good solid descriptions that tell you the area is full of dole-wallahs, single mums and state-registered invalids. For many of these students, as you'll soon discover, learning is *not* their forte.'

As we passed the staffroom she paused to scan the notice board before coming back to our conversation, one-sided as it was; 'We have roughly seven hundred students,' she informed me as I followed her. 'And we have a regular turn-around with the local Youth Offending Team. Mostly broken ASBOs, drugs, the odd knife incident, you know the sort of thing.' I didn't, actually, but she carried on talking as we strode through the school, 'Plus the odd pregnancy. Though not as many,' she winked conspiratorially, 'as the local convent school.'

She smiled, 'But don't worry, the kids here are usually fine.'

'Good,' I said, or it might have been God! as I scurried along in her wake, desperately trying to memorise the layout of the maze of corridors.

'You'll be taking over from Simon,' she announced.

'Simon?'

'Yes. Wonderful chap. Kids loved him. Terrible teacher though. Had to leave of course, after the incident with the sewage.'

'Of course.'

'But no one blames him...'

'Of course not.'

We stopped. '...and this is your room, Daniel.'

With a flourish, Judy opened a battered door to a room that looked like it had last been decorated in the mid-70s.

By punk rockers.

Glue-sniffing punk rockers.

'Any questions?' she asked me.

I noticed the room number. 101. 'No,' I muttered, 'This looks fine.'

I lied.

Judy looked me up and down, 'They'll challenge you, to begin with, of course. And they're well practised at mayhem.

But be firm, don't smile too much, give clear instructions, never change your mind and, of course, if you threaten to do something, make sure you carry it out.'

It sounded like she was explaining to me the art of training of pit-bulls.

'Remember, *you* own this room. Not them.' Then she added, 'And if you can do a bit of teaching between now and October half term, I'd be very grateful.'

I wasn't sure if she was joking.

I hadn't taught a lesson yet and already, the seven weeks until October half term, the full extent of my contract, seemed impossibly distant, strewn as it was with knife-wielding ASBO kings and teenage girls pushing prams.

'Have you got my timetable?' I asked, hopefully.

'Of course not,' she smiled at me indulgently, 'we'll be lucky if those get issued this next fortnight.' Then she said, 'But the kids will know where to go. In the meantime, whatever classes you get, if you get stuck, have them read chapter two of those text books on the shelf, copy out the questions… then answer them, of course.'

Copy out Chapter Two.

Of course.

And then I was standing alone, in my punk-rock classroom, all violent colours and torn posters of death-metal bands and a pile of text books that pre-dated punk rock, progressive rock and, I suspected, all forms of 'rock' as far back as the Cambrian era.

I walked around the class, dropping books onto desks. Then I dug a whiteboard marker from my teacher's-standard-issue worn leather briefcase.

I wrote on the board:

    1 READ chapter two
    2 COPY out the questions
    3 ANSWER the questions.

This was 1950s teaching of the kind I'd only ever witnessed on Channel 4 reruns of *That'll Teach 'Em*.

Feeling a tad nervous, I went to turn on my radio, hoping to hear the voice of Jim Naughtie making some politician squirm in discomfort. *Schadenfreude* was the surest way to make me feel better. Then I realised that my green, windy-up, ecologically sound, zero-carbon-footprint Dyson radio wasn't in this room, or this school, or even this town.

I felt like I'd accidentally left my life at a bus station, or in a taxi, and I couldn't find it. Somehow, my life had taken a wrong turn. I'd been set up for the next Head of Department's job. I lived with my successful wife Jenny, a child psychologist, and our wonderful son Joe, in a Victorian townhouse that had polished wood floors and was decorated in earthy colours and neutral tones and even had the original sash windows, sanded down to bare wood and lovingly repaired and repainted by me.

We both drove BMWs. Black.

Except that this wasn't a dream.

I was here.

And my old life, our old life, the life of me, my wife Jenny and our son Joe, was over. In the past.

I need to be free, she had told me.

And I said I'd give her as much freedom as she wanted.

I need to discover the real *me.*

You *are* the real you, I told her.

And she looked at me sadly.

The real me, without *you*.

The clatter of the school bell stung me out of my maudlin moment and suddenly I was here in my room, 101, wide awake and feeling very pissed off. There was a minute's pause and then the bell rang again. A longer peal this time, signalling that lessons were about to begin.

A burly fifteen-year-old wearing an oddly shaved haircut peered around the corner of the door. 'Hey, we've got a new one!' he jeered to his friends.

It's on, I thought. It is *so* on.

Being a schoolteacher is an act. A performance. In front of a hostile audience.

And you get to do the same act five times a day, forty weeks a year, for your whole life. So you'd better develop a good act, a damn good act. You'd better be seamless. And with that thought, I walked to the door to greet my new audience. I stood at the door, unsmiling as per instructions, allowing them in, but only on my terms.

Be firm, I told myself.

'Fasten your tie. Tuck in your shirt,' I repeated, quietly but firmly as they walked past. Ignoring the barrage of questions I sat them where I wanted them to sit, despite their protestations because, what happens, when kids see a strange teacher, is that all the naughty kids immediately go and sit at the back; weirdly, the naughtier girls usually sit to the left, and the naughty boys to the right. So I know that whatever deal we make right now about the seating arrangements is going to have to be about what I want, which is based on learning, not what they want, which is based on anarchy.

'Aww, why?' one of them whinged when I pointed to a seat at the front. 'Why you picking on me?'

'I'm not picking on you,' I said, getting a good look at his hair, which was shaved to the scalp either side of a heavily gelled, cropped white mohican. 'I want you at the front 'cos I like the look of you.'

'Sir's gay!' a boy shouted.

'You should be so lucky,' I said, adding, 'And you can sit at the front too. But on the other side.'

Then I did the same with the girls. But I sat the naughty ones (read: the ones with the most make-up and jewellery and the loudest shrieking voices) one row back, so they weren't directly opposite the naughty boys.

Then I pulled a chair front centre and sat down to face them. After a minute or so they grew silent.

'Good morning,' I said, keeping my voice as calm and quiet as my raging adrenaline would allow. 'I'm Mr Keane.'

The class waited patiently. They often give you a couple of lessons grace while they suss you out.

They wait to see if you're a bastard or not.

I said, 'You can call me Sir, or Mr Keane. Whichever you like.'

A small boy asked, 'What's your first name, Mr Keane?'

'Mister,' I responded.

A blonde girl near the front spoke up, 'Sir!' and I paused to look at her. 'Are you dead *moody*, sir? You look a bit angry. Or are you nervous?'

'Do I look moody?' I couldn't help but smile. 'This is my first day in a new job. Maybe I am a bit moody. Or nervous.'

'Would you like a fruit pastille?' she asked me. 'To raise your blood sugar. If you stress, out you might go into hypo.'

Nothing wrong with your knowledge of human biology, I thought, telling her, 'No thank you.'

'We're 11F,' she told me. 'Eleven *Fick.*'

'Eleven *Failures,*' another voice murmured.

'Bottom set!' a voice shouted. And the noise suddenly erupted. It took me a couple of minutes to get them quiet.

Someone shouted out, 'Are you permanent, or just a supply teacher?'

My answer would inform their behaviour, I had no doubt of that. So I lied; 'Don't worry, I'll be with you all year. I'm here to get you through your exams.' But I wasn't sure if that was true, and I was pretty sure I didn't want it to be.

'Don't bother, we're all going to fail,' the blonde girl said.

I looked at her; sometimes they *know*; they know exactly why, so I asked her, 'Why do you think you'll fail?'

The class grew silent, listening, as she mentally composed her reply. 'Well,' she said, 'we've failed all through school. For eleven years. We've got ASBOs, half of us are on statements, or drugs. Or Ritalin.' I didn't mention the fact that Ritalin was itself a powerful stimulant, and she continued, 'The lads are

8

unable to control themselves,' she leaned forward at this point, whispering conspiratorially, 'short attention spans, due to too much time spent playing video games,' and then she opened a compact and looked at herself in the small mirror, forgetting our conversation for a moment. Then, like the most artful of courtesans, she looked up and having ensured she had my full attention... she paused. 'And let's be honest, sir. We girls aren't going to learn *anything* from you, are we? Really?'

I looked at her; fifteen going on fifty going on fifteen, her identity wedged somewhere between the peroxide and the gum she chewed so nonchalantly. In reply I stood up and walked to the bin, picked it up and walked over to her. I said, 'I don't chew in class. Because it's against the rules.'

She looked a little defiant, but I wasn't directly challenging her so she didn't need to respond in kind. Didn't need to fight with me at this point. I held out the bin and she leaned over and spit her gum into it. Then I went to the board and wrote the number 30 on it. Below that I wrote the number 3. Then I wrote the number 7.

'Right,' I said, ignoring what I'd written on the board, 'We need to work out how much coursework you have to complete by Easter,' and I began to talk through what essays they had or hadn't written, making notes about what they had done, what they'd sort of done and what they hadn't yet looked at.

Grumbling, they went about the business of education, opening their text book at chapter two with heavy hearts and heavier expressions.

'Why're we doing chapter two? Why not chapter one?' someone asked.

'I don't like chapter one,' I replied. 'Chapter one *annoys* me.' I didn't mention the numbers on the board.

They managed about seven minutes of sustained work before curiosity and boredom got the better of them. Someone shouted, 'What are the numbers on the board for, Mr Keane?'

I paused, and then I approached the board to explain, 'Thirty is the number of weeks you have left in school. Three is the amount of lessons we have together every week.' I looked at them, adding, 'and it's roughly the average amount of bottles of wine I drink every weekend.'

'So you're ninety bottles of wine away from us leaving school?' someone suggested.

'Yes.' I rose and, next to the 30 I wrote /90. This got a giggle.

'Hey, that means I'm about 180 hundred bottles of Lambrini away from the dole!' someone else shouted, getting catcalls from his friends.

'You're quick at mental maths,' I responded.

'I can get you good wine, Mr Ken,' the large boy who'd been first to the door told me. 'Cheap Polish wine. Very tasty!'

'I'll bear that in mind,' I told him, adding 'It's Mr *Keane*.'

'OK, Mr Ken,' he replied.

Sitting next to the blonde girl was a raven-haired beauty whose hair was tied back so tight that, combined with her plucked and drawn-back-in eyebrows, it gave her an expression of permanent fury. Beautiful fury-eyebrows drawled, 'Mr Ken, what's the seven stand for? Your shoe size?' A fat boy at the back of the room said, 'It's not his *shoe* size, divvy!' and I could see with awful certainty exactly where this conversation was going so I took out my wallet, opened it and showed her a picture of Joe. She took my wallet, looked at the picture for a few seconds, passed it on.

My wallet got passed around the room before being handed back.

'That's Joe,' I told her, 'He's seven years old. He's why I come to work.'

She managed to raise an eyebrow an eighth of an inch higher, took out her mobile phone, switched it on, and showed me the picture on the screen; 'That's Micky. He's twenty-one. He's why I won't be in class tomorrow.'

The class erupted with laughter. Fair enough, I laughed too.

'But you're here now,' I said. 'That has to tell me something.'

'It tells you he's on night shift,' she replied, popping a wad of chewing gum into her mouth.

2

Wednesday, Lesson 4 – Room 101

'Hayley, put that *away* please.'

'I can't sir, it's my mum.' Again.

Hayley has torn her trousers, and I don't even *want* to know how; and her mum is texting her, telling her that she'll drop off a spare pair at reception. This is the fourth text Mum has sent in about nine minutes. To be honest, I think she just likes sending her daughter messages. Which is nice.

After only three days at this school, and despite its low-ability intake and reputation for chaos, it's taught me a real lesson; I've come to realise that the most revolutionary educational tool currently available is not the internet, nor is it Ofsted, BBC Bitesize, live-streaming *Big Brother*, or the interactive whiteboard. It's the mobile phone.

Schools have always been exclusive; self-contained; a world apart. There's a mystique about education – teachers have always had a power to *daunt* their students for decades after they leave school. And everything that went on in a school, or most of it anyway, stayed in school. It's part of a monastical tradition that goes back centuries.

But now, kids phone home. They phone each other. And they text constantly, to the exclusion of all else, especially learning. The tentacles of telephonic, satellite-boosted communication reach far beyond the school gates; they're global. And very personal. And, using their mobile phones, they film *everything*; they film fights and bullying; they film each other doing crazy stunts. They film each other having sex.

They film teachers, teaching, they film teachers not teaching and, apparently, they film teachers' breasts, when they're wearing low-cut tops.

With the advent of mobile phones, the lights have come up in the auditorium.

The magic is gone. School is just another place where young people hang out, and teachers are just people, telling other people about stuff. Stuff they don't appear very interested in.

West Bognor Technical College, it seems, has got a new student; me.

The next few days passed fairly quickly and I learned about the rest of the department, such as it was, from Judy. 'This isn't a large school,' she told me, 'and the full departmental complement is only five English teachers. We have three. Minus Carole, who is on maternity leave. Plus you. Plus whoever else we can drag in off the street.'

I wasn't sure if she included me in the 'dragged off the street' bracket. The departmental three were Judy herself, James Turner and Carole, on leave and expecting her third child at any time. I hadn't met James but, as a new member of staff, I didn't recognise anyone anyway.

Not staff, not students.

Despite its reputation, West Bognor didn't appear quite as awful as I'd imagined. The acting Head, Mr Sweet, did a couple of things right.

Firstly, he made sure that the staffroom was a haven of tranquillity, comfy seats and milky coffee, doled out for 10p a cup by Doreen, who also did a good line in chocolate biscuits.

Secondly, he was relatively successful in dealing with misbehaviour: if a student seriously misbehaved, he had them thrown out. Mr Sweet, a history teacher by trade, talked about the professional 'shield wall' we must throw up, in order to maintain control of our school. This shield wall pissed off a lot of parents; try to imagine being stuck at home with Wayne, six foot and fourteen stone of hormonal, bored teenager; his presence severely hindering your enjoyment of *Trisha* and *Cash in the Attic*.

And those year eleven's who consistently misbehaved were given a form to take home to their parent/carer/*whatever* that informed them that Bradley or Chantelle or Cherie (girls names at Bognor often began with a soft Ch, I discovered) or whoever was, from this moment onwards, to be *educated off-site*.

This meant that, when the paperwork eventually arrived some weeks or even months later, they were supposed to attend one of the work-related learning programmes (WRL – the whirls, as they were known) at a nearby college.

Of course, most wouldn't attend. They'd doss about at home, pissing off mum and her latest boyfriend.

But they didn't attend school either.

Result.

The consensus amongst staff appeared to be, let them go and bother security at the shopping mall, or eat themselves into a state of morbid obesity while watching daytime TV. Let them offer gainful employment to the solicitors down at the magistrates' court.

Just don't let them disrupt everyone else's education.

It was unethical, possibly illegal; certainly it was an affront to someone's human rights. Ofsted would have had a field day. But it worked. It allowed teachers to teach, well, after a fashion, and it allowed those students who wanted to, to study. I began to quite like Mr Sweet. Who wasn't at all.

Sweet, that is.

As a supply teacher it wasn't all good news though; any absent teacher would get their lesson covered by a supply teacher. And that would be me, then. The luxury of having three or four free lessons a week was quickly forgotten. On the plus side, it meant I had to quickly polish up on my classroom-management skills.

Theoretically, classroom management means ensuring that all students are on-task and learning to the best of their ability.

In practice, here, it meant keeping them in their seats. It meant stopping the riot that would inevitably follow if I lost control. But even the constant absence-covering wasn't too bad, and I quickly cottoned on that my main function at Bognor, within the English department, at least, was to ensure that Judy, the Head of Department, was not caused any hassle by my presence or my classes. For the next seven weeks, it appeared, my job was simple; to make Judy's job a little easier.

Friday, 12.20pm – School Hall

It's Friday lunchtime and there are only two lessons to go until the weekend. Having miraculously survived the first four and a half days, I'm standing in the hall waiting for the end-of-week lunchtime briefing to begin.

Like naughty pupils, the staff are drifting in, reluctant and late, and when they do arrive, they huddle at the rear; newcomers quietly shuffle their way in and stand in groups close to the door, rather than sit at the seats nearer the front. With no advance warning that this is classed as a 'working lunch' I'm sitting with a glum face and rumbling stomach as others munch on their sandwiches and pour coffee from flasks.

There are quiet mutters while Mr Sweet gives us a PowerPoint presentation on the results of last year's SAT examinations, using his laptop to scroll through sheets of statistics that indicate where we are, where we should be, and, crucially, where we are *likely* to be, target-wise, according to Government statistics devised in conjunction with local authority educational advisors, Head Teachers and panels of independent local worthies.

As the stats roll out, people are surreptitiously checking their phones for messages; some are openly texting, others chewing sandwiches and pies. One teacher whose name I don't yet know is sitting with a plate on his lap, loudly tucking into a plate of spaghetti meatballs. Being food-free, I'm forced to pay attention and it occurs to me that these stats have probably cost thousands of pounds and hundreds of man-hours to amass and yet what we have arrived at is, at best, informed wishful thinking.

Ten minutes into the session and about a third of the teaching staff still haven't arrived. Can't say I blame them; they're voting with their feet. Or rather, their stomachs.

Now we're listening to statistics about previous SATs achievement, targets for GCSE scores, added-value...

...Judy, my new Head of Department, sits down beside me, leans over and whispers to me, 'How do you add value to *shit*?'

She cracks up in silent mirth when I whisper the reply, '*Sweetcorn.*'

Noticing I am lunchless, she kindly shares her mug of tea and gives me a chocolate digestive.

By 12.35pm about a quarter of the staff still haven't arrived; thankfully, the PowerPoint presentation is over. I'm about to get up and leave when the Deputy Head, known to everyone as Big Cyril, takes the helm and launches into a monologue about raising student attendance, which is ironic seeing as staff absence is averaging around 20 per cent. Cyril pauses, mid-flow, to towel himself down with a handkerchief, and at that very moment, his eyes alight on a large, greasy and very satisfied-looking rat, perched on a vaulting horse.

We follow his gaze and stare silently at the rat.

In a stage whisper, Vic Hughes, biology teacher and union rep, says, '*Rattus Norvegicus,*' deciding, 'Well, it's *probably* not carrying bubonic plague.'

'At least he's turned up,' Big Cyril quips, which gets a titter amongst the staff. The rat scampers down from the vaulting horse, runs across the hall in front of the staff and disappears through a doorway and into the corridor.

'Looks like he'll be on time for lessons too,' Vic replies, as the bell rings.

The staff disperse in good humour and I go into the staffroom, dump my regulation battered-leather teacher's briefcase and put on the kettle; Judy's cuppa filled a temporary gap but I need to eat, and now. I've got lucky; I'm not asked to cover the lesson of one of the absent staff members, and I'm due a free period, or as they call it now 'non-contact teaching time' a phrase which is supposed to suggest that, though I'm not teaching, I'm not just sitting in the staffroom drinking tea either.

I pour boiling water into my cup, stir the teabag, take out my cheese sandwiches in granary bread and take a position in one of the comfy staffroom chairs to enjoy my lunch.

2.01pm – Room 101

Last lesson of the week is with a bottom-set year eight class, which can be a bit tricky; but this lot, though prone to anarchy, are surprisingly eager to please. I discover that most of them can read a bit, and I offer merits as a reward to those who volunteer to read out loud from the novel we've begun, though I end up reading most of it out myself, and then set them homework for the following lesson to do a presentation on their favourite animal or pet.

I've made it through the first week and this cheers me up no end; as they're packing up to go at five minutes to three I clap my hands together and say loudly, 'Smile everyone, this is last lesson on Friday, and the bell is about to go – it's like a mini-Christmas Eve!'

A tiny little girl called Nathalie tells me, 'Sir, you're nuts.'

'Crazy as a fox,' I reply.

'You wish,' comes the reply, followed by a gap-toothed smile.

The bell goes and they scarper, I pack enough books to keep me marking over the weekend, knowing I'll probably only do half of it, close the door on room 101 and pop in the staffroom on the way out.

I spy Judy in conversation with someone in a suit so I don't bother her but she looks up and winks and mouths *enjoy your weekend.*

Walking to the staff car park I'm feeling quite exhausted but not unhappy; my reluctant Toyota starts at the third attempt and I check my watch and work out that I have exactly eleven minutes to pick up Joe from his school. I put my foot down and speed out of the school gates in a cloud of blue smoke, touching almost 27mph by the time I get to the main junction half a mile away.

3.47pm

Ignoring the blaring horns of other drivers, I swing the car over to a parking bay and jerk to a halt outside a mini-market. This wire-meshed, CCTV'd establishment stands half a derelict mile from our new apartment.

Joe has his headphones on. 'Just stay here,' I nudge him.

Inside the shop, all is cool, and the smell of spices makes me feel hungry as I fill the basket with vital man-provisions: milk, coffee, white bread, brown sauce and cheddar. I know I'll have to buy proper food at some point but, so far, Joe and I are quite enjoying the diet of cheese on toast, biscuits and milk.

'You're new to the area?' the shopkeeper, a short burly guy with a big friendly face, asks me, as he gives me my change.

I nod, 'Yes.'

He proffers a hand, 'I'm Taz.'

'Daniel,' I tell him, shaking it. 'Me and the boy have just leased a flat off North Avenue.'

He forces a smile, but can't hide the expression of horror that flickers briefly across his face – an expression that takes what I'd said, adds italics, and sticks a couple of slightly horrified exclamation marks at the end.

North Avenue!!

I feel like I've just met the local undertaker and he's whipped out his tape measure.

'You got a son?' he asks me, no doubt hoping to retrieve the situation; I am, after all, a prospective long-term customer. Or perhaps he's checking to see if I am a newly arrived cigarette, alcohol and sliced-bread smuggler, looking to steal his business.

'Yes, Joe. He's outside in the car.'

He glances doubtfully at the Toyota parked on the kerb outside the armoured windows of the shop.

'I've just started working at West Bognor Technology College,' I continue.

'You started work at Bog Standard?' The surprised tone and shocked expression takes what I've said and repeats it back to me, in italics, with added exclamation marks, overlaid with a tone of horrified regret.

Bog Standard Technology College!

'Bog Bloody Standard!' he mutters, 'Good luck mate! They don't study for GCSEs at Bog Standard; they take GNVQs in anti-social behaviour orders.'

With conviction born, no doubt, of experience, he walks to the front door and lifts a sign to show me what it says.

No More Than 4 School Pupils At A Time.

Then he turns over another sign, written twice as large, in red ink and underlined, which tells me,

<u>NO BOG STANDARDS ALLOWED! EVER!</u>

Smiling ruefully, I pay him and say goodbye, the bell above the door ringing dolefully as I leave, as though to tell the neighbours to bring out their dead.

'Good luck mate,' I hear him shout after me.

4.01pm – Bainbridge Close

There are only four houses in Bainbridge Close, a very short Edwardian street off North Avenue, where we now live; three of the houses are boarded up – as locals say, the window cleaners use sandpaper – and the last house, ours, is converted into four flats. We occupy the basement.

The street used to end at some sort of industrial railway line, which has long since been dug up and replaced with a prettified embankment, with small trees and shrubs that sit in graffiti-daubed pots dotted along its length as far as you can see.

To park anywhere near our flat, you have to manoeuvre past a bricked-up burger van, edge round a council-yellow road-grit container and then pull in tightly behind a discarded skip.

Cursing as I again manage to scrape the car bumper against the skip, I get out and inspect the damage. Superficial, thank-fully. But on a car like this there is a law of diminishing returns; the more knocks, scrapes and dings it receives, the less I notice each one. I could see me getting to the point where I'd begin touch-parking, like a blind man, gauging distance by whether or not I collided with the vehicle in front or behind.

Joe and I got out and carefully walked down the mossy concrete steps to that lead to our front door. I held my breath against the smells of nettles and cat pee while I struggled with the dodgy Yale lock, eventually giving the frame a kick that frees up the door with a pop.

Inside, the sweet tang of cats was replaced with the dull odour of mildew and the sight of heavily flocked purple wallpaper. 'Teatime,' I said, and Joe hurrayed loudly.

While the electric oven warmed up I went into the bathroom, resplendent with its purple suite, gold hardware and mirrored ceiling, washed and changed out of my regulation chino-ish pants, blue shirt and nondescript tie and into a t-shirt and shorts.

Back in the kitchen I placed four slices of bread under the grill and began putting the groceries into the scumble-washed, hand-stencilled cupboards, on the off-chance I might at some future point use them for making tea.

I paused in my unpacking. I was confused. How do you decide what foodstuff goes into what cupboard? Are there a set of guiding principles for this sort of thing?

Until recently it had never been a decision I'd had to make alone. At university I simply used whatever space was left in the kitchen I shared with four other students and, after a few weeks, learned never to leave food in the kitchen anyway. And when I began living with my (now ex-) wife, she decided where to put stuff.

Now that I at last had the prerogative to stash foodstuffs wherever I liked, I was stumped.

I knew that under the sink is where the cleaning fluids and cloths and stuff go.

And I know what a fridge does, obviously.

But beyond that, who decides what goes where? I was very puzzled. Was there an unwritten rule, I asked myself? Like, left to right. Big to small? Tins on top? Or perhaps, bread then tins then... I dunno.

After almost three weeks we were still living on toast and takeaways.

'Dad, I'm starving,' a voice informed me from the living room; I looked in and said, 'Soon,' and glanced at the clock perched precariously on the MDF fireplace, above the two-bar electric fire 'with flame effect'.

It struck me with a guilty pang that I hadn't asked Joe how he'd enjoyed his first week at his new school. New schools can be a nightmare for kids and as someone in the trade, so to speak, I knew just how easily a new kid could be lost, ignored or simply not noticed in the first place by teachers. Or worse, the teacher could get irritated by too much enthusiasm, too many raised hands, too many attempts to answer questions. I visualised a hundred horror scenarios, each of which ended with Joe staggering away crying; a broken child.

And me forever branded a bad dad.

Worrying about this, and about the order in which you are supposed to fill up cupboard space in a kitchen, I decided to make a proper meal for the two of us. He could munch the toast while I cooked a proper meal.

I began to look around the apartment, specifically at the pile of removal-van boxes stacked up against the back wall, trying to remember in which one I'd stored the tins of ready-to-eat food. Eventually, after emptying the contents of four or five tea chests onto the floor, I found a carrier bag containing dry spaghetti, tins of sauce, mushrooms and suchlike.

Yeah, I thought. These'll do.

All I needed to do now was keep Joe happy with the toast while I cooked the pasta, which would take at most, half an hour. That, and some of that blue fizzy drink that all the kids seem to really like, and hey presto!, tea fit for a king.

'Here,' I said, handing him some heavily buttered toast. He mumbled something about it being burnt but shovelled it into his mouth anyway. 'How was your day?' I asked him.

'Fine,' he said, between mouthfuls, and went back into the living room.

'We've put in a full week,' I congratulated him, us, me. But he didn't hear me, so I went back to the spaghetti and laboured for a good twenty minutes to produce a plateful of healthy goodness, containing all the stuff that I've read is good for people; wholemeal pasta, tomatoes, mushrooms, green peppers. Stuff like that.

Proudly, paternally, I spooned out a healthy plateful and took it in for Joe, who I discovered sitting with his mouth open, snoring softly. Sound asleep.

Quietly, I put down the plate, went into his bedroom and fetched a quilt.

3

Thursday, Lesson 2 – Room 101

I'd asked my bottom-set year eight class to prepare a talk on their favourite animal or pet and after a couple of false starts I kicked off proceedings by talking about the cat I had when I was a kid. After asking a number of questions the pupils worked up the confidence to speak formally to the rest of the class.

It went well.

But a pattern began to emerge after the fourth presentation on Staffordshire bull terriers, the third presentation on Japanese akitas, two more on specially imported, and technically illegal, American pit bulls, and one on a Canary dog, which isn't yellow, by the way, and is reputedly very tough.

And it's this: the less literate the child, the more expensive the imported fighting dog they're likely to own.

Monday – School playing field

Sarcasm.

Let's face it, for teachers, it's a guilty pleasure. But as an alternative to violence, suicide or complete nervous collapse, it serves us well. And I've always believed that PE teachers have it best. They don't need to resort to sarcasm – simply launching straight into verbal abuse as and when the occasion demands it. This is a tradition that stretches back generations to when PE teachers were deemed to be Not Very Bright. So they were allowed to be rambunctious and coarse and, well, loud. They were allowed, in fact, to dish out quite a bit of abuse. Still are, in an unofficial sort of way.

However, my faith in the sheer *unwarranted* level of verbal cruelty emanating from the PE department was given a severe dent on this particular morning.

I'd been warned in advance that I'd be doing a lot of PE cover lessons this week, in order that I arrive at work in appropriately sporting attire. My second week at Bog Standard, therefore, saw me wearing tracksuit, and whistle hanging from a cord, as per the cliché. I searched in vain for a bunch of keys to hang from my whistle cord, as I'd noticed most PE teachers do. Though I've no idea why.

My first PE cover lesson was just after break on Monday with a lively bunch of year nine boys who would be playing football. Mick Talbot, stalwart of the PE department, explained that all I really had to do was blow the whistle to start the match, blow it to end and, if anyone was rendered unconscious by a heavy tackle or a clash of heads, blow it very loud and he would come over and administer First Aid.

'They'll be lively at first,' he told me. 'Straight after break and they've probably downed about a thousand calories of Coke and sweets and chocolate in under ten minutes; they'll have a sugar rush that'll last about fifteen minutes. Then they'll flag a bit. Quieten down.'

'Seems daft to sell coke and sweets to kids,' I said. 'Wasn't all that supposed to get stopped a while ago?'

Mick nodded. 'Yeah, but the Coke machine pays for the school minibus.'

I had no more PE lessons that day but caught another cover the following day. Mick greeted me like a veteran.

'All by yourself?' I asked.

'Steve is off with stress,' he told me.

Stress? It occurred to me that being a PE teacher was one of God's professions. It couldn't be more pleasant. I said something to this effect and Mick said, 'Try doing this in

February, with a bottom-set year eleven class. For the rest of your life.' Then he said, 'We're doing hundred-metre sprints.'

I looked at the approaching gang of surly teens. 'More year nine's?'

He nodded. 'Just hold the stopwatch. Start it when I drop the flag,' he told me, adding, 'and stop it when they cross the line.'

We began, timing each student and recording this information on a sheet. The National Curriculum requires that each student shows a linear progression in their physical prowess, which is silly really. Children, especially teenage boys, don't grow at a uniform rate. A class of fourteen-year-olds will contain boys of under five feet tall and weighing less than seven stone, while others are approaching six feet and weigh over twelve stone. And one or two fat kids weigh even more than that.

We stood and watched one.

'Look at him,' Mick said in disgust, as he clicked his stop-watch on a chubby, red-faced boy who collapsed in a heavily sweating heap at the finish line.

'Twenty-one seconds, Pavarotti!' Mick shouted. 'That's rubbish!'

He stalked up to the prone figure and, in an ostentatious double-take, noticed that one of the boy's feet was still not quite over the white line. 'Clock's still ticking,' he shouted down at the boy, at the top of his voice, and at a range of about three feet.

With a look of anguish, the boy limply dragged his offending, Nike-clad foot over the line.

The other boys jeered.

Mick turned to me. 'I'm toughening him up,' he said. 'He'll need a thick skin for all those years he'll spend arguing with the staff at the DSS, when he's making out his disability claims.'

Mick bent down and, in a mock-conciliatory whisper, told him, 'If you can do that run again, in eighteen seconds or less, I'll give you a Mars Bar.'

'Really, sir?' the boy asked, suddenly regaining some of his life-energy.

Mick nodded, fiercely. 'Really. Or a mince pie.'

The youth dragged himself to his feet and, surprisingly quickly, it seemed to me, went back to take his place on the starting line and limbered up.

'I'm ready, sir,' he told Mick.

Mick nodded, and I think he was quietly impressed with the boy's mental fortitude as he waved his arm for the other lads to forego their turn. I handed him the stopwatch and he held it out and began a countdown, 'Three, two, one...GO!' he yelled.

Chubby took off and lumbered down the track at a surprising lick.

The other boys were chanting, 'Pies! Pies! Pies!'

'I think he'll make it,' I said, glancing anxiously at the stopwatch.

Mick nodded, and yelled, 'Meat Pie! Coming through!'

As the boy crossed the line, Mick clicked his stopwatch, checked it and then showed it to me.

22.1 seconds.

I looked at the watch. I looked at Mick.

Mick looked at me.

'I think I started the clock a bit early,' he said.

'You think so?'

'Yes. It was probably nearer 17.1 seconds.'

'You're telling me that you started the stopwatch a full *five* seconds early?'

Mick looked solemn. Then he gave me a wink and nodded, 'About that, yeah.'

Thursday, Lesson 5 – Room 101

At Thatcham Grange Grammar School the boys played rugby and I was used to seeing sixth-formers with blacked eyes or with their noses held straight with gauze and an aluminium splint. They'd smile ruefully at mention of their 'war wounds'. Sporting injuries were seen as manful.

The girls at Thatcham Grange didn't really do injured however. They did careers, they did ambition, they did older boyfriends with sports cars. But no black eyes or anything.

Overall though, I thought I knew something about the rough and tumble of school life. My first taste of *real* violence, therefore, came as something of a shock.

It was the third week of term and I thought that I was settling in, I thought I had it sussed. Nice kids. A bit dim, some of them, and a bit naive, but OK really. Charming, in their own way.

And as I stood explaining to 11*Fick* exactly why Mercutio was one of the greatest of Shakespeare's characters, so great, in fact, that he needed to be killed off so as not to unbalance the structure of the play, I suddenly noticed that Beth Kendall was furiously tugging out her earrings, quickly followed by her lip-stud.

The she pulled back her hair and quickly tied it tight with an elastic band.

Her phone was switched on and sitting on her desk and I could hear someone shouting on the other end of the line.

Only later did I realise that Beth knew what was going to happen about a half minute before it kicked off. And the scary thing was, considering what happened next, she didn't run. Or ask me for help. She just took out all her piercings so that they couldn't be torn from her flesh. Then slipped on two sovereign rings for the very opposite reason.

The first I really knew about what was happening was when the door burst open and another girl dashed in, still holding the phone she had been using to hurl abuse, and launched herself straight at Beth with both fists flying. Two seconds later they were rolling around the floor fighting as I desperately dashed between the desks to split them up.

Only, they wouldn't split.

I've broken up a few fights, between boys, at Thatcham

Grange, and generally when a teacher approaches they give up, or just hold on until they're pulled apart. They're relieved mostly. It's just posturing.

But Beth and her opponent weren't posturing, they were trying to *maim* each other, and I was unable to prise them apart, entwined as they were in each other's hair, slamming punches, kicking, tearing, gouging and howling like banshees. Screaming incoherently, bellowing and shrieking as they assaulted each other.

'Get Mr Sweet!' I shouted. 'Quickly!'

At this point, Beth bit the other girl in the face and blood began to dribble between her teeth as she shook her head like a terrier with a rabbit in her jaws. The girl screamed even louder, but not in a traumatised way, more a sort of increased level of fury way, and she raked Beth's face with her French-manicured nails.

Some of the boys were egging them on now. Tables were going over. And chairs.

I glimpsed at least two kids filming the whole thing on their phones and a small but insistent voice told me I'd be on YouTube by teatime. And I don't think more than ten seconds had passed since the door had burst open.

If they'd been boys I'd have dragged them apart but, being girls, I was reluctant to make any physical contact with them, so I tried to simply insert myself between them. They fought round me, and through me, like I wasn't there, kicking and punching, gouging and biting, and all the time howling. As we staggered round like three drunken sailors I was worried that it was going to degenerate into a three-way tag match. Thankfully for me, help arrived in the form of three members of staff: Judy, Mr Sweet and the teacher from whose class the other girl had bailed. Between us, we managed to prise them apart in a blur of hair and blood and squeals of fury, and the girls were led away to separate rooms, still hurling threats of violence and mayhem.

More staff arrived and phones were temporarily confiscated,

despite protests, so my fears about taking a starring role on YouTube were allayed, and the class was settled down by Judy while I went to the bathroom to wash the blood from my shirt as best I could; a runner was sent for twenty-eight statement forms, and each student required to write out a statement.

A half hour later the bell rang and the students, a little subdued, left the room, dropping their statements onto my desk as they left.

I stayed at my desk, staring numbly at the bloodstains on my shirt, as aches and strains of battle, having arrived by stealth in the heat of combat, made themselves known as I cooled down.

A fingernail had gouged a deep scratch through my shirt and into the flesh of my forearm. I'd strained my neck.

I took out my wallet and opened it to look at the picture of Joe.

That's Joe. He's seven. He's why I come to work, I heard myself say.

He was also why I didn't walk out of room 101, there and then, and never *ever* return.

Saturday, 2.16pm – B&Q Superstore

'Couldn't knock a nail!'

Joe and I had driven up to the new B&Q superstore, hoping to buy replacement taps for the purple bathroom suite, and Joe was playing his favourite game of quoting his great-grandma, Alice, a woman for whom the ability to build, fix and/or renovate things, using copious amounts of heavy tools, was the absolute prerequisite to becoming a *proper* man.

It followed, therefore, that her greatest insult was to look some man up and down and, as he departed, utter the phrase, 'Couldn't knock a nail!'

Joe liked to do this too.

And he liked to use her other favourite insult, *narrowback!*

In fact, he was wandering around, looking for weekend DIY

enthusiasts in front of whom he'd stand, hand on hips and give a searching look, and utter one or other of those damning phrases.

Looking at taps for bathroom suites, purple or otherwise, probably doesn't make it into my top three thousand in a list of favourite things to do, coming somewhere below putting out the bin, changing light bulbs and putting cutlery into the correct compartment in the drawer.

'Put that back, please,' I asked Joe, who'd arrayed himself with a toolbelt and was busy loading it with expensive hammers, chisels and the like. He looked at me for a moment, then reluctantly began divesting himself of all his carpentry tools.

'I want to be a chippy when I leave school,' he informed me. Then, out of the blue, he asked, 'Why did you want to become a teacher?'

I paused from checking the stainless-steel bathroom fittings. Why indeed?

About twenty years ago, my dad, Joe's grampa, had asked me pretty much the same question. Dad had been pretty surprised, well no, actually, he'd been *stunned*, when he discovered that I was, in his words, 'acadeemic'. None of our family were *acadeemic*. We were artisan stock, and proud. My dad, his dad and so on back for generations were all carpenters; they were handy. OK, there'd been a Great Uncle Hector who'd worked as a gardener. But that was shortly after the Great War; he suffered from shell-shock, so it was alright. He was a loon.

So when, at the bright and cheery age of fourteen, I arrived home one evening with a letter from the head of year that explained that because I was academically inclined, I should be steered toward 'A' levels and beyond, my dad was rendered speechless.

For about a week.

Mum had to bring him round. She had to sweet talk-him. Explain that it wasn't anyone's fault; some people were just born that way. No one could have known.

They didn't encourage it or anything.

'Too much bloody reading,' Dad announced, over the dinner table. Then he threw my GCSE options sheet over to me, with his signature on it.

I think he'd have preferred it if I'd been gay. Or left-handed. There being absolutely no such thing as a good left-handed carpenter, apparently.

And there I stood, in B&Q, being disparaged by my son for not being handy enough. Possibly I was guilty of the worst crime of all, of being, in Joe's eyes, a narrowback! Wryly, I reflected that he was probably right. I left school neither handy, nor qualified. While I would catch up on the academic front some years later, part of me had to acknowledge I'd never be truly 'handy'.

We stopped at a café for a sandwich on the way home, and were flicking through the catalogues I'd picked up.

'What do you think of that?' I asked Joe, who was munching on a tuna sandwich. He gave it the once over, then shrugged.

'That good, huh?'

Between us we weren't working up a huge sweat over bathroom fixtures, or any of the taps, shower-heads, plugs and other accessories.

Plugs.

Who knew there'd be such a selection of bloody bath plugs?

But Joe had taken quite a shine to a particular set of ornate, gold-plated taps and, while he was studying these in awe, silently mouthing the description written in the catalogue, I went back to the counter and ordered another coffee.

I turned. 'Want anything more to eat?'

'Tuna sandwich.'

Another one? 'OK.'

I ordered the second sandwich.

Then I took the food and drink back to the table. Joe demolished this one too, all the while looking toward the counter and smiling whenever the assistant caught his eye.

'You not eating any more, Dad? You should buy some more food.'

'Why?'

'It's good to eat.'

'I know.'

'Buy more food then,' he insisted.

I shook my head. 'I'm not seven years old like you.'

He smiled past me at the assistant.

Then he winked.

'What are you doing?' I asked him.

He looked at me, wide-eyed. 'Nothing.'

When we left, he turned to the woman behind the counter one more time. 'See ya,' he told her loudly.

'Later, gorgeous,' she replied, giving him a wink.

In the car I said, 'Joe, you're too young to be chatting up women.'

He looked up from the bathroom tap catalogue with an expression that clearly said, 'One of us had better start.'

4

Sunday, morning – Bainbridge Avenue

I have this recurring dream; I'm in a classroom and I'm attempting to teach, but they're not listening. Not simply *not listening*, but paying me absolutely no attention.

Blanking me. Like I don't exist.

I'm shouting at the top of my voice and it's having zero impact. They're laughing and chatting, doing each other's hair, texting friends, wrestling on the floor.

In my dream my voice rises to a shriek as I try to wrest order from this chaos, but it's not making a blind bit of difference; I'm shouting as loud as I am physically able to now, and they're still blanking me; some of them get up and wander out of the classroom and I shout at them to remain in class but they simply don't acknowledge me. Or they side-step me like they would a car parked on the kerb.

I shout and shout and shout until my voice is hoarse. They're not fazed.

I don't exist.

Of course, in reality, it's never quite that bad. I manage to retain some degree of control in even the most unruly of classes. And in most I usually manage to hang on to at least 51 per cent of the power. And a shred of dignity.

But I've seen teachers in other classrooms reduced to incoherent shouting; they stand, invisible to every pupil in the room, bawling and screaming at young people who have zero respect for them and no interest in what they say.

And they do this day after day, week after week. For years; whole careers.

I'm awed by their staying power. If I was reduced to that state I'd leave the profession. If I lost control that badly I wouldn't last two days. And the fear is always there. Teaching isn't the worst job in the world, in fact, some days, it's the best job in the world, but at all times you know that you're working on the edge of total disintegration. You know that at any moment something could slip out of your control that could cost you your job or, worse, your mental health. In a good school the structures and the discipline that exist enable teachers to navigate this possibly treacherous path with a good deal of success but, in a poor school, where discipline and behaviour are breaking down, the stress levels are huge because, due to the lack of control, the risk of catastrophe is huge.

Working in this sort of environment is exhausting. And in a school like this, it's self-perpetuating – the worse the behaviour, the greater the turnover of staff, the lower the expectations of those who remain, the less the students, and the staff too, subscribe to the concept of *education.*

The staff in this school can be divided into three roughly equal-sized groups: the full-time members of staff, the temporary staff, like me, and those staff on long-term sick leave.

Discipline, already poor for reasons that exist way beyond the boundaries of the school, gets worse. Those who remain become deeply, bone-achingly weary, not from teaching, not even from the mountains of stupid paperwork that seems to have invaded the classroom, but from the daily grind of just holding it together. And the wage bill is 50 per cent bigger than it should be because the school is not only paying teachers who are ill, but also the supply teachers who step in to take their place in the shield wall.

When I first started teaching, about once every term I'd spend a few minutes thinking about the possibility of a different career. After a couple of years, this had dropped to once a year, usually just before the end of the summer holidays. Now, the thought occurs to me almost every day.

I'll stick at it though, I've got responsibilities, but I can't blame those new teachers who manage only a year or two, or sometimes a day or two, before quitting. In a sink school like this teaching is less about education and more about crowd control. And it makes people ill. I'm determined not to succumb…but the fear is always there.

Joe was tucking into beans on toast, a meal that has the redeeming properties of being both nutritious and easy to prepare. I was sitting perusing the jobs page in the *Times Educational Supplement*, not exactly sure what or where I was looking for employment but, as the song goes, open to persuasion.

Blame it on post-break-up cynicism but it seemed to me that the job advertisements were composed entirely of what can charitably be described as euphemisms. Nothing new there, I suppose. But then I realised that, like all good euphemisms, we all know what is *really* being said.

But the first rule of job club seems to be that we don't talk about it.

A few phrases stuck in my mind, and like the English teacher I am, I jotted down translations in the margins:

Collaborative Leader	All of the permanent staff have left
Clear vision	The Head has fascist tendencies
Challenging environment	The kids are nuts
Innovative new buildings	We knocked down the old school, but it doesn't matter, the kids are still nuts
Enthusiasm required	Must be desperate
Expected to develop and deliver the whole school strategy	Don't worry, there's no actual teaching involved

I closed the newspaper and put down my pencil. It struck me with the sort of clarity that can only be brought on by months of exposure to corrosive levels of stress and emotional trauma, or powerful hallucinogenic drugs, that I was completely adrift. Most of my friends had been *our* friends, Jenny's friends really, and when she left me, so did they. Or they'd been colleagues from Thatcham Grange, to whom I was now the career equivalent of a Dead Man Walking. And I was living with my son in a grotty flat, working as a supply teacher in a sink-estate school.

I felt like the hapless male character in a TV comedy drama.

Bugger! I thought.

I'm Jimmy Nesbitt.

Friday 12.37pm – School Hall

'…so the pre-OfSted inspection reclassified our primary intake,' Terry Calhoun, ambitious assistant head teacher, read carefully from notes he'd taken at the meeting.

'…and it appears that instead of being of 'below average' academic standard, our kids are '*well* below academic standard', at this point he gave a wry, almost apologetic smile, 'which is good news, in a way, as it means we're not expected to do quite as well as we otherwise would have.'

He paused again, turned a page, looked over his spectacles at the collected staff sitting listening, 'So the pressure is off, a bit.'

He looked over at Big Cyril, who nodded and stood to face the staff. 'As a consequence of this, and other criteria, the local community is in the running to receive funding from the Government *Respect* programme.' Cyril went on to list the benefits that derived from living in a designated disadvantaged area, his voice rising in cadence as the list rolled on; 'this is a whole-community regeneration package – extra Police Community Support Officers, parenting classes, new build for some of the worst affected council-owned properties, vigorous implementation of ASBOs, respect training and, of course,' his voice rose to a triumphal pitch, 'extra money for us.'

Staff shifted in their seats, and despite Big Cyril's obvious excitement, this clarification had not excited staff as much as might have been hoped for. It appeared to have bored some of us. But I could tell Terry and Big Cyril were excited by it, so leaned forward a little and continued to listen.

Terry cleared his throat as Cyril took a seat again; he explained, 'We don't know *exactly* how much we'll receive but, hopefully, it'll allow us to employ extra classroom support, behavioural mentoring, specialist staff for the Learning Support Unit...' he paused mid-sentence to acknowledge Cliff Baines, who had raised a hand.

'Yes, Cliff?'

'I don't think I'm alone in thinking, well *asking* really, will there be any money in all this for more *teachers*?'

Terry checked his notes, took a sip from a glass of water, and then replied, 'Not directly.'

Cliff nodded. 'Well, when this big pot of hard-earned taxpayers cash comes rolling out of London, will there be any *indirect* money for teaching staff?'

Terry smiled wryly at Cliff in a passable attempt at saying *we're all in the same boat Cliff.*

'I know what you're getting at, and I sympathise, but I don't think any money has been ring-fenced for that purpose.'

Big Cyril shifted uncomfortably in his seat.

Cliff said, 'So this jackpot we're in line for ...'

'Nothing's been confirmed,' Terry cautioned.

'...well, as a teacher of Human Geography, I think I can *confirm* that this area is in economic, social and cultural decline but, yeah, OK, I'll rephrase the question – this unconfirmed jackpot that we might be in line for, on account of us being a shit-hole in the neck end of nowhere, there's money for support staff, and for the bad kids who spend most of their time in the Cuddle Club...'

'The Learning in Isolation Unit,' Terry told him.

'Well, I stand corrected,' Cliff demurred, 'but getting back to my main point, with all this theoretical cash floating in our direction, and this establishment being a *school* and everything,' he smiled ironically as he laid extra emphasis on the word school, 'are you saying that there's no actual cash allocated for teachers?'

Terry glanced at Big Cyril, who looked away, a touch disconsolately, I thought, then he looked back at his notes, took another sip of water, and then said, 'No.'

Cliff nodded and smiled grimly, then turned and said something to a colleague next to him.

This is why school management never want to have meetings with teaching staff.

2.30pm – Science Cover Lesson

The bell signalled the end of the lesson. Kendra put her file into her Jane Norman bag and said to me, 'I've got Miss Smith now,' and her frown told me she wasn't happy.

'Miss Smith is a good teacher?' I asked her.

She nodded, 'Yeah, she is, but we aren't allowed to talk in her lesson.'

'Ah.'

She nodded.

'But you learn a lot?' I asked.

Kendra nodded, 'Sure, we do really well. I'm targeted for a C but I might get a B.'

'So she's a good teacher?'

Kendra shrugged, a little smile; 'I suppose.'

This is the weird thing; kids enjoy chaotic lessons but chaotic lessons don't make them happy, or proud of themselves. They don't enjoy lessons with strict teachers but, if you look on the Friendsreunited site (and, saddo that I am, I do, regularly), everyone talks fondly of those martinets who dragged them through their exam grades and forced them to achieve.

Kids naturally tend toward chaos but, crucially, they have no respect for those teachers who allow chaos to happen.

If I remember back to my own schooldays, they included French lessons every Tuesday and Thursday, with Mrs Rigby, who could not control us. On the mornings of Mrs Rigby's lessons we'd all visit the nearby fruit shop and buy bags of cherries, purely in order to throw them at each other during her class. She was a young, slender, red-haired woman, and probably a newly qualified teacher too, now that I think of it, and despite our horrendous behaviour, to a pupil, we loved her dearly. She was great.

But her lessons were absolute disasters and we often made her cry. And still the cherries flew around the room.

Now I can't speak French, not a word. Well, perhaps a word. And while I think of Mrs Rigby with fondness, it's tinged with a real sadness for what we put her through.

And while others were singularly unpleasant to her in a variety of ways, here's the worst thing *I* did, a small act of spite and bullying for which I am eternally ashamed.

One Wednesday evening in our final year at school we had a school dance and some of the teachers were there to keep an eye on us. Which was nice of them, considering it was unpaid and we could be stupid. And at one point, with the music blasting and people dancing, and lights flashing, Mrs Rigby was standing next to me. And I felt her bottom.

Gave it a real squeeze.

She had a nice bottom, but that wasn't why I did it. I did it because I could.

I did it because I knew she couldn't stop me. She had no defence; not a single word or technique that she could have used to stop me. And when I did it, she gave a sigh of disappointment that I heard over the noise of the music, and she just walked away.

She just looked sad.

So kids love chaos in a classroom; they embrace it. But it

doesn't make them happy, or better behaved, or respect the teacher who allows it to happen.

I watched Kendra and her friends walking out of my classroom, giggling, chatting with the boys, flicking through their texts, and I asked myself again – what exactly am I supposed to be achieving here?

In the grand scheme of things, I'm still not quite sure what we teachers are supposed to be doing. I don't think *anyone* actually knows for certain – educate? Socialise? Prepare them for work? For life? Or simply keep them occupied until they're old enough to stop acting stupid?

There have been so many models of 'good teaching' over the last few decades that I don't know for certain that I'd recognise if I *was* a good teacher. There's no official Gold Standard. No one really knows what constitutes a good teacher.

There are targets, standards, behavioural models, student-centred teaching, didactic teaching.

There are carrots.

Sticks.

Ofsted.

The Government, LEAs, Governors, teachers' unions, the media, observations from Head Teachers – no one knows for certain when we've got it right or how we'd recognise it when we do. No one can agree. No one has the nerve to say, 'This is good. This is how it should be.'

So we can't blame the kids for adapting, and learning to swim comfortably and happily in this ocean of vague, apologetic and negotiable values; they recognise what works. They'll work when they have to, and they're happy to exploit an easy lesson when it appears. Until I know for sure what it is that would make me a good teacher, and no one in a position of authority can currently agree on that, I'll just continue to try and teach them a bit of English. Maybe encourage them to read a few books. Even the odd magazine.

And I don't insist on absolute silence in class, which makes my lessons a little more bearable for the students, but it makes life harder for me.

(By the way, Mrs R, you have my *deepest* apologies.)

Wednesday, Room 101 – Detention

'Sir, have you got any brothers or sisters?' Dicka asks me.

'Two brothers and a sister,' I tell him.

'Are you the oldest?'

'Middle,' I tell him. 'You?'

'Only child,' he says. 'A couple of step-brothers, but that's all.'

Then he asks, 'Did you fight with your brothers?'

'All the time.'

He looks thoughtful, like he wants to say more, but he's too cagey to give too much away.

Paul Dickson, aka Dicka, is on detention for disruption. *'Citizenship: Relationships III – family and siblings'.*

Once they got their heads around the word 'sibling' (it took a while) they were quite keen to discuss the good and bad (mainly bad) things about families. But Dicka just wanted to ask stupid questions; maybe he feels it is his role to be class joker; maybe he's just a fifteen-year-old boy having a laugh.

Now he's sitting in my class asking more questions. School finished forty minutes ago and I'm a captive audience. He looks slyly at me, 'Mr Ken?'

'Yes?'

'When you were at home, did you ever see your sister?'

'Of course.'

'Butt naked?'

I could be at home now, sitting with my kid, eating tea and watching *Eight Simple Rules* on Disney, a programme too old for him, too young for me, and just about right for both of us. I look at Dicka. 'You don't leave until you complete two sides.'

'Side and a half?'

'Two.'

'Go on. Side and a half.'

I shake my head. 'Two.'

I glance at his sheet. He's completed about a third of a page.

'What you doing?' he asks me, after completing a couple of more lines.

'Writing.'

'Writing what?'

'My journal.'

'What do you write in your journal?'

I pause, put down my notebook, say to him, 'It's a translation from Greek of a four-thousand-year-old treatise on the rights of man.'

I nod at his sheet of A4. 'Write.'

Jimmy, the caretaker, comes in and begins to rearrange the desks, wiping them down as he goes.

Fifteen minutes into the lesson and we're discussing sibling squabbles. Dicka tells the class that there are some family problems that can only be solved through violence. I disagree, I tell him, selling him the party line. All situations, however intractable they may appear, can be solved through communication and negotiation.

He thinks deeply for a moment or two, the class is quiet, waiting for his riposte; expectant; then his eyes slowly light up and I get a little afraid of what he's going to come up with. 'What if, right, what if the siblings were Siamese twins?' He pauses for half a beat before continuing, 'And one was gay. And they shared the same arse.'

He looks around at the class, 'There'd be trouble. It'd *definitely* come to blows.'

Tuesday, 12.41pm - School Foyer

Judy fixed her steely gaze on him as he left; she watched him go and then said, 'Jake Dixon,' nodding to herself. 'Oh, I *know* him alright,' she told me, 'I taught him about, oh, fifteen years ago. He was a jumped-up little shit back then, and he still is.'

'Well, according to him I'm picking on his son.'

'Son?'

'William Crick,' I said. 'Well, his step-son, I suppose. I've been giving him detention and making him complete his GCSE coursework.'

Judy snorted, 'That's kind of you. But don't worry about Jake; he won't last. Janet Crick's the mum. I taught her too. She goes through men on a quarterly basis. This, in point of fact, might actually be Jake Dixon's second bite of her particular cherry.'

Judy turned her gaze away from the school gates and smiled at me in that way I've come to recognise as a message saying This Subject Is Now Closed.

I watched Mr Dixon climb onto his full-suspension Raleigh mountain bike and pedal away, his shaved head bobbing as he worked his way up the hill, the flab of his waist wobbling over the sides of his pants.

The sight of skinheaded thirty-something men in grubby tracksuits, cruising the streets on BMXs isn't unusual around here. It seems that their maturity begins to stunt around the age they start smoking, and for a lot of them it has totally ceased by age fifteen. All notion of contribution or obligation or ambition disappear in clouds of cheap marijuana smoke.

It's almost quaint. But sad too. It's like a war happened and all the proper men got killed. And in the absence of any financial, moral or practical reason for the nuclear family unit to exist, for *men* to exist, women are coalescing into matriarchal family units of grandmother, mother, children.

I thought of Joe and me; the opposite side of that particular coin. I wondered if these matriarchal women missed having men as much as I missed having a woman in my life. Perhaps I should mimic their behaviour and set up a conveyor belt of short-term relationships with unsuitable women.

Easier said than done.

Teachers aren't babe-magnets. Telling a woman that you've just met in a bar that you're a teacher will never provoke passion, no matter how you dress it up. I may have a few letters after my name but none of them spell Pilot or Doctor or ex-professional Footballer.

Most people don't have great memories of school and in a bar/woman/date situation I suffer by association. And teaching has always been seen as one of the caring professions. Not exactly a tough, manly occupation.

I once told a woman that DH Lawrence was a schoolteacher.

She looked blank and asked, 'Who?'

To me, being a teacher is a funny, interesting and satisfying job. It's never dull. But for Ms Right, on a night out with her pals, planning the next phase of her career in HR or fire-fighting, downing her third pint of lager and patting the glass-collector's bum as he passes, teaching is a bit worthy. It doesn't thrill.

As for mentioning my single-parent status, forget it. While sympathy may flow for a moment or two, accompanied by coo-like sounds, on any adult level the shutters have already come down and she's working out how to escape into the arms of the nightclub doorman she met earlier.

I'm going to get another career. A date-friendly career. A babe-friendly career. Maybe a plumber. Or a rock climber. Kick-boxing would be good. I can see it now: 'Yeah, I'm a kick-boxer, I just do a bit of teaching to make ends meet between bouts…back to your place? Sure. I'll just call in to let my, uh, coach know I'll be out late.'

In the meantime, I'm working as a supply teacher in a sink school on the worst estate in town.

It's not exactly cagefighting.

But it's close.

5

The Wenkel brothers transferred in from a school about ten miles away. When they arrived they indicated via sign language that they could not speak English, so the school arranged tutors and special lessons.

But then we got a message from their previous school telling us that they *could* speak English. And we learned that they'd been permanently excluded for dealing drugs and selling stolen goods.

Elya Wenkel looks to be about eighteen years old, Iwan Wenkel twenty four.

They don't attend lessons.

And I don't even think they're brothers.

'Carl Armstrong.'

'Yeah.'

'Yeah *what?*'

A pause, then 'Yeah…er, Mr Ken.'

'Mr *Keane*,' I correct him, automatically.

'Cherelle Bennet.'

'Here Mr Ken.'

'Chantelle Brown.'

Silence. Chantelle hasn't shown her face in the five weeks I've been here. I click a box on the on-screen register.

'Junior Donkin.'

No response. Absent as usual. Last year, apparently, Junior's mum went away on holiday and left him at home for the week with twenty pounds to spend on food. She had to leave him at home because the dogs needed walking. Rumour has it he spent the week camped out near the beach. Him and the dogs: bull mastiffs, I seem to recall. He only came into school for his free dinner before disappearing again.

As the kids say, Junior likes to 'jump the fence'.

'Liam Francis.'

'Yo!'

I pause, look up, 'Yo what, Liam?'

He looks confused, turns from his card game, someone whispers, 'Yo Mr Ken?'

'Mr *Keane*,' I say, and nod.

'Hassan Khan.'

'Yes sir.'

I say, 'Take off your baseball cap, Hassan.'

He grins, 'Aw Sir, I can't. It's me religious thingy.'

I ask, 'What religion involves wearing a baseball cap in school?'

He points at the logo. 'Manchester United religion.' Then he takes off his cap, still grinning. 'Deal me in,' he says, turning back to the card school.

I trawl through the register, dragging good manners from the mouths of teenagers who have never said please or thank you in their lives. Who treat everyone in the same way they treat their peer group, because that's all they know how to do. This complete inability to adjust their approach to circumstance is chronic to the point of being a disability.

I go through the Cherelles, Chantelles and Charlenes, the Liams, Connors and Carls, ignoring the hubbub of students who are ignoring my instruction to be quiet when I'm taking the register.

Some of the kids are sweet though: 'Toni MacErlane' is a friendly girl who also happens to be quite bright.

'Present, Mr Ken!'

Some are a bit funny: 'Michael Murphy.'

'Totally switched on and focussed, ready to begin the next full day of education, Sir.'

'Elya Wenkel.'

'Wagging it!' someone tells me loudly. I tick a box on the screen. 'Dealing smack!' someone adds.

I look up, sternly. 'At this time in the morning? I doubt it.'

When I've completed the class register on the laptop I fill in a paper copy too, and then I send Toni and Shivon to the school office with it. There, our Welfare Officer Jane awaits the list of non-attenders and attempts to contact each one by phone to establish the reason they're not at school.

Registration is a complete pain in the arse; keeping them quiet for fifteen minutes, insisting on a proper response when I call out their name, insisting that they take off their coats and hats, don't eat crisps or drink coke. Don't apply more make-up or give each other tattoos. Don't smoke. I've given up trying to stop them from playing cards, as it appears there is no rule against it, so long as they don't actually have money on the table.

And my collar is now resolutely unfastened.

Period 2 - Room 101

Script writing.

It isn't in the syllabus. It isn't measured. It isn't even easy. So the smart money says I shouldn't ever attempt to do it in class. But I like my year tens to have a go, I like to show them just how much they can control their own language. I want them to understand just how much language creates understanding.

We start by inventing characters and devising backgrounds for them. We look at age, gender, education, family and so on as we develop a profile, a person, about whom we will begin to write a script.

'What about IQ?' someone asks?

'Good idea.' I turn to the rest of the class; 'Michael has suggested we consider IQ when we are creating our characters.'

As is normal when a new stimulus appears, the class

immediately go off task and instead of discussing character traits, they're all discussing their own IQs.

Except one.

'What's IQ Mr Ken?' Cherelle asks.

'It stands for Intelligence Quotient,' I tell her and write it on the board. Then I say, 'To be honest, it's a bit limited as a way of measuring how smart someone is. The questions can be random, or you can be asked to say which one is the odd one out from, say, A, B, C or D.'

Cherelle looks a little startled, then fixes me with a determined eye. I can see her mind working.

'Is it B?' she asks.

Thursday Lunchtime – Staffroom

'Well, it turns out they were both seeing the same boy.' Sarah looked around the table, 'Well, *man*, I suppose. He's about twenty-four.'

'Twenty-one,' I corrected. 'I think I've seen him,' I said. 'Really?' The staff sitting around the table looked at me. 'Yeah, Beth showed me a picture the first day I was here. He looked a lot older.'

Sarah nodded. 'Well, the rumour has it that Chanelle, that's the girl who burst into your class –' she looked at me and I nodded, my memory of Chanelle still clear – 'She had attempted to steal Beth's boyfriend.'

'Not a good idea,' Viviene, head of MFL, decided. 'Beth Kendall doesn't mess about.'

'Exactly!' Sarah agreed. 'So Beth arranged a particularly nasty form of revenge.' She looked around the table conspiratorially, her voice lowered. 'It seems that part of Chanelle's play for snaring Beth's boyfriend involved her setting up a webcam link, and she'd been well, putting on a sexual *display*, online, for his pleasure.'

We all looked suitably awed by this news.

Sarah continued, 'But Beth found out about it, and because she had access to the boyfriend's computer she downloaded the whole bloody film. A total of ninety minutes of her rival, *sorting* herself out.'

Viviene snorted, 'No wonder she never gets her coursework finished. She's spending all her time starring in her own on-line porn shows.'

This got a few laughs from around the table.

'Yeah, well, after Beth had downloaded the film, she set up a website called something like, I think www.chanelle-slut.com or something.'

Sarah's smile was Cheshire-Cat wide; nothing, absolutely nothing, beats the *schadenfreude* experienced by a teacher when a horrible pupil comes a cropper; she managed to compose herself and explained, 'And then she told everyone about it. Half the kids in school have been going on-line and watching it.'

'Hence the fight,' I said.

'Yeah. But *we* only discovered what was going on when the IT technicians were doing a random sweep for downloaded porn.'

'Is that why Beth was arrested this morning?' I asked. Two uniformed officers and a woman in a suit, who I'd taken to be a detective but might have been a social worker, had taken Beth out of class during lesson two.

I'd assumed it was drugs, or theft or something.

Not sex crimes.

'Yeah; not for the fight. For the website. It's a child-welfare issue now. The boyfriend's been arrested too.'

'Chanelle is only fourteen,' Viviene told me.

'They've placed her with foster parents,' Sarah told us. 'Her mum says she can't cope.'

I closed my eyes for a moment, yawned and stretched in the way that, so I've read, men do on the eve of battle. Truth was, just like Chanelle's mum, at this moment, I wasn't coping too well either. It was bad enough that the lessons careened from one extreme to another, but the job front appeared to be a complete washout and in two or three weeks I'd be staring down the barrel of unemployment.

'You alright Daniel?' Viviene asked me, noticing my glum expression.

'Yeah,' I nodded. 'Fine.'

She gave me a wry smile, uttering a phrase I hadn't heard in fifteen years. 'Fight the power, Dan,' she told me, 'Fight the bloody power.'

Wednesday, Lesson 4 – Room 101

If a student behaves really badly, like the occasion when Tommy Smith threatened to kill Big Cyril using his knuckleduster knife, or if they are very naughty for a sustained period of time – say six months – the Inclusion Team might arrange a trip to Alton Towers for him and other 'challenging' students.

This school is an *inclusive* school and, whatever the no doubt laudable motives that underwrite the Inclusive Ideal, in practice it means that discipline in the school resembles a toilet that never flushes.

All nutters welcome. No questions, no expectations and no real prospects either.

Tommy Smith has ADHD.

What he *needs* is a dad, a stable home life. Affection. Boundaries. Lots and *lots* of exercise. Decent food and lots of sleep.

What he *gets* are burgers, electronic games that keep him awake 'til three or four most mornings. No boundaries, no social skills. Ritalin.

And Inclusion.

And his mum gets an extra £40 a week on top of her state benefits because, by definition, ADHD is a disability.

'Sir,' Malcolm puts up his hand a millisecond after shouting out the word.

'Yes?'

'If I tell you to fuck off, can I go to Alton Towers too?'

'No. And don't use bad language in my class, Malcolm.'

'I was only quoting Tommy. And you said that quotations are evidence.'

'Well, don't use evidence in my class.'

'Sir,' Malcolm persists, 'If I threaten to *stab* someone, can I go to Alton Towers then?'

I think for a moment. The truthful answer, I've come to realise, would be yes.

And your mother would get more money. But Malcolm is a good kid, he's quick and funny, and I'll try to keep him on the straight and narrow, so I lie and tell him no.

Friday, 3.35pm – Room 101

'Are you religious, Daniel? Judy asked me at the end of my observation.

'Me? No. I'm post-religious.'

'Really? And what does that mean?'

'I do believe in a higher being; I'm just not overly impressed with the choice of Gods currently on offer.'

'Well, don't hold your breath waiting for something else to turn up,' Judy was still scribbling notes as I waited for my debrief, 'but I was impressed by your description of Samhain; I think it scared the students too. Well done.'

In preparation for Halloween I'd told the students a short tale about Samhain, the pagan festival over which our present Trick or Treat night is thinly pasted. I'd concluded with a description of the area in which they lived three thousand years ago; this area; all forests and monsters and scared villagers swinging lanterns in front of their dwellings to ward off spirits.

Judy looked down at her notes again, then back to me: 'I think all religion is complete bollocks, to be honest. We live, then we die. Beyond that?' She shrugged. 'Who cares?'

She completed writing her sentence and put down her pen, 'So long as I have gin and tonic, I can do without a "higher being".'

I nodded.

'Ready?'

'As I ever will be.'

Oh yeah, I nearly forgot, Judy popped her head in a little over an hour ago and asked if she could observe me teaching 8Z4. And now we're talking about gin and God and I'm thinking this was an ambush observation, with a crap class, last lesson on a Friday, the week before half term, with the intention of finding a reason to get rid of me.

I didn't think I was *that* bad, but then I don't know what Judy's agenda is.

8Z4.

Z is the lowest band.

4 is the lowest set.

It follows then that any class designated Z4 is bottom class in the bottom band in a low-achieving state school that serves a deprived area. This means, in practice, bedlam. And the Head of Department has sprung an observation.

And let me repeat. Last lesson. Friday. They don't sack people in education, they just observe them, with a shit class.

Let me demonstrate how this class goes: I say, 'Be quiet, please.'

Bedlam.

'Quieten down, please.'

Bedlam.

'I'll add a minute on to the end of the lesson for every time I have to ask you to be quiet.' Bedlam continues unabated; their grasp of deferred gratification doesn't stretch to a full hour. They simply can't comprehend that what they are doing now bears any relation to what might happen in the future, so talking about what is going to happen in fifty-five minutes time is useless.

Judy, sitting at the back now, scribbles notes.

In desperation, I reach into my drawer and take out my borrowed PE whistle and give it a bloody long blast.

Silence descends.

'Give me a go of your whistle, Mr Ken.'

'At the end of the lesson; if you're good.' I look around slowly, getting as much leverage out of this respite as possible. 'Sit down and be quiet,' I tell them all. 'That includes you,' I tell one child. 'And you. And you.'

Eventually they're sitting in their seats.

'Today is Friday,' I tell them, to muted cheers. 'And Friday is like…'

'Christmas Eve!' someone volunteers.

I nod. 'And why?'

'Because the weekend starts in an hour.'

More murmurs of approval.

'But for the next fifty minutes we're going to learn stuff.'

Groans.

I go back to first principles: 'Why do we come to school?' I ask them.

'To learn!' comes back at me from more than one mouth.

I pause. 'What do we mean by "learn"?'

Silence.

I look around again, my knowledge of the verb 'learn' allowing me to assert some dominance. 'My job.' I tell them, 'is to make you lot smart.'

Judy glances up from her observation sheet.

'I am going to help you be smart, so that when you grow up you can get a good job and earn lots of money.'

'I'm going on the dole!' a kid shouts out.

'I'm going on inability pension!' another one adds.

'It's *invalidity*,' I correct, 'But at least I'll teach you how to write really well, so that your dole money doesn't get stopped.'

'They can't stop your dole. It's the law!'

I ignore this. I say, 'Can anyone think of a job where you don't need to be able to read and write?'

Various professions are shouted out: Bin man. Soldier. Window cleaner. I explain how even a bin man needs to read his route, how soldiers need to follow written instructions in order to shoot the right people. Window cleaners need to keep records so that they know who has paid. I explain how reading is a skill that everyone needs, and that I am going to help them improve.

'So you're going to help us earn lots of money?'

I nod. 'That's my job. To help you get smart, and earn money and have a good life.'

They all seem to be in agreement with this concept.

'Right. Let's start at chapter two.'

Groans of incomprehension.

I mentally scale back my expectations and simplify my instruction. 'Open your books at page eighteen.'

Some manage to follow my instructions, but most still don't have a grip on what they are supposed to do. I simplify my instructions even further.

'Open your books,' I tell them in a clear voice.

This they understand.

'Now find page eighteen.'

'I can't find it…'

I ignore this and remind them, 'Everyone who reads …'

'Gets a merit!'

I say, 'But I'll read first.'

I offer to read first because if I ask them directly, they'll refuse, but they love to join in. Hands shoot up and I choose one of the many volunteers.

Despite their enthusiasm, and the previous six weeks of intensive work, we haven't yet reached page twenty; the next bit is painful to watch and listen to, as various twelve-year-olds struggle to read simple English. But they look to me for support, and I try to give it.

I glanced at Judy, who was taking notes as Cherri struggled over the word 'ceiling'. I allowed her three attempts and then gave her the first bit: 'Seeee…'

'Seeeeee ling.' Cherri laughs nervously. 'I thought it might be that,' she said.

'Good girl, I knew you'd get it.'

After a few volunteers, plus a couple of paragraphs from me, I see we've read for twenty minutes, and we're at the end of chapter two. I get them to begin writing a chapter review. As they're a bottom set, I have to explain to them what to write, and allow them the option of 'storyboarding' the chapter. Which is kind of like drawing, instead of writing. I'm aware that it isn't quite English.

With less than a half hour to go now, the kids can understand the concept of the 'end of the lesson' and this allows me to crack the whip a bit, which I need to because this class hate writing. Even when it's only drawing pictures about writing.

I spend most of the rest of the lesson playing Meerkat. In some schools it's called Mole, but the rules are the same. You bat down each kid as they pop up their disruptive little head, answer questions crisply and clearly. And say 'no' a lot, with a smile on your face.

Every lesson should inspire and educate. Every child should leave every lesson knowing more than when they entered. Progress should be clear and measurable, both to teacher and student. Cherri starts to have a fight with Lee, slapping him across the head, but it's only in fun, so far as I can see.

I deal with it.

Then Dean begins to make a paper plane, so I deal with that.

And half the class are now talking. I deal with that.

And Joleen wants to go to the toilet. And so does Terri. And Conner. I deal with that.

I used to think I could teach. But now I need a chair and a whip. Or tear gas. Meerkat stops being fun after fifteen minutes.

Then, without warning, the bell goes and we haven't finished; we haven't done the 'plenary', in fact we haven't collected in the books, or tidied up. As they scramble to leave the class I ponder, bleakly, on what they *might* have learned from this lesson. And what Judy has learned about me.

These thoughts leave me with a sinking feeling, and then I'm sitting wondering why Judy is asking me about religion and higher powers and the medicinal effects of gin.

Room 101 looks like a bomb site.

Judy says, 'I'm surprised Liam Jones was in class. He's been caught smoking four times this week. He's supposed to be in isolation.' She looked at me. 'To be honest, I heartily approve of the underclass taking up smoking. I'd give them cigarettes with their benefits. And cheeseburgers. Cull them.'

She gave me one of her looks and said, 'Well, if Liam has foregone the joys of the "Cuddle Club" to come to your lesson, that's a vote of confidence, of sorts.'

'So, the good news first,' Judy began. 'If this was the 1950s you'd be the best teacher in the school. You're didactic; you set high standards, you teach from the front and you lead the class clearly through the lesson. Apart from the end. Which didn't. End, that is.' She gave me a short smile. 'But this isn't the 1950s.'

Silence hung in the air.

She looked back at her notes. 'The students like you, that's clear. But that brings its own problems, because then they don't know how to behave with you. If they hated you or were scared of you, they might behave better,' she said, conceding, 'or worse.'

Then she said, 'They'll take longer to work you out, because you're friendly, but you want control too.'

'Is that good?' I feel like a trainee again.

She looked down at her notes. 'It's interesting.' Then she erased something from her sheet. 'Sometimes,' she said, 'the only thing the students learn is how to sit still for ten minutes without demanding someone's attention.' Then she looked at me. 'You try to teach too much. These students have an average reading age of six or seven years old; some lower than that. You're expecting them to be able to read like thirteen-year-olds. I know they *are* almost thirteen, but they're the bottom set in a difficult school in a town where unemployment is a way of life and lessons are widely seen as social events. And learning is something to be avoided. Or, at best, endured.'

She closed her file. Then she smiled at me. 'Slow it down. Break it into bite-size chunks of fifteen minutes. Reward them copiously.'

Then she said, 'It's half term in a week.'

'I know.'

'Well, do you want to stay on here until Christmas? Or have you got something else lined up?'

'Sorry?' I was confused. 'No. Er, yes?'

'Was that a yes or a no?'

'Yes. 'Til Christmas. That will be fine.'

'Good.'

'I thought you were going to pay me off.'

'Why?' She looked at me with the air of a patient parent with a dutiful but stupid child; 'You've survived, and that's qualification enough, but if you want more reasons, you're smart, the students enjoy your lessons *and* you turn up every morning. That's more than a lot of people do round here.'

I must have looked more confused because she went on to explain: 'I chose this lesson because I wanted to see you at your worst; unprepared, bottom set, last lesson of the week. Not because I wanted to see you *fail*. Because I wanted to see you *survive*.'

'Right.'

'Christmas, then.'

I nodded.

'I know you'll be looking for a better job, Daniel. And I'll give you excellent references. But it'll be nice to have you 'til then.'

'Right.'

She stood up. 'Enjoy your weekend.'

Right.

Daniel Ken

Bainbridge Avenue – Half Term

I spent the whole of the following week teaching on autopilot, fighting an unsettling feeling that in agreeing to work another half term at West Bognor I had signed my name to an open-ended contract, and one that wasn't written with my best interests in mind. But then, my whole life at the moment seemed to be a series of bad choices and expensive bargains. I wondered how many more bad moves I could afford to make before everything fell apart.

On the first Saturday of the holiday I rang my parents.

'So they kept you on then?'

'Yeah.'

Walking to the window to get a better signal, I glanced across at Joe who was attempting to cut every piece of his dinner into tiny bite-sized chunks prior to any attempt at actually eating it.

'You can manage alright with the kids in this school?'

'Sure, Mum. It's my job. I'm good at it.' *At least, I used to think I was.* But I was thinking about trying to teach my bottom set year eights to read. And the fight. And citizenship lessons with 11 *Fick*. The truth was, I'm ashamed to admit, I was feeling a bit sorry for myself too, thinking, here I go again, disappointing the folks, screwing up, snatching defeat from the jaws of victory.

And I was knackered. Physically, mentally and emotionally. A half term at West Bognor had totally drained me.

'Well, so long as you're alright,' she said, adding, 'I'm not sure that leasing that apartment was a good idea.'

'It was a bargain.'

'Jenny been in touch?' she asked.

'No,' I said.

Subject closed.

'Joe's OK?'

'You OK, Joe?' I asked.

He looked up from his diced meal, 'Sure!'

'He's fine.'

57

'Good,' Mum told me. 'Come over and visit, soon.'

'I'll have to go,' I told her. 'I've got lots of marking.'

'Lindsey said she'd baby-sit, if you ever want to go out.'

'Thanks Mum.'

I hung up.

You grow out of your parents, I thought; you leave home and become an adult, and their continuing care becomes bothersome. And you grow out of their house too; you cease to fit and you can never return; even their furniture and decorations belong to an earlier decade, though your parents' house always remains *home* in a very fundamental way. And every other home you live in is judged against your first.

I watched Joe cutting his chips into even tinier slices. 'Are you going to *eat* some of those at, some point?' I asked, slotting the phone back into the charger.

'Sure!'

I wondered what Joe would be like when he grew up; what *home* had I provided that he would be able to look back on and compare.

We𝑠t Bognor Technology College

Motto: Failure is just success — travelling in the wrong direction

6

Saturday, 10.45am – Bainbridge Avenue

On the Saturday morning after half term, I decided to go into school and make a start at cleaning up my classroom; maybe it was because my contract had been extended that I felt I should make more of an effort; make it feel more like *my* classroom. Whatever it was, I wasn't able to stop back and do it on an evening for having to pick up Joe so I'd have to do it this morning.

I went into his room, 'Hey, how do you fancy breakfast at McDonald's?'

In reply, he leaped out of bed and was dressed in about four minutes. We drove into town, did the deed at the Golden Crescents, or Triangle or whatever they're supposed to be known as, picked up double cheeseburgers, and then we went to HMV, where I bought some posters. Then we went to a branch of Dixon's and I bought a radio. Then we drove to school.

As a community school, West Bognor Technology College, as it's known by the School Governors and the Local Education Authority, is open for business on Saturdays for pensioners' groups, yoga classes and the like.

Proudly I showed Joe up to my room, unlocked it and we went inside; the first thing I did was unwrap and plug in the radio. Joe volunteered to tune it in; at seven years old, he's a musical fascist, and though I wanted to listen to Jonathan Ross on Radio 2, he insisted we listened to a dance-music station.

'Auntie Lindsey has this on in her car,' he told me, singing along to Amerie's 'One Thing'.

'Ooh Gobble gobble gobble,' Joe sung.

'I'm not sure if they're the right words, Joe…'

'They are, listen!'

'Well, you can repay my eardrums by pulling down all those death-metal posters, and putting them in the bin. Joe willingly got stuck in, in the sort of haphazard, slapdash way that seven-year-olds do and soon there was a pile of torn paper on the floor next to the bin, which was overflowing.

And then he found a pile of comics featuring various ninjas chopping heads off other ninjas, and sat down happily to read them instead. I continued, finding myself singing along to various dance tunes. Tearing posters off the wall is easy, it's prising out staples and drawing pins and peeling off old sticky tape that's a pain. But in an hour or so I'd cleared the walls fairly well and I discovered that the lurid paint scheme only really applied to the window wall. The rest of the room was painted an interesting shade of battleship grey.

I decided we needed a five-minute break before deciding what to do next.

'Fancy a wander?'

'Yeah.'

I was still getting used to the shape of the school building, which was vaguely figure-8 in shape, and on two levels. The two inner quadrants were decorated with decrepit pieces of weather-blasted 1980s sculpture, empty pizza boxes, and odd remnants of graffiti, most of which said things like 'Nikki Y2K' or 'Toni is a slag – true!'

The entrance to the school was in one side of the waist of the figure-8, while on the other side was a rotunda, currently cordoned off due to asbestos being discovered in the walls and ceiling. Judy had told me that the library had been closed for about a year but I was curious to have a look at it, possibly pilfer some decent books. 'Let's take a look around,' I said.

If you can judge a school by its library, then West Bognor was sadly deficient. At Thatcham Grange Grammar we were proud of the fact that we held a good proportion of the canon of English Literature. And a good chunk of French too. And American.

The library was huge. Oak-panelled. And quiet.

West Bognor's library was a puny split-level affair, the shelves were bare, or piled with old magazines. And from somewhere above came the unmistakeable sound of Metallica.

The two floors were connected by a spiral staircase and I held out some hope that there might be a few good books upstairs. I'm biased of course, being an English teacher, but I know that reading books is the quickest way for a child to become intelligent. I have faith in books and in reading and I know that, despite the billions spent on IT over the last few years, it doesn't help you get smart at all. It's a red herring. Kids teach themselves IT; it's the lingua franca, the pidgin, of the modern world. Teaching IT is like teaching TV, and come to think of it, we do that too. But the kids know more about using IT than we ever will. We can't teach them anything about IT that they don't already know. But we insist on trying, via squandered millions, and meanwhile, I thought sadly, as I reached the top of the spiral staircase, we're letting libraries disintegrate.

And literacy is dipping below third-world levels.

Joe shouted out, 'Hello!' and I followed his gaze upwards to a woman who was hanging at a precarious angle from a ladder, just below the ceiling, above a twenty-foot drop down the spiral stairwell, stapling posters onto a wall. She was dressed in a black sleeveless t-shirt and a long black skirt that seemed an uncomfortable choice for clambering up ladders; she had pale, bare arms I noticed.

'Hey kid,' she greeted Joe, turning down the speakers on her iPod and looking down at him. 'Could you pass me that poster?'

Joe went to fetch it and then clambered up the ladder until he got high enough to pass it to her.

'Thank you,' she told him and stapled the poster onto the wall. Then she glanced down at me and said, 'Hi, I'm Merlene. The new school librarian.'

'Daniel Keane. English teacher.'

'Aah. Mr Ken,' she said knowingly.

'Keane,' I said, adding, 'We're just in decorating my room, and I thought I'd check out the library.'

She nodded, still banging in staples. 'Sure. Come back in a few days, when it's up and running.'

I took that as a signal that she was busy so I said, 'Come on Joe, let's leave the librarian...'

'Merlene,' she corrected me.

'...let's leave Merlene to do her work.'

'Bye Merlene,' Joe said, staring intently at her.

'Bye Joe,' she replied, adding 'and Mr Ken.' with a tone that I can only describe as a mixture of a drawl and a smile. As we left I heard the sound of Metallica, turned up loud again.

Back in the class I began tidying up the mess, and pinning up some new posters but Joe was eager to talk about the new librarian. 'Merlene is so cooool, Dad...'

A couple of months ago, when it finally hit Joe that me and his mum weren't necessarily going to get back together anytime soon, and with the inner resilience of a child, he simply decided that he had to find me a new partner. And he's been attempting to fix me up ever since.

'Merlene is too young,' I told him. And too pretty, I thought.

And, like the boy said, too coooool.

'She's nearly the same age as you.'

To Joe, anyone over nine is roughly the same age. I said, 'When we've put these posters up we can go and eat.'

Hopefully, he suggested, 'Can we invite Merlene?'

'Just us lads,' I told him.

'It must be difficult to climb a ladder wearing that dress,' Joe suggested. Then he told me, 'I like mini-skirts,' giggling raucously. 'You can see girls' bums!'

'Joe!' I admonished, though I added, 'Maybe that's why she wears a long skirt.'

'Naah. It's 'cos she's cool,' Joe informed me confidently.

'You are way too young to be looking at girls' bums.'

'They're all squidgy!'

Dismayed, I thought maybe it was the breakfast club ruffians he was mixing with, having a bad influence. Then I thought, maybe it's Joe who's a ruffian. Maybe I'm becoming one of those feckless parents who don't notice their own child turning into a monster. Maybe he's not hanging about with a bad crowd, maybe he *is* the bad crowd. I looked at him and he looked back at me. He has a gaze so honest and clear, I thought, it could tear down mountains. He has huge green eyes and long black lashes.

Joe is seven. A beautiful boy. Give him another eight years, I thought, he'll be breaking hearts.

Mine already.

Wednesday, 10.02am – Corridor

'Here, take my arm, let me help you.'

Harriet leans against me, her grip soft on my arm as she negotiates the stairs, the stiffness of her legs causing her to roll from side to side as we slowly and deliberately descend.

'Nearly there,' I tell her, encouragingly. Then, when we reach the bottom I ask, 'Do you want me to come with you to the office?'

'No thank you, sir, I can manage.'

Harriet has a high-pitched voice, a child's voice. She's fourteen. She suffers from a particularly aggressive form of kidney disease which means her body struggles to deal with its own waste products, and minerals that should be disposed of naturally are silting up her internal organs and joints, which swell and stiffen and deform, and she finds it difficult to climb up and down the stairs unaided. There are lifts, and I can get a key from the caretaker, but she prefers not to cause a fuss.

Harriet is small and bright, she's polite and she smiles a lot, but she suffers chronic pain, and the steroids she takes to control the disorder cause her to become plump and moon-faced.

Despite her condition she's always pleasant and she works hard and she wants to learn. Harriet is one of my stars; one of those children whose presence turns teaching from a job into a vocation.

A leaflet she produced for a project we completed shortly before half term, entitled 'Welcome to West Bognor', is displayed on my classroom wall.

I stand at the foot of the stairs and watch over until she reaches the double doors by the office. I watch her push open these doors; she's leaving early and her mother has come to pick her up.

Then I go back to my classroom.

11.34am

In the midst of what might be politely called the hurly-burly of life at West Bognor Technology College there is at least one oasis of calm and reasonable behaviour.

This oasis is Mr Turner's class – Room 119.

I discovered Room 119 by accident on my way to do a last-minute cover-lesson for a teacher who'd just gone home sick. Many of the classes in this school sit back to back with each other and have adjoining doors and I was trying to take a short cut.

The door said **Mr J Turner – English – Room 119** and my floor-map indicated it backed onto room 18.

I'd come across James once or twice in the staffroom, usually as he left for home about three minutes after the bell went, but I'd never been into his classroom. Life as a supply teacher meant that I was constantly covering for absent staff, and meant that I rarely had any free time to pop and chat.

I knocked and opened the classroom door. 'Is it alright if I pass through?' I asked. James looked up from whatever he was reading and nodded.

I passed through.

As I did, I felt like time had slowed down, like I was in some parallel universe; the lesson had started only two or three minutes ago and yet class was working, in silence, text books out, heads down, scribbling away.

'Thanks,' I said, and James Turner nodded, went back to his book.

I closed the door quietly behind me with a snick.

In my cover lesson the class was pretty much what I'd come to expect; loud, unmanageable, barely working; paper balls were being thrown about, and I feared chairs might follow; various kids indulged in their latest fad, bursts of face slapping, accompanied by yelps, cheers and laughter.

But I wasn't as appalled as usual. In fact, I wasn't too interested. I was still thinking about James Turner's classroom. Had I hallucinated? In the middle of this Bog Standard chaos did he really manage to have a silent, hard-working class?

Sue Lishman, the classroom support worker, arrived about fifteen minutes into the lesson and she was a godsend. Having worked in the school for a number of years, she had a handle on crowd control that I didn't and, between us, we settled the class long enough to get them to open their books.

'Sue, what do you know about Mr Turner?' I asked her, when we'd eventually prised the class away from their favourite activity, chaos, and got them working; well, sort of.

'James?' Sue said, lightly placing her hand on top of a male pupil's and whispering to him *no more slapping;* he nodded mutely and got back to his work as she continued talking. 'There's not much to say. He never asks for support. In fact, he turns it down if he's offered it.'

'His classroom is quiet,' I said.

Sue nodded, 'Yes, it is, isn't it?' She smiled. 'Very quiet.'

Then she asked me, 'Do you wish your classes were like that?'

'Sort of,' I admitted. 'At my last school they were. Well, maybe not *silent*. Not like in Mr Turner's classroom. But fairly quiet, yeah.'

'James is a one-off. He has complete classroom control. The kids never, ever misbehave.'

'Weird, isn't it?'

'I think it's just what they've come to expect from him,' Sue said, then turned away. 'Nichola, don't put Adam in a head-lock please,' she said, and went to deal with a minor fracas that was developing at the back.

'What the kids expect?'

She turned and nodded. 'Yes.'

Eventually, the bell went, the chaos subsided and I went back to my own room.

12.31pm

One of the things we don't do at Bog Standard is celebrate traditional events like Halloween or Bonfire Night. I'll be taking Joe to a municipal bonfire and firework display next week but, although every street corner within a three-mile radius of our apartment has sprouted its own half-ton pile of pallets, car seats, planking and mattresses, it's one of a number of things that have slipped out of fashion in schools.

We don't have prayers in assembly either – we have 'Thought For The Day' messages emailed to us every morning. But since I don't yet have a log-on facility, my tutor group, 11*Fick,* can't share in the wit and wisdom of whichever senior member of staff has had the misfortune to have to do a Google search for this morning's 'Thought'.

Instead, the card-schools and the make-up sessions continue.

2.56pm

I'm discovering little tricks, doing all of this cover work, dotting around from class to class, trying to pick up and run with the jagged end of some absent teacher's lesson plan. One scam is to send a particularly disruptive kid on a message. For example, a fruitless search for an unavailable book: 'Try the library, and if not there, go to the Geography classrooms and ask there,' I'll tell Liam, or Conner or Sharnice.

And if you add in a detour to the back of the PE block for a cigarette, that'll get rid of them for at least thirty minutes. I suspect that they know it's a scam. I suspect I'm rewarding bad behaviour by letting them out of class, but the alternative is to have them *in* the class.

I mused on this news as I returned to my room, opening the door on my own temporary little kingdom. Room 101 is starting to look a little tidier; it's not the fact that I've straightened the desks, thrown out a couple of decrepit filing cabinets or stapled some very cool posters onto the wall, nor is it the 'how to write a formal letter' instructional displays, or even the examples of students' work that I've spread around in a desperate attempt to make the place look pupil-friendly. No, it's the gaggle of year seven girls who've taken it upon them- selves to come to my room every break and lunchtime and tidy up. But before you accuse me of child-slavery, misogyny or anything else I have to say, in my defence, they *volunteered* for this. And I'm beginning to suspect they get more out of the deal than I do.

For a while I thought they were just being kind, or useful, or that they pitied me for the state of the room; perhaps it was an early manifestation of the nesting instinct. I didn't mind. But over the last three or four weeks I've come to realise, via the music they've begun playing, the lunchboxes they're now bringing, and consuming, and the absence of much actual *tidying up* being done, that actually, what they're doing is *annexing* my room.

It's got to the point where I'm beginning to think it's their room not mine, and I'm feeling uncomfortable when they're there, like I'm trespassing. I have to make excuses for my presence, 'Sorry girls, I'm just planning a lesson, I'll be out in a minute.' Or, 'I'll just be a moment,' as I heft a pile of books that need marking. 'That's Ok sir,' and they'll smile at me and their smile will gradually water down, the eager expressions diminish into some sort of impatience, as they watch me, eagle-eyed, waiting for me to depart.

Lessons two and three, the lessons before the girls arrive, have begun ending earlier and earlier; the kids have put away all of their books and are standing by the door waiting for the bell. This is in order that I can quickly prepare the next lesson and then vacate the room before the year seven girls arrive, and occupy it.

I've begun doing my marking in the staffroom.

Other teachers think I'm showing off, sitting ticking books at lunchtime and stuff. They're wrong; I'm stateless.

I'm hot-desking.

Just a lowly contract worker, without a base to work from.

But when I'm in my classroom, rather like the pensioner who cleans her house before the home-help lady arrives, I'm finding that the presence of these girls, and their willingness to do odd jobs for me, is forcing me to do more for myself just so that I don't have to prise them away from whatever they're talking about, or whichever dance they're practising, and make them feel that they have to actually *do* any jobs for me. I'm not quite sure why I let them in in the first place, but now they're here I can't bring myself to throw them out. These girls aren't the popular kids, they aren't the academic elite; I think they just need a bolt-hole, a place where they can relax. The bad kids can lurk behind the PE block and smoke; the handful of Goths that are enrolled here hang around the music block; a lot of kids sit in groups in the yard, enduring the rough and tumble, the maliciously booted footballs, the name calling. Others just sit in the canteen munching down chips and cheese 'n' gravy butties. Followed by two or three cans of Coke.

School can be a loud, demanding and unforgiving place and I suspect that the girls who have taken over my room every lunchtime and break aren't well equipped to deal with it. So I don't mind that they have scammed themselves a haven; I don't mind that they've cuckooed my room; they're safe here.

And anyway, it's forcing me to make my presence felt in the staffroom.

More of which, later.

Thursday, 10.41am – Room 101

'Sir, look at my Nano!'

For a moment I thought Carl was offering to show me his intellect, but no, it's his new iPod, bought, apparently, with the extra benefit money that Mum has been receiving since he was officially categorised as suffering from ADHD. No matter that Carl is so far beyond morbidly obese that the only active part of his entire being is his vigorous sense of righteous indignation; he's hyper. It's official.

Which means we've got to cut him even more slack than we already do. And that's a whole wagonload of slack. And Mum gets a bit extra from the DSS. And Carl gets a new Nano. Or an Adidas hoodie. Or Nike running shoes. Which, incidentally, he doesn't use for their stated purpose. The belly got him years ago.

But Carl is fun, so long as you don't intend that the class should actually learn too much when he's in the room; he's engaging, reasonably intelligent and, weirdly, for such a naughty boy, desperate to please. Of course, when he blows, which he does most days, he becomes a snarling, foul-mouthed fifteen-year-old ball of righteous fury.

He blows when he is given instructions. He blows when we say no. He explodes in anger if he is asked to be quiet. He throws chairs.

Punches people.

Runs around.

Carl already has a police record: vandalism, anti-social behaviour, violence, theft, drunkenness. Small stuff, of course. But give him time.

And that list of misdemeanours means that apart from the Educational Welfare Officer (EWO), the Head of Year, EdPsych, various learning mentors and support assistants, Carl now has the smiling beneficence of the Community Bobby and Social Services beaming down upon him.

There is, in fact, a small army of people who are employed solely to stop Carl doing whatever he wants to do, whenever he feels like doing it. To whoever happens to be in his way at the time.

And then I read somewhere that David Cameron wants me to give Carl a hug. Well, apart from the fact that if I did, I'd likely be suspended immediately, pending an investigation, or given a full Zidane right on my kisser, I don't actually want to hug him. I have a son, who I hug lots, and a mum, who I hug at weekends, and I'm looking for a nice woman, who might want to hug me back.

But hug Carl? No thanks.

I don't need to hug him. I don't need to understand him, unless it's in a Sun Tzu 'know your enemy' sort of way. And the way things are at the moment, I have no way of actually teaching him. Because that would involve someone using the 'N' word to Carl. The word that no self-respecting liberal dare use in polite society.

The 'No' word.

Carl doesn't need a hug. He needs boundaries. I was reminded of this simple fact when I saw him being led into the Head's office to make a statement about an incident when Carl and a couple of friends had stoned a minibus carrying kids from another school to a football match with our Under 13's.

That was a couple of days ago. He's still in school. Still giving staff 'verbals'. Still disrupting classes. What's scarier is he's not the only one. We've got loads of Carls. And we have them for five years each.

But I know what Cameron was *getting at;* if we don't understand these kids, if we don't get to grips with them on some level, our society won't just have them for five years, we'll have them for decades, or at least until global warming mistakes their lazy, obese figures for walruses and sweeps them out into the ocean.

And let's be honest, being Carl must be pretty sad in a lot of ways.

He's fully Ritalin-ed. Obese. Friendless. Family life is chaotic; Mum is a tattooed biker chick; when he's not at school or on the streets abusing passers-by, he spends most of his time at his gran's house. He's a desperate kid looking for something to get his teeth into, and we're feeding him a physical and mental diet of pre-chewed mush.

Carl is fifteen years old.

In less than a year he will be looking for paid employment.

A couple of weeks ago Carl was in my class, showing pictures of his latest 'dad' to his friends. One of them, known to all as 'Toad', took a good look at the picture and said, knowledgeably, 'Yeah, we've had him. He's crap.'

It almost made me want to hug him.

But not quite.

7

'We need a Twankey.'

Oh-oh. I'm not thespian material.

With this thought I listened glumly as Sarah Cross from the drama department enthused at length about how much fun it would be for me to get involved in the annual school panto. Like most dyed-in-the-wools, my main professional concern in deciding whether or not to volunteer for anything is working out exactly how much of my precious non-teaching, non-planning, non-marking time (known colloquially as 'a life') this particular activity will eat up.

'Well, I could always do some scene-painting or something, I suppose.'

Sarah smiled archly, 'Is that because Merlene is doing the set design, Daniel?'

I hadn't realised that my secret fondness for Merlene had become public knowledge; I've only spoken to her three times after all. Then again nothing is secret for long in a school. But I also realised that if I denied all knowledge it would immediately sound like a lie. So I said, 'Well, what else can I do?'

'Can you, erm, *perform*?' Sarah asked brightly.

I shook my head firmly.

'The thing is – ' she paused, a smile seeping across her face – 'we need a Twankey…and, don't take this the wrong way, but I think you'd be perfect.'

I pondered on this; was I giving off the wrong vibes? Had I

been too quick in expressing my feminine side? Did Sarah think I was gay? Or just ageing queen-like? Was I, in fact, the Quentin Crisp of Bog Standard?

'Twankey is always better played by a man,' she explained. 'Last year Jen had to play Twankey.'

'Jen?'

'Jen the cleaner.'

'Oh right.'

Jen the cleaner is one of those old-school incorrigibles; a combined cleaning whirlwind, early-warning system for the best gossip in town, and general non-teaching matriarch. She also runs the sweepstake and collects for weddings, funerals and the like.

'She just played herself,' Sarah told me. 'Went down a storm.'

'Why not ask her again?' I suggested, but Sarah pulled a face. 'Try *directing* Jen, Daniel. Not fun.'

'I don't know;' I stalled desperately as I thought of a reasonable excuse, then played my Ace Card; 'Anyway, I have commitments,' I told her.

'So do I,' she replied, 'but I'm still doing it.' She gave me her most winning smile. 'Bring him *along*, silly. He'll love it.'

I gave in. 'OK.'

'I knew you would!' she told me. 'I knew if I went on about it enough, you'd give in.'

This is how I end up on stage, in drag, wearing drag-queen make-up, screeching dubious lines to a, hopefully, hysterically laughing audience. Not with a bang, not even a whimper, but with a string of crap excuses and ending with a lame 'Go on then, if you can't find anyone else to do it.'

Oh no, he's not.

Oh yes, he is.

'What night do we rehearse?' I asked her.

'What *night*?' she repeated back to me as if I'd asked the most stupid question. '*Every* night.' She patted my arm reassuringly, 'Well, maybe only three nights for the next couple of weeks; then toward the end of the month, it'll be Monday to Friday in leading up to the show. We'll be getting off timetable for a couple of days in December for the dress rehearsals. Plus time to do performances for the local primary schools.'

'So it's a bit of a skive?' I ventured, hopefully.

Sarah smiled, a little too vague to warm my heart with the thought of lots of free time; 'Well, you *could* say that.'

Tuesday, 12.44pm – Staffroom

'I'm fucked.' Dale sat in the staffroom staring blankly at the pink statement sheet in front of him.

'What's happened?' I asked, sitting down beside him at the table. He looked downcast. Defeated even. I wanted to draw my shield closer to him; to close whatever chink had appeared in his armour.

'We've just had a modular exam for the GNVQ.'

I nodded.

'But there are kids on the course who don't do *any* work. You know what it's like.'

I nodded again; I'm finding out.

'I've written letters home to parents, spoke to management. Threatened detention. But they still don't work,' he smiled wryly. 'And they don't do their detentions either; we get complaints from parents, if we complain, and the only way they get anything done is if we spoon-feed them the work.' I pursed my lips and nodded slowly in what I hoped was a sage and supportive manner; it didn't matter, he wasn't looking. It was fairly common knowledge that the IT department 'encouraged' their students through the course. Because in secondary school, the pass grade is all.

Not much else is asked of you.

This 'assistance' was a cause of some grumbling, even within

IT, who weren't happy with what they were expected to achieve and how they had to go about achieving it.

I reached over and turned down the radio. 'So come on, what's happened?' I asked again.

'Well, we can't let anyone fail, can we? No matter how crap they are; they *must* pass.'

'Yeah, I know, it's like a law or something.' And, I reflected, it's one of those laws that is self-defeating. Because they know they really can't fail, they just don't bother.

'Well, half of my class walked out. During the exam,' Dale said flatly.

I nodded slowly, appalled, as this information sunk in, 'How many?'

'Eleven. Out of twenty-one.' He shuddered. 'It was choreographed: after five minutes, one of them stood up and walked out, then a couple of minutes later, another, and another. Like bullets from a shit gun.'

I let out a whistle, this wasn't nerves, it was a mass protest. Insurrection.

'Do you know why?' I asked.

He nodded. 'I know what they're *saying*,' he held up the statement sheet, 'on these bloody forms. And I know the *real* reason too. They hadn't done any bloody work. All term. All of last year either.' He put the form down on the table. 'But this way, they don't have to admit they didn't do any work; they can just blame me, or Mike or whosever class they were in instead. Doesn't matter. They're all in my department. Look at this.' He picked up the sheet and handed it to me. I glanced over it; the statement said that the undersigned did not understand the test because they had not been taught the subject properly. At the bottom were about fifteen names.

'The little shits,' I said.

'The *lazy* little shits,' he corrected me.

If this was believed by senior management, this could be a career-ending move by Dale's pupils.

'So they don't do any work, then they blame you?' I said.

He nodded.

'But you've got records of all the phone calls to parents, copies of emails and stuff?'

He nodded, which was good. Because if the kids weren't getting the right grades, the school couldn't be relied upon to defend him. Lesson number one in teacher training should be 'Cover Your Back'.

'So they can't touch you, can they?'

Can they? I thought.

He took a deep breath, 'Well…'

At that point the staffroom door opened and Big Cyril looked in; 'Dale, can I have a word?'

Dale nodded and stood as Big Cyril left the staffroom.

'Fight the power,' I whispered, as he followed.

He raised a clenched fist and gave me a tired smile.

At times there's a real Orwellian feel to the politics of teaching; it may be that this is the case in all public-service jobs, maybe just all jobs. Whatever the case, teaching is no longer about education, it's about meeting targets. We've become target-focused data collection consultants. Since the league tables arrived, all schools have desperately tried to increase their 'percentage of students gaining at least 5 GCSEs grade A–C' which is the gold standard of teaching. This has meant that some subjects, where it is hard to get a decent grade, where you can't *fake* it, GCSEs in subjects like French or Music or Chemistry, have withered, whereas others qualifications like, say, GNVQs in IT or Leisure & Tourism, have expanded massively.

There's a kind of triage at work too, in this obsession with statistics; those students who are barely literate, who are going to get grade G or F, are not really worth saving, and those who are going to get As and Bs are flesh wounds, and can look after themselves. The only students on whom it's worth expending real effort and logistics are those borderline grade Ds. Because they are the ones who, if they get a grade C, will make the school look good.

And they are the ones who, if they don't, will make the school look bad.

I've been to dozens of meetings, both here and at my previous school, where we discussed at length the various techniques available to help us raise grade D students to a grade C. But I've *never* been to a meeting where we discuss how to help the functionally illiterate, that is, those who will perhaps scrape a grade G, learn to read a bit better. Nor have I, in ten years, ever discussed how to get the high flyers from an A to an A*. Because there's no profit in that.

But the Government, in its wisdom, decided that a GNVQ in Information Technology is equivalent to four GCSE grade Cs, so many schools, including this one, it seems, have pushed a huge amount of otherwise low-attaining students toward this subject. The typical GNVQ is equivalent, in theory, to getting, say, a combination of English, Maths, Chemistry and Physics.

Except it's not.

One GNVQ in IT, plus woodwork or Media Studies or something, gets the pupil, and the school, its magic score of five A–C passes. No matter that the child can't read, write or spell correctly, can't add up, multiply or work out percentages in their head. They've got their five, and that's all that counts.

Five years ago, Bog Standard's '5 GCSEs at A–C' stood at 21 per cent. For a school catering to mainly poor white kids in a post-industrial small town, this is absolutely typical. This is a male *and* female average. The boys by themselves scored below 15 per cent. Because no one achieves less than poor white boys. But with the adoption of the GNVQ IT course the A-C scores rose quickly to 58 per cent and the school was elevated 817 places in the league tables in just three years.

IT was the bee's knees.

The cat's pyjamas.

And Dale Wilson, Head of IT, was the star of Bog Standard. But this year the Government has decreed that the 'percentage A–C' must include maths and English. So the IT/GNVQ scam doesn't work any more.

The short cut has been blocked.

And Dale, while not exactly under pressure, is no longer basking in the warm glow of management beneficence. If he fucks up, he gets nailed. Just like everyone else.

And kids understand this. They're willing to exploit it, if it means they can get away without doing any work. So they chose an IT exam to walk out, in the knowledge that no harm or punishment will come to them. Someone else will take the blame, Dale, probably, who has three small kids, is good at his job and well liked by fellow staff.

I sat back and took a deep breath. Relax, I told myself.

This is not your battle.

2.38pm – School Field

'Mr Calhoun doesn't usually come out onto the field, sir,' Curtis tells me. Terry Calhoun is the assistant head with responsibility for technology in school. Like all of school senior management he is, nominally, listed as teaching five lessons a week. And like senior management throughout the world, he rarely actually shows his face on the shop floor. Or in this case, the playing field.

Teaching staff cover for him when he's got a meeting to attend. Which is often.

And on those days when he simply fails to arrive, the kids just go out and play football by themselves.

'We pick squads and have a kickabout,' Curtis continues.

He's standing beside me, giving a running commentary on the players on the pitch; Curtis is a member of the U16 squad, a possible future pro, signed to a local club, but a knee injury has curtailed his season. 'Marv's just big and slow,' he points toward a vigorous boy who is bullying around the ball, trying to get possession. 'Powerful kicker, but no real skill.'

I nod.

'Wren's skilful, but he's a smoker and he got dropped last year for his fitness.'

I watch Tom Renton, aka Wren, fending off tackles with ease but it is clear he hasn't got the heart, or possibly the fitness, for an extended intervention in this match. Like a lot of teenagers, Curtis is clear-cut and serious about good and evil, and for an athlete, cigarettes are bad news. He frowns deeply as Wren gives up a 50/50 chase for the ball.

As we watch the makeshift game run its course, Curtis shows me some of the exercises he has to do every day to help repair his knee ligaments. 'This one is difficult for me,' he explains, squatting low on one leg.

The ball shoots past us and the goalie runs to retrieve it.

'There aren't many on the pitch,' I observe.

'Most of the lads got sick of just having a kickabout every lesson; they're doing trampolining in the hall.'

The kids at Bog Standard, surprisingly, love trampoline lessons; maybe it's something about that repetitive, explosive release of energy that appeals to these otherwise disaffected fifteen-year-olds.

You can get a GCSE in trampolining.

Then, from some smoke-riddled corner of the school, Elya Wenkel suddenly appears in full football kit and jogs past us and onto the pitch; he is quickly absorbed into the melee that is passing for a football game.

'Wenkel's good,' Curtis tells me. 'Smooth and skilful; really tricky on the ball.

Elya Wenkel is barely five feet tall, slightly hunchback, and wiry, but he is skilful; he's light on his feet, perceptive, tricksy; there's a sense of humour to his game. Sometimes he is pushed off the ball by one of the bigger lads but when he gets it back he is surrounded by cries of 'Here Wenkel,' or just 'Wenkel!' as everyone vies to be the recipient of one of his scalpel-like passes.

With ten minutes to go before I blow time on the game, some of the lads are wandering off the pitch and in the general direction of the changing rooms. I let them go, eyes fixed on

Wenkel and his silky skills. The Wenkel brothers have a reputation as felons and ne'er-do-wells, and this is mostly justified, if you believe the rumours. I know they bunk their lessons, and they don't wear anything approaching a uniform, and I have experienced things 'disappearing' when they're in the room; I know that they're usually seen skulking behind the PE block, smoking, taking playful swipes at fellow students with torn-down tree branches and generally just lurking in the shadows. But they haven't committed any major crimes since they arrived here.

And they're starting to fit in.

Elya's been here for a couple of months now; the kids have him sussed; they know what he's good at, they know where to go to see him, or to avoid him. They're getting his humour; he's beginning to understand their language and their jokes.

It's the same with me, I suppose.

I check my watch.

'Can I blow the whistle?' Curtis asks me.

I hand it to him; he blows loudly on the whistle, twice, jogs over and waves them off the pitch. He watches them as they walk or jog back to the changing rooms. Then he comes back over to me.

'You ever thought of becoming a PE teacher?' I ask.

He shook his head. 'I'm signed to Man City. Youth squad.'

If Curtis stays on their books and turns pro, by the age of eighteen he could be earning four or five thousand pounds a week, and that's before he ever makes the first team.

He asks me, 'You'll be here after Christmas?'

For a moment I don't know what to say; it never occurred to me that I'd be here in November and now it's a racing certainty that I'll be here in the New Year.

'Of course,' I tell him.

'Good,' he says.

3.44pm – Room 101

I crumpled up the letter and lobbed it toward the bin. It skipped off the rim and fell back onto the gum-stained carpet.

This job-seeking business was not going well.

'Why don't you go into primary school teaching?' Jenny once asked me. 'The kids are more manageable, plus the career prospects are excellent. For a man.'

Oh yeah, what do you call a man who works in a primary school?

Head Teacher.

And if there are two men?

Head Teacher and Caretaker.

Three men?

You don't usually get three men working in a primary school.

'You never will though,' she told me. 'You're not ambitious enough. You *like* what you do.'

And her tone let me know she considered this to be a bad thing. But she was right, I thought, and now, even though a move into primary teaching would probably be a good idea, would certainly be an avenue to get me out of *this* place, I wouldn't consider it.

I like my job; I like the energy, the buzz. Sometimes, being a classroom teacher is like being a kind of drug addict – the highs are huge and the lows are crushing.

And in the long term it can destroy you.

But you can't stop.

I picked up the rejection letter, carefully uncreased it and flattened it out on the desk. Re-reading it, I realised I hadn't even got past the initial sift. Should I be more ambitious, I thought? After all, Jenny had left me for a high-flyer.

Was it even remotely possible to find a job where I'd be allowed to continue just *teaching*? And maybe in a half-decent school.

Was that too much to ask?

I thought that, maybe, it was.

8

Monday – Food Technology Cover Lesson

Jimmy, the school caretaker, is a scrawny guy with a wispy beard and tatty dreadlocks; he usually wears sandals and torn jeans, he's so thin you can almost see his ribs through his t-shirt, and he has a strange metal stud that pokes out between the dreads at the back of his head.

The kids call him Jimmy Jesus.

If someone is sick in the hall or in a classroom, or wets their pants or bleeds or spills something, the kids all start chanting JIMMY! JIMMY JESUS! JIMMY! JIMMY JESUS!

When he arrives, bucket and mop at hand, and starts sloshing clean the mess, they go strangely quiet. Embarrassed, I'd almost say, if that was an emotion they understood.

They watch him intently.

This morning Jimmy was called to a cookery class where I was doing a cover lesson; the teacher had become sick after tasting a student's food. The kids began their chant of JIMMY! JIMMY JESUS! and, as per usual, became strangely mute when he arrived to perform his cleaning routine, paying close attention to their books but glancing sideways at Jimmy as he scrubbed clean the kitchen floor.

When Jimmy had gone I looked sternly at the class: 'I wish you wouldn't call him Jimmy Jesus. It must be very embarrassing for him you know.'

Nelly Porter piped up, 'Sir, but he *is* Jesus. Honest.' I shook my head, giving her the 'more in sorrow than anger' look, as though to end the conversation, but she carried on with her explanation. 'He's poor and he hasn't got any clothes except his holy jeans and t-shirt.'

'And he does good deeds,' Alfy Bates added, 'Wiping up sick, and stuff.'

I glared at them. 'That does not make him the son of God,' I said.

'The son of Man,' Alfy corrected me, ever the student of theology. Then he said, 'Anyway, we've all seen the proof, haven't we?' and there was a murmuring of agreement.

'Oh, really?'

Alfy nodded, pointing to the back of his own head, where Jimmy had his strange metal stud. 'Stigmata,' he whispered across to me. 'Techno Stigmata.'

Despite quibbling over Jimmy the Caretaker's divine status, or otherwise, I must admit there is something *alternative* about him. And it's not just the dreadlocks. His presence has a benign effect on things.

Sometimes I think that in education, our value-free pick n'mix attitude to religion leads to a desire to allocate supernatural powers to the most unlikely sources. Our 'God-shaped hole' is filled with random bits of superstition, prejudice and hope. This translates into a systemic distrust of whatever we can't measure, evaluate, number or control. Simple 'difference' is labelled chaos, and is seen as some sort of *enemy;* the antithesis of learning.

And it often is.

But occasionally it assumes a mystical status.

I considered this while watching Sammy Wildish stroking the school cat, Coochie.

Sammy is thirteen.

Tattooed and pierced, with multi-scrunchied hair that scrapes back her eyebrows into the *de rigeur* arch of fury, Sammy is truculent at best and raging at worst; she has a facility for incandescent fury that is truly wondrous to behold.

'Hey Coochie, who's a *gorgeous* boy then?' she purred, fingers runing down his arched spine.

And Coochie purred back, appreciatively.

Sammy destroys classrooms on a biblical scale. But here she is, cooing and stroking Coochie. The school cat.

Everyone loves Coochie; especially Sammy, who sometimes, very badly, needs someone to love. And strictly speaking, Coochie belongs to the school caretaker, Jimmy. Or perhaps Jimmy belongs to Coochie. No one is quite sure. For health and safety reasons, Coochie shouldn't even be in school; we aren't allowed to keep sentient mammals on site – Ok, we allow chavs, but we're required to by law and, anyway, I don't want to get embroiled in the whole chav/sentient issue. I'll leave that for a rainy day in the staffroom.

If we get raided by Ofsted, which is due any time now apparently, we'll have to quarantine Coochie in Jimmy's house. As it is, the management turn a blind eye to Coochie's presence. Especially now, when we're going through a period of severe rat-infestation.

But it's at this point I'm going to lose my credibility, because I'm going to tell you about how Coochie became a yogi.

You won't believe it, but it's true. Honest.

Because, a couple of months ago, Coochie got banned from the Monday night yoga class, held in the school hall. He had taken to wandering into the hall during the yoga session, settling down on a chair and watching the students go through their asanas. If the mood took him he would drop down onto the floor and, in his own feline way, join in – stretching and rolling in parallel with the class. Coochie is a natural born yogi. But ten or fifteen minutes into the session, he'd usually be spotted by Jimmy the caretaker as he did his rounds, and Jimmy would come quietly and sheepishly into the hall, pick him up and carry him out of the hall, shutting the door behind him.

Jimmy told Coochie one evening, 'This is a *woman's* yoga class Coochie, not for men.' But strictly speaking that was untrue; back in November a couple of men joined the class and they'd arrive with their leotards and mats and towels and join in with the rest of the class. And in the way that these things do, the Coochie situation developed a momentum of its own; after conversations over après-session lattes, Nina, the yoga instructor, being decidedly equal-opportunities in outlook, decided that Coochie should be allowed to stay. So when, the folllowing Monday, during the warm-up routine, Coochie entered the room as usual, and sat in the middle of the hall, cleaning himself, Nina paused and said, 'We appear to have a new member of the class.'

She went to her kit bag and took out a small Coochie-sized mat, laying it out on the floor before continuing with the session.

Coochie went and sat on a chair to watch the proceedings.

He watched them complete their warm-up. He watched them begin their Sun-Salutations. Then he dropped down onto the floor and sauntered over to the Coochie mat, sniffed it a bit, walked around it a couple of times, and then lay down on it, contentedly. Now, no one is actually claiming that Coochie took an active part in the yoga session, but it has been confirmed that he stared intently at the yogistas (or whatever yoga practitioners are called), and in his own way, began to mirror their movements; rolling, arching, stretching languidly, pausing to watch and check he was doing it right.

I'm not sure if this makes him a visual, or a kinaesthetic learner.

And since he was allowed to join the yoga class, his attendance has been 100 per cent, he is enthusiastic, he doesn't disrupt or challenge. In fact, Coochie encourages and models positive behaviour for difficult pupils, so after only a few weeks of yoga class, he shows clear evidence of learning.

Given a class of Coochies, my exam pass-rate would soar.

Lunchtime

As a prelude to the forthcoming parents' evening, I'm sitting here completing student reports for the denizens of 11*Fick*, and wondering how many times can I use 'challenging' as a euphemism for being 'utterly badly behaved', before I go insane?

How many ways can I write 'appears to lack focus' when what I really mean is that 'Michael is an idle sod who doesn't have the gumption to fasten his own shoelaces of a morning, can't hold a conversation with anyone beyond the four teenage boys in his peer group, and has less classroom presence than my mouldering paperback copy of *The Wildlife of Rural Gloucestershire* (3rd Edition 1951)'? Can you think of a phrase that puts the words 'has a tendency to react with extreme violence to the merest perception of a suggestion that perhaps, they might attempt to follow teachers' instructions' in a good light?

Nope.

Neither can I.

What about the suggestion to Clyde's mum that Clyde should perhaps stop bringing in his charge sheets to show off to the more impressionable members of his tutor group. I do understand that it makes him look cool, but heading toward an ASBO by age fifteen cannot really be counted as a legitimate career path. Not in school anyway. Not yet.

To be honest though, I do get some satisfaction in writing reports, and it's not simply the chance to tell Cherelle-Marie's mother that she should persuade her daughter to wear more skirt and less eyeliner and oh, here's a thought, perhaps consider for one moment the possibility of bringing a pen to class. And doing her homework. No, what I enjoy about writing reports is the chance to praise good kids, of whom, surprisingly, there are a quite a few in this school.

I'll come clean: despite my protestations to the contrary, I am forced to admit that Bog Standard Technology College is full of kids who are often quite nice and sometimes work fairly hard in class. One or two of them even, I've discovered, are bloody marvellous. Writing reports gives me the chance to tell them that I think they're good people, without the background noise generated by the whining, stroppy, can't-do/won't-do, reluctant 10 per cent who occupy 90 per cent of my teaching time.

Writing reports gives me the chance to tell the parents of good kids that their child is normal, decent, and not noticeably stupid. Which is always a good message to put across. And a message that is usually, in my experience anyway, gratefully received.

So I soldier on, trying to invent new and different ways of telling parents that Thomas is a chancer and a cheat, that Bobbi skips any lesson that occurs after lunch and that Kelly is, basically, a bit thick. So, if I have to write the odd bland phrase, or neglect the chance I'd promised myself to write a scathing exposé, and perhaps make the odd euphemistic remark instead of searing the page with the burning flame of my truth, well, I will.

Besides, I'll savour those moments when I get to say that Charlie is a joy to have in class or Nicole *should* consider applying for a scholarship despite her gothic make-up, dyed black hair and multiple piercings, and that Michaela is bright, interesting and should do well when she leaves school. Because school is all about young people learning, and being around that, being able to contribute to that whole system in some small way, no matter how haphazard it seems at times, is a good thing.

It's entertaining.

It's challenging.

And although I don't want to be quoted on this, it beats working.

Wednesday – History Cover Lesson

'What do you know about the Cold War?'

Silence.

Wind whistles softly in the background as a metaphorical tumbleweed rolls across the classroom floor.

I'm doing a GCSE History cover-lesson with 11A, allegedly the school's top set. I continue, 'Come on, does no one…'

A hand rises tentatively.

Ruth Murdoch.

I nod toward her; she says, 'Does it describe the political relationship between the communist East and the democratic West in the period between 1945 and 1989?'

'Good answer.'

The rest of the class stare disconsolately, not knowing where this conversation is going to lead but sure it will include their having to do some work.

As a mainscale teacher I'm supposed to get two or three free lessons a week but, because I am a supply teacher, this is not the case.

'I'm Mr Keane,' I tell them, 'and because my free time coincides with your history lessons, and because Mr Kirkwell is on long-term sick-leave, you'll be getting me between now and Christmas.'

They whisper and giggle amongst themselves, one or two groan. I can't decide if they are pleased or not.

'We aren't doing the Cold War,' Ruth tells me, helpfully.

I nod, 'Right.' Ruth is obviously a Bright Kid.

'Listen up!' I say loudly to the class, keeping their attention by using the very phrase that Gill, my former teaching tutor, hated, and told us we must never, ever use. 'The relationship between this class, GCSE History – 11A, and me, Mr Keane, mirrors certain aspects of the Cold War.'

I go to the whiteboard and, using the only marker I can find, write 'MAD' in big letters.

Then I turn and eyeball some of the students.

'See that?' I ask one girl. She nods. 'What about you?' Another student nods. 'Right, that is an *acronym*,' I tell them, repeating slowly, 'Ac-Ro-Nym. Does any…'

Ruth's hand shoots up again. I smile; she says, 'It's when you take the first letters of every word in a phrase or sentence and make a new word.'

'Correct.' I look around the class again; no one wants to meet my eye in case I ask them a question and they're obliged to answer. 'And the letters in this word stand for what *might* occur in this classroom if we don't get along.'

They're watching me now, thinking *I'm* a bit mad.

I've got to get them in line in the first ten minutes of the first lesson or it will be hell for me for the next three weeks. But I'm over-talking, I need to conclude soon.

'Mutually Assured *Destruction*,' I explain slowly. 'Because, if you make life unpleasant for me, I will make it very unpleasant for you. And we will *all* suffer.'

I pause; this performance is all nuts and bolts stuff for a teacher, and it is a *total* bluff, but it can work on a higher set class, where the students might actually care a bit about their education, might subscribe to the idea of self-improvement, and can therefore be scared into behaving well.

'However,' I continue, 'this will not happen. MADness will not occur.'

Clear statements work best with boys, and with low-ability kids, which is why, in this school, I've got used to using them a lot, but this being a top set and, therefore, girl-heavy, I'm not sure if it will succeed quite as well; I plough on regardless. 'We are going to have, what they called in the Cold War, a Non-Aggression Pact.'

I pause again, pace around a little, making eye contact, not too much though, or it will make me look nervous and provoke a challenge; it's like working with tigers.

Or bears.

'If you do your work, do it quietly, and allow me to do my

work, *I will not bother you.*' I emphasize these words clearly. 'I will let you get on with your coursework.'

Quick on the uptake, someone asks, 'If we're good, can we go to the library?'

'*You* can,' I tell him, rewarding his initiative, saying to the whole class, 'If you get on with your work, I'll allow four people to work in the library, every lesson.'

The boy grins widely, stands, and picks up his book, so do three of his pals. 'Only two boys allowed. And two girls,' I say to the boy I gave permission, 'So pick a learning partner and get lost.'

A girl puts up her hand, 'Sir, can me and...'

'Do you have your coursework with you?'

'Yes.'

For some reason I don't believe her; she's shifty. 'Show me.'

She looks down, pantomimes looking through her Jane Norman bag and then, blushing, admits, 'I can't find it.'

I look past her, 'Any other *academics* want to go to the library?'

A couple of hands go up, I check to see if they have work to do and I send them to the library with a note.

'The rest of you can get on with the work written on the board.'

They know the routine; Mr Kirkwell went off in April and they've been working independently pretty much since then.

After five minutes someone asks me if I can put on the radio.

I nod.

Sure.

We have a non-aggression pact.

Room 101 Friday, 2.39pm

11*Fick* are doing their weekly PHSRE (Personal, Health, Social and Religious Education) lesson; this week's module is entitled: 'Appearances, Culture and Self-Esteem.'

It's basically about not calling people names.

The topic provokes an instant onslaught of cheerfully disparaging comments, insults and barracking. Insults fly, remarks and comments of the deepest purple are scattered around like confetti at a civil ceremony.

'Pepperoni-face!'

'Kipper-mouth!'

'Moose!'

In the midst of all this Teri looks at herself in the mirror; 'I've got a bum-chin,' she says, touching her dimple with a painted fingernail.

Dicka shouts out, 'One-Ton's a blockhead!'

'Put your mirror away,' I tell Teri, 'and Paul, stop the insults please.' Though, truth be told, Scott Walton, known to all as Won-Ton, *does* have a fairly large and very square head.

But they're all off again, now abusing each other's head shapes.

Some of these I've heard before; blockhead, pinhead, horsehead (I draw the line at 'dickhead' though Paul 'Dicka' Dickson argues loudly that it's OK for him to be called that).

Some of the insults are new to me (and hopefully will be new to you):

A *Dorito* is someone with a pointed chin and a wide forehead.

A *Gilbert* is someone whose head is shaped like a rugby ball.

The insults fly back and forward but it's fairly good natured and, as no one is perfect, no one comes out on top. As the energy dissipates and the conversation dies down a little, I ask, 'What shape is my head?'

A silence descends.

Beth Kendall tells me, 'Sir, you *really* don't want to know.'

Fair enough.

2.37pm – Room 101

'Sir! I'm stuck!'

'Sir! I don't know what to do!'

'Sir! I haven't got a pen!'

'Sir! Sir! Sir! Lauren called me a cow!'

'Sir!'

I was surrounded by a baying crowd of anxious, mildly hyperactive eleven-year-olds, all shouting repetitively, and bouncing on the balls of their feet, hands raised, desperate to catch my eye, catch my attention. I felt like a barman, and someone had just phoned in to say that the drinks were on the house. All night.

It wasn't just a massed attack, it was a *soviet* attack. Reckless, relentless.

And I was going under.

I rubbed my eyes, stood up and looked over the tops of their shouting heads; my shoulders ached, my eyes watered, my stomach churned.

I'd been feeling unwell for two weeks, sleeping ten hours a night, rising from my bed with the utmost difficulty. I had toothache, bellyache, swollen glands, a stiff neck and I was very, very tired.

All attempts at marking had stopped. Lesson planning, even in its most rudimentary form, stalled last week. Teaching had ceased to occur. Last night, in desperation, I'd Googled my symptoms.

It appeared that I was going through the menopause.

'EVERYBODY SHUT UP AND SIT DOWN!'

The room went quiet.

I don't shout much, so occasionally letting rip still has some effect. The eleven-year-olds went meekly back to their seats.

'DO NOT SPEAK!' I ordered them, rising unsteadily to my feet. I paced back and forward, glaring at them, but behind the thin veneer of fury my mind raced as I desperately tried to remember what we were supposed to be doing. 'LISTEN

TO MY INSTRUCTIONS!!' I told them. I glanced at the electronic whiteboard for enlightenment. It stared back whitely. I remembered, it wasn't working. Then I remembered what they were supposed to be doing, and pointed at the work listed on the old blackboard propped in the corner; the work I'd spent a patient twenty minutes going through, discussing, illustrating, giving examples, and generally unpicking the process of what they'd be doing, and why, going as far as listing alternative approaches, writing a choice of descriptive phrases, handing out photocopied sheets of word-banks.

And at the end, before they started work, I'd asked, 'Does *anyone* not understand what they have to do? If so, raise your hand.' And they'd all stayed silent. And their hands were down.

And they had all, it appeared, ignored *everything* I said.

All of it.

Including the instruction to raise their hand if they didn't know what to do. They'd all ignored me right up until the moment I stopped talking. At which point they all jumped up and raced toward me, wanting to know exactly what it was they had to do.

Because not a single, individual member of the class had listened to a single word I'd said. Each one must have thought something along the lines of, 'I'll wait until he's finished talking, then I'll go and ask him what to do.'

And now I'd shouted at them. I'd gone all 'silver-back' as Gill would have said.

On my post-graduate teacher-training course, Gill, the chief lecturer, was an unreconstructed 1970s-style feminist; she was also a staunch Roman Catholic. Her view of men was appropriately skewed – the course itself was female dominated, the women outnumbering male students 20/4 – this weighting was, according to Gill, 'a way of restoring the gender imbalance in education'. The fact that 80 per cent of English teachers were already female didn't seem to matter.

Nevertheless she was an engaging, if slightly madcap, lecturer, with a fund of education-related stories that she would recount at length, and often at the expense of any study occurring. The main theme of Gill's stories tended to be her own heroic struggle to defeat the mythical Alpha-'silver-backed'-male, the battle against which, most of her adult, feminist, life seemingly had been devoted. And I dare say she'd won.

Any of Gill's lectures, from War Poetry to Classroom Management Techniques, could, and often did, morph into a rant on the subject of the fascistic iniquities of the paternalist system. And these lectures would end, no matter where they began, in powerful statements of feminist fact and post-masculine intent, along the lines that 'men need to be relieved of their impulse to dominate' and 'the silver-back-male syndrome is ever present, even in the mildest-mannered of men'.

Then she'd stare at me. I was never really sure who this mythical silver-back was, but I knew he was a bad 'un.

I worried.

Was he one of us, the four male students in class? Could he be, in some metaphysical way, *all of us*? Was I, in fact, the silver-back male? Whatever the answer, every time Gill uttered that damning phrase and fixed me with a steely glare, I felt the guilt and shame of centuries of misogynist repression weighing on my shoulders.

At the end of the lesson the kids trooped out, and I sat back at in my chair and closed the lid on my laptop. I was still feeling off-colour, still needing sleep, but the quiet of a classroom at the end of the day was like a warm quilt, making me feel all cosy and relaxed. I stretched out my legs beneath the desk.

The adjoining door from room 102 opened and Clare, a teacher, came in with a sly smile on her face. 'Was that you *shouting* Mr Ken?'

I nodded. I'd given up trying to correct my name, 'Afraid so,' and I tried to explain, 'I lost my loaf a bit...'

But she shook her head and said, 'Nah, it's good to shout now and then,' adding an appreciative, 'And you *do* have a loud voice.'

'I silver-backed them,' I said glumly. 'I'm an unreconstructed, masculinist...'

She nodded toward my classroom door, 'Well, *whatever*, Tarzan, but if you can stop beating your chest for a minute, you might remember that you've got bus duty.'

'Shit!'

I'd totally forgotten.

I jumped up and dashed outside to the main road, just in time to watch the 133, my designated bus, packed to the rafters with riotous children, pull away from the bus stop and into the traffic.

Big Cyril stood at the gates.

He too had watched the 133, my designated bus, packed with riotous children, pull away into the traffic.

Then he turned to look at me, frowned and, very theatrically, checked his watch. Big Cyril, I noted, had short stocky legs, and as he swaggered away back into school, his long arms swung loose at his sides. With his dominant glare and balding pate, I suspected strongly that a sly peek at his broad back would have revealed a thick silver mane.

9

'Wipe it, *pencil*-penis!'

I frowned, 'Shona, students don't insult each other in my class.'

'Sorry sir.' she looked away from Paul, the allegedly slim-todgered object of her derision, and went back to her work.

Paul muttered to himself, I looked at the paper ball he'd been about to throw and nodded in the direction of the bin. He smiled sneakily, drew back his arm to lob it in, but I shook my head and he stood up and walked to the bin, dropped it in and went back to his desk.

There's an argument that says that if a student can do reasonably well in a bog-standard secondary school, that's equivalent to doing *very* well at a high-flying grammar school.

Well, I'm not sure if it equates academically – having an excuse as to why you don't know stuff isn't the same as actually *knowing* it – but I do think that it gives you skills that serve you well through life; being able to study in a behavioural shit-storm, just having the ability to focus on something while the world around is in meltdown, that's got to be useful if you become, I don't know, a politician or a phone-monkey or something. But, as some sort of spurious argument for the defence of low-achieving schools it's hollow because you could argue equally that schools like this teach a lot of kids that you can get away with just about any level of bad behaviour and no one will ever stop you, in fact they'll probably be nicer to you. And they rapidly learn that being stubbornly stupid is a useful negotiating ploy, and that if things get *really* bad, you'll actually get more attention from people whose job it is to clear up the mess you make.

So the *Tom Brown's Schooldays* model of learning through adversity doesn't work too well here, though for those who can endure, and learn, this place provides some useful life-lessons.

But generally, I'm not totally convinced of the practical usefulness of equating moderate achievement in a shit situation with raging success elsewhere.

Courage under fire, it's not.

However, some kids seem immune to the slings and arrows of outrageous behaviour that fly around the typical bog-standard class. Shona is one of them.

A tiny, freckled girl, she sits in class generally ignoring the stupid comments that fly around, and she puts quiet effort into completing every task she's set, she smiles when I speak to her, and if one of the boys tries to disparage her, she nails them with some sharp response, usually containing a visual description of the person she's attacking suffixed by the word 'penis'. Like the one she just made to Paul.

So, mainly, they leave her alone; she's one of them, she wears the same clothes, speaks the same dialect, has the same phone. But she wants to work; it's her default setting, this quiet concentration, and the other kids accept this in the same way that they accept outbursts, paper planes and the despairing shouts of the teacher. They accept that little Shona just gets on with stuff without being told.

But it's unusual and it intrigues me.

So when the lesson ends I spend a few minutes looking at her work, checking her target grades; this class is set four of five and looking at the quality of her work indicates that she doesn't deserve to be here. I muse that, notwithstanding the occasional smart retort, her generally quiet and docile approach to learning, combined with her chav-ish appearance, has meant she is overlooked, and that she's been left to stew in this low-ability set. I decide that I want her moved up, to set three or even two.

If this means the class is diminished through her absence then that's OK. Anyway, on the good-news front, I've managed to skive off last lesson in order to do some last-minute rehearsals for the panto.

And here's the good news; I get paid to do it!

12.44am – Room 101

With fifteen minutes before the next lesson, I paused to check my lunchtime text from Joe:

m-k j.

Which, roughly translated, means he's not been involved in any life-threatening events, hasn't been permanently excluded from his primary school for head-butting his teacher (though I'm not sure that's an exclusion offence any more) and isn't in the hands of terrorists, religious fundamentalists or radical educationalists.

All of which you probably *can* find in schools up and down the country, I reflect.

With a rehearsal 'til about half six, I text back;

> Gran will pick you up.
> See you at home.

On principle, I write it out in full.

I'm still racking my brains, trying to come up with a sentence that will require use of a semi-colon or parenthesis when I'm interrupted by the sound of whimpering coming from behind the filing cabinets. So I press the green button and switch off my phone. I'm one of about four people, out of the thousand or so in this school, who bother to turn off their phones during school hours.

Halfway up the half-staircase there's a veranda above the main foyer where a number of filing cabinets stand, and it's there that I find Toad, squashed in between two cabinets, body twisted away, face looking at the wall, and he's weeping.

Toad is one of those characters who you quickly get to know when you begin working at a new school; he isn't blessed with intelligence, good looks or a winning personality; he's a pain most days; he's a runner and he's a liar.

But there's a gentleness about him, a feebleness almost, that is endearing. And he's inserted himself in this small space and he's crying quietly. And I can't walk away from whatever it is that has driven him there.

I walk over to the cabinets, lean against one of them, and say to him, 'Hello, *Thomas*, you in trouble again?'

He sees me but doesn't look at me. 'This place is full of freaks,' he says, between sobs. His eyes are full, and he's in pain and he looks like a wild animal, trapped and uncomprehending.

I stand there for a moment or two longer; he says to me, 'Mrs Robson *hates* me,' and launches into a story about how it wasn't his fault, and how he got blamed and how he's going to get his revenge and…well, he's full of bile and venom, but it's of a particularly inoffensive strain. I wait for the tirade to end and then ask, 'Do you want to come downstairs and help me do a job? I'm going to the library.'

He rubs his eyes, nods.

'I've got some photocopying to do,' I tell him. 'Panto scripts.'

'You in the pantomime?' he asks with a sly smile.

I nod. 'You want to be in?'

'No way!'

'Well, can you watch the machine for me while I go and run a couple of messages.'

'OK,' he replies.

We go downstairs, walk along to the library, and he sits on a chair while I load up the machine; I press copy and say, 'Switch off the machine when it's finished will you?'

He nods.

Then I go for a walk, pop in the staffroom, check my mail box to see if there are any missives from the Government, local education authority or Big Cyril.

None.

Good.

But there's a letter from a school telling me I *haven't* got an interview at James Reed Technology College and sixth Form Centre.

I bin that.

I return to the library a few minutes later to find Toad refilling the machine with paper.

'Ran out?' I ask.

He nods. 'But I asked Merlene for some paper,' he tells me as he fills it up. I watch him to make sure he's doing it right but don't interfere. His eyes are red but no longer tearful.

He slams shut the paper tray and looks at me.

'Press the Copy button,' I suggest. He does, and the machine burps into life with a whoosh.

'You should get a job as a photocopy technician,' I tell him.

He looks at me as though to say, *yeah*, and I say, 'Really, people do that; it's a real job.'

He says, 'People do some strange jobs then.'

Tell me about it, I think.

The bell goes for period four and, for me, that means two hours off timetable to rehearse for the panto.

2.45pm – School Hall

Sarah shakes her head disapprovingly; 'You *haven't* learned your lines, Mr Ken.' The other cast members on stage beside me, word-perfect twelve- and thirteen-year-olds the lot of them, titter and nudge each other.

Despite my initial misgivings, pantomime rehearsals are not too demanding, and the combination of dress rehearsals plus the offer of doing a performance at a local primary means I'll get a couple of days off lessons. The only fly in the ointment is the fact that I simply cannot remember my lines.

I've tried reading through them last thing before bed; I've tried learning a page at a time; I've tried repeating each individual line thirty times, in the belief that if you do something thirty times it becomes ingrained.

No good.

I'm useless.

Oh, I can shriek like a panto dame, I can spout risqué jokes, sing badly and appear outraged on cue. I can get a laugh from the other members of the cast.

But only with the script in my hand.

As I pause, mid-scene, to glance at my script, I see Sarah shake her head sadly.

Three weeks left to learn the script…and I've discovered I have a learning difficulty.

Wednesday, Parents' Evening – School Hall

'I'm not really persuading you, am I?'

Tara's mother fixed me with an unimpressed, mildly dismal, stare; 'No. I'm afraid you're not.'

'I'm sorry I can't help you more on this.'

She stood up, said goodbye, and left.

The problem is, Tara's mother has unrealistic expectations about what her child can achieve in a school like this. Actually, she has *very realistic* expectations.

I'm trying to explain that Tara will still do well, so long as she works hard for the next couple of years, but she's not buying it. She's not buying our behaviour policy, our academic record or any of the other stuff I've been selling her for the last fifteen minutes. And she's right not to.

The other problem is that Tara's mother really didn't want her in this school in the first place, she wanted her to attend St Cuthbert's, the recently built faith school situated about five miles away. Most decent parents don't mind that their kids have to carry bibles, and they really don't mind about the 'two-inch rule' on skirt hemlines (FYI: that's a minimum of two-inches below the knee). The important thing is that, Religious Education, History and Geography lessons notwithstanding, St Cuthbert's gives a decent education, and the kids get excellent exam results.

This is because they have good discipline. When they have a kid who does misbehave, they chuck them out. And usually these excluded kids filter down to schools like ours.

But, to be fair, all the bright kids in the region go to St Cuthbert's. But Tara didn't get in. She's bright enough, and her mum's affluent enough, but they're a single-parent family, and that's a bit frowned upon up at St Cuthbert's. In a 50/50 situation, St Cuthbert's will go for the brightest kid. The religious kid. The well-behaved kid. And the nuclear family.

Tara only scores two out of four.

I'm almost finished with parent's evening; it's been fairly quiet. At a grammar school, all the parents turn up; they have questions, complaints, expectations; some even have bar charts.

At a parents' evening at Thatcham Grange, one parent sat down and opened his laptop. 'Look,' I said, 'Shouldn't we just chat a bit first? Discuss the big picture?'

'Just have a look at these predicted grades,' he replied. 'Tell me where you think you've gone wrong.'

But at Bog Standard, two thirds of the parents don't seem to turn up. And those who have arrived don't seem to ask too many probing questions. Apart from Tara's mum, who is right and, quite rightly, doesn't accept my party-line bullshit.

I take advantage of a parent-free lull to take an official-looking letter out of my regulation schoolteacher's battered leather briefcase; I'd discovered this letter lying at the back of my pigeonhole, scrunched between two flyers and an invitation to become a GCSE marker. I tear it open. The letterhead informs me it is from River View Arts College, a decent secondary school situated about eight miles from here; as its title indicated, it specialised in art, music, drama and theatre but, unlike Bog Standard Technology College, which wasn't very technological, River View did exactly what it said on the tin.

'Dear Mr Keane...' it began. I scanned it excitedly, looking for the punchline...*application* blah blah...*interview* blah blah...*23rd November* blah blah...

What?

My scanning screeched to a cartoon halt. I went back to the date of the interview.

23rd November.

Bollocks. I'd missed it.

It looked like the last of the parents had dispersed and I began to quietly pack my bag; the pantomime begins next week and I'd like to spend at least an hour, for at least a couple of evenings, with my son before he goes to sleep. It seems like he's spending all of his time with his Aunt Lindsey.

'Hiya!'

I looked up from my half-packed briefcase to see a small, spiky-haired, lip-studded, generously tattooed woman smiling across the table at me.

And by her side was Carl.

Fat Carl.

Ginger Carl.

Angry Carl.

'Hello,' I replied, and smiled at Carl.

Carl frowned.

'I'm Carl's mum...' she said. 'How's the little bastard doing?'

10

Friday, 9.02pm – Pantomime – Backstage

I'm sitting backstage wearing pancake make-up, false eyelashes, a wig, Day-Glo-striped stockings, and a yellow and pink dress that features a huge bustle.

I've got my script in my hand and I feverishly read through each scene until the moment I go on.

Feverish is an appropriate word. I'm feeling ill. The low-level but manageable ill-health I've suffered from for the last two months has chosen the final night of the school panto to take a turn for the worse.

I can barely speak. I'm wobbly. I'm drinking a cocktail of Diet Coke and Night-Nurse from a plastic bottle.

Fortunately my hoarse, croaky whisper sounds sufficiently dame-like to get a few laughs on its own. And when I get to stand centre-stage, take my fake bosoms in both hands and sing 'We're a Couple of Swells' it goes down well. On those frequent occasions when I did forget my lines and Sarah shouts them in a stage whisper from the side, the audience are so amused by my dramatic uselessness that they've begun applauding my mistakes, or shouting out the lines on my behalf.

'I knew that line!' I shout back at one point, to a tumultuous round of applause.

I turn to the audience, 'I did! I did!'

The final performance ends, as they always do, to mass applause, a huge bouquet for Sarah and bottles of wine for adult performers.

'Well done, bro,' Lindsey tells me after the show. She's brought Joe backstage, along with her own two sprogs, Matt and Chris.

The performers are dispersing and the manic energy that kept me going through two hours is dispersing too. Lindsey watches me disrobe. 'You look like shit,' she says, wiping the pancake from my face.

'Thanks,' I reply.

Sarah, sitting on a chair opposite, drinking wine from a paper cup, concurs, 'You do too,' and then she asks Lindsey, 'Is he yours?'

Lindsey turns up her nose, '*No*. Just my brother.'

'So he's still on the market?' Sarah asks Lindsey.

'On the shelf more like.'

'Do you mind if I have a go at him some time?'

Lindsey shakes her head, 'Be my guest.'

I look at them both. 'Hey, I'm still here you know.'

Sarah tells me, 'Go home, Danny, you look ill.' Then she says, 'Give me a call sometime. When you feel better. We'll go out.'

Thursday morning, with a mixture of reluctance and justified relief, I rang in to say I was sick and wouldn't be in for a couple of days.

And so, a week before Christmas, I only got half pay. And while I was convalescing I received a letter from Big Cyril asking me if I'd consider working there for another term.

Here we go again, I thought.

Bainbridge Avenue – Sofa – Convalescing

As part of my convalescence, Joe and I were sitting at home, on our lime-green 1980s sofa, watching *Scrubs*. He's at that age where TV programmes are really, really interesting, and he was engrossed. Most of the programmes on the Disney channel feature semi-dysfunctional families whose issues usually get resolved by the end of the programme via arguments, pratfalls and a spot of soul-searching.

Joe gets a kick out of watching these families struggle. Plus he thinks angry people are funny.

'Do all teachers get divorced?' Joe asked.

'No, silly,' I told him, rubbing his head. 'It's not like a *rule* or anything.'

'You and mum did.'

'We weren't very happy, Joe. Plus we're not quite divorced yet.'

'Was it me?' he asked, ignoring my hair-splitting.

'No,' I smiled at him, but inside I felt quite odd, 'it wasn't you.'

'Was it because you were both teachers then?'

I shook my head. 'Mum's an educational psychologist. She lives with a teacher now. You remember Paul?'

He looked back at the TV programme. 'This is the best bit Dad, *look*.'

One of the *Scrubs* characters was dressed up like a WWF wrestler and was acting very, very angry.

This put Joe into fits of laughter.

Later we were eating tea and he brought up the subject again, saying, 'I'd never marry a teacher.'

'Don't speak while you chew.'

He swallowed theatrically.

I asked, 'Why won't you marry a teacher then?'

'You're all rubbish at being married,' he said, adding, 'Miss Hall got divorced last year too. And her baby is only one year old!'

Miss Hall is Joe's teacher.

Joe was six years old when his mum left so, to him, being in a similar situation at the age of just one year old, it sort of makes Joe an elder statesman.

'Are you going to advise Miss Hall on what to do?' I asked.

He shook his head. 'No. Teachers never listen to advice.' He looked at me and smiled: 'Do you?'

I leaned over and kissed him on the forehead. 'Nope. Too busy dishing it out.'

Last Day of Term – Room 101

Today is the final day before the Christmas break and I have tutor time with 11*Fick;* we're supposed to be discussing 'Citizenship', or something, but I've given up trying to teach this topic because Chantelle Brown has brought her baby boy into school to show off to her friends. I'm not sad to abandon 'Citizenship' and, it appears, neither is the class. Lessons abort for an endless variety of reasons; a fight, snow falling outside, crap teachers, a wasp in the classroom. All are guaranteed to destroy classroom equilibrium.

It's Christmas.

And a baby has arrived.

In this neighbourhood, that's *anything* but a miracle.

One of the most obvious career moves for an under-educated, unskilled working-class girl is to have a baby. So, for probably the only time in her life, Chantelle is ahead of the game, and she's determined to enjoy her temporarily elevated status. The child is wrapped in soft clothes and a powder-blue blanket; he is asleep and his expression is angelic. Perfect. Chantelle herself glows.

I ponder the latest Government-issued statistics that tell us that girls like Chantelle are unlikely to develop meaningful skills or get decent careers, and will probably remain on benefits until such time as her child leaves school.

I looked at Chantelle, plump-cheeked, pink-skinned and healthy; doing exactly what Mother Nature intended her to do at this age. Maybe we're missing something, I thought. And maybe, on some primordial level, Chantelle has already voted with her feet.

'He's called Daniel,' she told me as I watched the girls pass him round.

'Nice name.'

They stroked baby Daniel's face, cooed over his downy hair, his clothes. Even some of the lads paid attention to him. Oddly, Beth Kendall and a couple of her friends paid little attention to

Chantelle and child. I'm not sure if it was a competitive thing or whether Beth simply didn't approve of the whole baby-mother thing.

Teri, the girl who'd offered me a fruit pastille on my first day at Bog Standard, chatted at length with Chantelle, asking her the details of how she coped with the demands of parenthood.

'My mum helps a lot,' she said.

'And do you feed him yourself?'

Aware of the mixed audience, Chantelle nodded, shyly.

'Ouch,' Teri said.

'Do it now!' one of the lads says eagerly, but two or three girls hit him across the head and he shut up, red-faced.

The lesson is aborted so I don't even attempt to stop some of the kids who are listening to their iPods, texting each other, or using their phones to film the baby, though I frown when someone throws a paper ball across the class.

As the boys chat and the girls coo I wander about and make some end-of-term effort to tidy up room 101 while the class enjoy this welcome, and hopefully permanent, break in teaching and learning.

When Chantelle eventually leaves the room to show off to some friends in another class, I allow a couple of girls to accompany her, and I have no inclination to make the rest of these proto-adults complete their worksheets on 'Citizenship III – Cultural Diversity in the Workplace.'

'Let's watch a video,' I tell them.

'Sir, you are *sweet*.'

'Thank you Mr Murphy.'

'You're most welcome Sir.' Murphy likes to talk; he says, 'I've got a copy of *Evil Dead II* in my bag, if you want to borrow it.'

'Thanks, but no.' I slide a DVD of my own into the slot in my laptop. A moment later the image flickers clearly onto the whiteboard screen.

'Mr Ken, can I take this opportunity to wish you a Merry

Christmas and a prosperous New Year?' Murphy says to me, somewhat formally.

I pause, look at him and say, 'Well thank you again. May I wish the same to you and yours.'

He nods, leans over, proffers his hand. We shake.

Paul Craig leans over too. 'All the best Sir,' he tells me as we too shake hands.

'You too.'

Charlene complains, 'It's stuck on *Pause*! Press Play Mr Ken!'

'Mr *Keane*,' I correct her. Then I press Play.

They're happy.

A half-hour later, the bell rings and they're leaving the room, some of them wishing me a Merry Christmas but most of them just piling out of the door as quickly as they can; I watch them go, thinking that this is their last Christmas as school pupils. Once again, I wonder what we've taught them.

Only Teri pauses at the door; she asks, 'Well, Mr *Keane*. Have you enjoyed your term with us?

I nod, smile and tell her, 'Yes. I *have* enjoyed it.'

She giggles, 'We're not as bad as you thought?'

'Worse.'

'Aww. Would you like a fruit pastille?' she offers, opening her bag.

I shake my head.

'Merry Christmas, then.'

'You too Teri.'

She leaves the room.

Then I'm sitting alone in my classroom.

My classroom.

And I'm not thinking about what I've taught them, but what they've taught me.

We st Bognor Technolo gy College

Student Syndrome of the week ODD – Oppositional Defiant Disorder

11

Sunday – Bainbridge Avenue

'Watch this kick, Dad!'

I'm waching Joe in the new footy strip he got for Christmas, kicking a ball around the street. Like all seven-year-old boys, Joe is obsessed with football. And last year's World Cup didn't help. Much like everyone else, I enjoy watching tournaments, hoping that *this time* we get to stuff Johnny Foreigner in a penalty shoot-out, but in general I don't get it; this obsession with blokes kicking a ball. OK, it's fun to have the odd game with your pals, but I don't understand the *obsession* people have with it. Besides, I'm reliably informed that people pay real money to attend football matches.

I have this theory that being good at football, being *really* good, for a boy at least, is like being absolutely beautiful if you're a girl. It's a gimme; a get-out-of-jail-free card. You simply don't *need* to be good at anything else. But most of us realise at some point that we're not particularly beautiful, or that we're pretty useless at footy, so we develop personalities to compensate.

Despite his enthusiasm, Joe is hopeless at football. He can't kick, can't dribble, can't tackle. Can't throw in. He usually doesn't even know which direction his team is playing. I take this to indicate that when he's older, he'll be smart, funny and a great conversationalist.

First Day back School Hall

'...*eight domains... Collapsed into an umbrella... consensus... edict... hiatus...*' The speaker was Tom, a stringy, bearded, educational psychologist. He read from his notes in a low monotone voice that invited everyone to mentally switch off within the first five minutes. He'd been talking for two hours.

Tom paused to make some smirking reference to a former minister for education that was supposed to bring us on-side. Or on-message. Or, well, I really don't know.

Whatever it was, we didn't.

If I'd wanted to endure an all-day party political broadcast on behalf of the Ineffectual Party I'd have subscribed to the *Wishy-Washy* channel. But instead I was learning to empathise with the youth, and, '*bearing in mind the practical truth of Bakunin's dictum*,' share their pain and anger.

Today was a Staff Training Day.

'Prozac by Powerpoint,' Judy calls it.

First day back after Christmas and the teaching staff of Bog Standard were seated in rows on plastic chairs in the main hall listening to a man who didn't teach, and whose children didn't go to state schools, tell us how to do our job. Time that could have been profitably spent planning, marking or just sitting in the staffroom complaining (*reflecting*, as it's known) was being criminally wasted listening to a smug, overconfident and, worst of all, non-teaching representative of the DfES explaining how, if we could only empathise with the underclass, we would be able to teach them better. No one asked if it was possible to make them *learn* better. Because it wasn't.

Like some hippy throwback, a relic of the 1960s, Tom patiently explained that violence is '*simply a learned cultural response that, through the provision of viable behavioural alternatives...*' and so on.

And so on.

And *so* on.

I tried to pay attention, I really did, but my stomach was rumbling. The school had committed the worst crime imaginable, they'd arranged a staff training day and not provided morning coffee. Or biscuits!

'...*and after completing your on-line SEF, simply hyper-link to your ECM, allowing you to work out the necessary provision. Then contact your LEA Inclusion Consultant...*'

My thoughts drifted to that day in November when I'd been on bus duty, and a hail of alco-pop bottles had suddenly rained down on staff and students from the trees over the road. 'It's just high spirits,' I'd been reassured later, as I turned my half-forgotten first-aid training to good use, applying compression to the small but deep flesh wound of a year eight girl.

'...*morphing the SEBS/SEAL into three waves... the Danish model...*'

I thought of the boys who returned to class after lunch, red-eyed and giggling from the weed they'd smoked, sleepy, quietly snacking on Mars Bars and chocolate digestives. And how I didn't bother to report them because

a) nothing would be done and

b) I didn't really mind because, to be honest, they were better behaved.

'...*workface reform agenda...*'

Workface? I flicked through the booklet. I counted all 101 pages of wisdom, wit, advice and website references.

'...*the tolerance of ambiguity...*' the speaker droned, '...*and note the golden triangle* within *the circle*,' he then advised.

Hello, I thought, we've gone all Pagan; perhaps we'll simply burn the bad behaviour out of the kids, but no.

'*diagnostic tests of construction,* not *destruction...*'

Then I heard a trumpet blast. Tom smiled as he held aloft a small electronic gizmo: 'That is the signal for lunch,' he told us. I looked over to Judy who had muttered, 'Thank Christ for that,' rather too loudly.

'When the trumpet blasts again...' Tom was waving his gizmo.

'Let's hope it's judgment day,' she interrupted again.

'... it will be time to resume the session,' he confirmed. But all I could think was Coffee! Biscuits!

Wahey!

After a couple of mugs of intellectual relief, I popped into my classroom. Looking up at a poster of Ant 'n' Dec that I'd stuck on the wall in a vain attempt to add a touch of levity to the atmosphere, I whispered a prayer: I'm a teacher... well, you can guess the rest.

There was still no luck on the interview front.

Back in the staffroom, people were hanging around, seemingly reluctant to re-enter the hall and have to endure more of Tom's self-help insight and wisdom. Jimmy the Caretaker was busy taking down the Christmas decorations and disposing of the empty bottles of good cheer and contraband confiscated from the year elevens and subsequently drunk by the teaching staff on the last afternoon of term. The corridors and rooms felt bare and quiet, contemplative even, without the noise of the energised hordes of teenagers who are usually racing around shrieking.

They'll be back tomorrow, no doubt dressed in brand-new Berghaus and Sprayway jackets, phones welded to their ear, accompanied by the bling-bling of cheap gold jewellery hanging from their wrists and necks.

I settle down to spend the final five minutes before I have to go back into Tom's 'personal-learning-arena' having occupied the only spare comfy chair in the staffroom; I pick up and start flicking through some brochures. Not the educational pamphlets that tell me about the latest classroom-management courses that are available (chair and a whip, anyone?), but the holiday brochures telling me where I can escape to when the sun returns, sometime after mid-June.

Vic Hughes is sitting at one of the bank of computers that

the management have had installed in the staffroom over the holidays, 'You know what this means?' he asks me, pointing at the PCs.

I look up from a brochure, quizzically.

'It means that Big Cyril and the rest of the senior management team don't actually have to set foot out of their offices ever again; instead they'll just email us constantly on trivial subjects while avoiding the nasty business of actually walking around, showing the students who's in charge.'

'Yeah, but if they did that,' I say, 'they would have to acknowledge the fact that they're *not* in charge. And then they'd be forced to deal with it.'

Vic nods vigorously; he loves this sort of talk and I'm happy to humour him, if not to actually stir him up into outright rebellion. But he's right, and he's an excellent teacher, which completely forgives his tendency to complain.

And to be honest, being able to teach is the *only* yardstick that we use to measure each other by.

Can you teach?

It's the gold standard.

You got a PhD in educational psychology? Great. But can you control a difficult class? And make them learn?

You're an Ofsted Inspector? Very good. Well done. Now do you want to show me how well *you* teach?

I've been here just over a term now, and though I've had one or two wobbles, I think I've proved I can teach. The first term, I decided that my job was to make sure Judy's job wasn't made any harder. This term, I feel better placed to do a half-decent job of educating young people. In the distance I hear the trumpet blast of Tom the Guru's gizmo, calling all teachers back to the 'learning-arena'.

Friday, 10.43am – Room 101

'What did you get for Christmas?' I ask one of my year sevens.

'A new mobile. Plus a Berghaus. And Rockports. But the phone, that was my main present.'

I ask a few more kids and the answer is the same every time. 'Put your hands up if you got a new mobile phone for Christmas,' I ask them. Every one of them puts up their hand.

The first days back after Christmas sees the kids at Bog Standard bedecked in sportswear from head to toe; no matter that the school uniform is clearly stated in the glossy pamphlet given to all new pupils and staff, the kids wear their new Adidas and Nike over, under and often in place of their uniform. The girls, of course, are bedecked in low-carat gold jewellery and absolutely everyone has a new mobile phone. They'd be bullied if they didn't.

Charlie lists his presents proudly: 'iPod, new phone, new bike, laptop, clothes, a keeper ring.' He lifts his hand to show me the eight-ounce ring he's got wrapped around his middle finger.

Charlie gets a couple of grand's worth of presents. I spent less than two hundred pounds on Joe.

I remember reading an article in one of the broadsheets that said that transient and insecure cultures tend to display their wealth; it's portable and it's instantly recognisable as a badge of worth. On the other hand, settled cultures invest their wealth, there's no need to put your wealth on display – everyone you know knows your worth and, to some degree or other, values your presence.

West Bognor used to be a pit village, steeped in Methodist values of sobriety, hard work and cleanliness. Now? It's steeped in cheap gold and sportswear and brim-full of kids like Charlie.

I know, from reading the behavioural reports, that Charlie's step-dad won't allow him into the living room at home. When he returns from school he goes straight to his bedroom where, usually, his mum brings up his tea while he's watching

Neighbours. He spends most evenings playing video games or sitting in chat-rooms.

During the holidays he stays with his gran.

2.03 pm

'Dan, can I ask you to do me a big favour?'

Big Cyril is at the staffroom door and he's waving me over; I go to him and he explains the situation: 'We've got a supply teacher in Maths who has just walked out; she's refusing to teach a GCSE class who've been horrible to her; chairs thrown about, swearing, threats of sexual violence.'

'The usual,' I say.

He nods and continues, 'Do you think you could you pop in there and settle them down a bit?'

11*Fick* are doing their work experience this week and I have a free lesson.

I stop myself from asking him why Cyril, a senior member of staff, doesn't do the cover lesson himself and then I remember that he's a senior manager and that's a sure sign he doesn't like being in the classroom. I also remember my temporary contract; Christmas was expensive and I have an overdraft that isn't going away if I become unemployed.

Besides, I've had two weeks off work and am feeling fresh and in need of a challenge.

Plus, after yesterday's training session, I'm all fired-up to employ the three E's – Empathy, Excellence and, er, Ecstasy.

But despite these, I'm not sure if I'm any good at dealing with riots. Not with a class I don't know. In a classroom where they have already established control.

I walk along to the maths area; there is currently only one full-time maths teacher in the school, the others having left for new jobs, retired and not been replaced, or just gone on the sick.

It's loud when I walk into room 71; I recognise a few kids,

and smile 'Hello,' as I put my paperwork on the desk. They go a bit quiet. Sometimes you impose order on a class, sometimes you negotiate. Sometimes you just go with what works.

'You lot need any help?' I ask. There a few murmurs. 'We don't know what we're doing,' one of them tells me.

'Why is that?'

'The teacher can't control us,' one suggests.

'Do you think that, perhaps, you might be a bit responsible for that?'

Someone says 'no' and another says, 'It's your job to control us!' but generally they seem more listless, more *pissed off*, than angry.

I say, 'Look, I've got a free lesson now, and 'cos you lot have frightened off the supply, I'm going to have to sit here with you and keep an eye on you.'

'You don't have to!'

I nod, sadly, 'I'm afraid I do.' I point to a wodge of forms I've been filling in,

'And look at these. Reports. Some of them are *your* reports. Due in on Thursday. So if you will do your best to get on with your work I can sit here and get on with mine. OK?'

The class settle down.

Grudgingly, they begin to work. I look at their names in the mark book; they're a top set, targeted with grade Cs most of them, one or two higher than that. They haven't had a regular teacher for two terms. I'm surprised that they acquiesced so easily.

Perhaps because it's their first day back they haven't worked themselves into a total frenzy yet. And with it being before lunch most of them probably haven't eaten yet. With the younger classes, lesson three, the lesson after break, sees them arrive all sugared up and super hyper. The older kids, girls especially, are schooled in the art of starvation and, the lesson before lunch, they're often more listless than wired-up.

Nevertheless I allow myself to feel OK about my growing ability to control a class in this school. Fifteen minutes later the door crashes open to announce the arrival of Mr Sweet. 'You can go,' he tells me with a grim smile that never manages to stop being a frown. I pick up my paperwork and leave the room.

As I walk back along the corridor to the staffroom I hear Mr Sweet's voice, shouting, telling them exactly what would happen if there was ANY REPEAT OF THIS SORT OF BEHAVIOUR...

...the rest of his tirade is drowned by the bell.

I reflected on a few things. Firstly, they deserved it, really, being told off by Mr Sweet. Just because they'd been OK with me, it didn't excuse their behaviour with the supply teacher. But, secondly, they deserved better than what we supplied them with – I couldn't really fault their being restless.

But thirdly, more prosaically, I knew they would think fondly of me, at least in comparison to Mr Sweet... and that could give me a bit of leverage for the future.

2.22pm

Even the bad boys around here are clueless.

I quietened the class and introduced the topic for our Citizenship Tutorial – 'Equality and Respect in Relationships' – which is as scintillating a read as it sounds.

Mikey, a fat, surly boy with badly cut hair, shouted out, 'I don't need to read this. I don't need to know about multi-cultural equality in my relationships with a woman, because I'm going to be a pimp!'

I smiled at him, in the way a teacher really shouldn't smile at a clueless fat boy. 'What?' I spoke with gentle sarcasm, 'You're going to persuade young women to fall in love with you and then, *because* they're so besotted with your good looks, your charm and your persuasive manner, they're going to go around sleeping with perfect strangers for money? And *then* they're going to hand over that money to you?'

Mikey's gaze shifted nervously around at the class, aware of the hate-filled glares coming from the girls, any one of whom could have torn him limb from limb, either physically or verbally. 'Er, yeah.'

'Dream on, sackless.' Cherelle hissed.

'Cherelle, we don't abuse each other in my class,' I told her.

'The only abuse he gets is from himself,' Chantelle muttered.

I stifled a laugh.

Mikey countered, 'Well, I'll be a drug dealer!'

Inwardly I groaned, but I was determined to attempt to shed some light on the fallacies that lay behind his dreams so I asked him, 'Let me get this straight. You, Mikey, at fifteen years old, are going to enter into business with brutal career criminals. You're going to be buying and selling class A drugs from men who carry guns and knives, men who *excel* in the use of violence? You're going to successfully avoid the attentions of the police, and the associated risk of long-term jail sentences, and not only are you going to survive in this world, you're going to *thrive*?'

He nodded vigorously. '*And* I'll be driving a Porsche.'

I looked past him at the class, glared again at the poster of Ant 'n' Dec – 'You're supposed to get me out of here!' I groaned, inwardly.

Like they tell you on those adverts for teachers that get shown on TV, you know, the ones with the urban jazz music and the cool monochrome images and the voiceover by Ewan Macgregor or someone, teaching is never boring.

12

Friday, 12.34pm – Staffroom

The Wenkel brothers are still in school, despite their being caught dealing marijuana again. Apparently the Governors decided that the quantities were small, 'for personal use only', and the fact that they were selling it was mitigated by their being refugees from the Czech Republic.

'How can you be a refugee from the Czech Republic?' Mick from the PE department asked, as we sat in the staffroom during lunch. 'It's really nice there, and it's part of the EU. People go on their *holidays* to the Czech Republic. What are they seeking refuge from?'

Tim, lead-learning assistant in the 'Cuddle Club', the guy the kids call 'Crazy Frog', explained, 'They suffer persecution from the authorities because, as Romanies, they're labelled as thieves and criminals.'

Mick shook his head; 'Those two *are* thieves and criminals.'

'But they're Romanies,' Crazy Frog responds, as though this is a defence.

Which, I suppose, it is.

Tuesday, 10.08am – Room 101

'Isn't he cute!'

'Aww, little sweet-pea!'

A year seven runner was standing by the door, holding out a sheet of paper; he'd brought me a message, which informed me to read out the following instructions to the class. And now he was being barracked.

'Leave him alone,' I told the girls, who were continuing to make comments about the little runner. 'He *is* cute,' I conceded, 'but that doesn't allow you to embarrass him.' I rubbed his hair and said, 'Get lost. I can take it from here.'

'I need my sheet back,' he said defiantly.

'Well wait around until I'm finished reading it out.'

I'd recently developed a guttural sound effect, halfway between 'Hey!' and 'Hoy!' that reminded me of the grunt made by Mr Miyagi when training the Karate Kid.

'Ouy!' I said, and the class gradually looked toward me. 'Here is A Message. From Ms Hopwood, deputy head of this school, so LISTEN!' I scanned the message, which was about half a page long, and decided to summarise; 'You may be aware that it has been snowing.'

Five kids run to the windows. I grunt 'Ouy!' and they return to their desks. 'It says here,' I continue, in my normal non-Miyagi voice, 'if you want to throw snowballs, do it on the school field, *Not in The Yard.*'

'I like throwing snowballs in the yard.'

'Well don't,' I said, 'Or you will be disciplined.'

'What does that mean?'

I shrugged, tempted to say *nothing,* but instead repeated, 'You will be disciplined. So don't throw snowballs in the yard, or at staff cars. Ms Hopwood will be on duty to ensure that you all comply with this instruction.' I gave the runner back his note and he left the room accompanied by various comments from the year tens.

At lunchtime I was walking toward the staffroom when I spied Miriam Hopwood returning from her yard duty, covered in the evidence of a full and thorough snowballing attack.

Miriam is the new deputy head with specific charge of the pastoral side of school life; Miriam is a committed Christian who believes in showing the kids unconditional love, sharing her liberal values, and giving everyone a second chance.

She was drenched.

She was a white-out.

She looked defeated. I thought she might cry.

But she didn't notice me as she passed, ice dripping from her unkempt hair, shivering as she shook snow from her collar. Her skin was pinked where, it appeared, she had taken a full-force snowball to the forehead.

She peeled off her coat, unfurled her scarf, and gave both of them a good shake, and then she went into her office, closing the door behind her, leaving a puddle of melted ice on the floor below the sign that said 'My Door Is Always Open'.

With a sharp click, I heard her door lock shut.

I was tempted to go and knock and ask her if she was OK, or just ask her for a new merit stamp or something. Start a conversation. See if she was still breathing.

But I didn't.

Instead I went into the staffroom, logged onto one of the new PCs and checked my mailbox.

Wednesday 12.32pm – Room 101

Grace and Amerie are officially New Best Friends.

It began after October half-term, when Grace joined from another school. Although she is quick-witted, friendly and very bright, Grace is also socially awkward and quite immature.

Amerie on the other hand, is just plain dim. In mitigation, I could use the current terminology and explain that she comes from a 'chaotic' family background.

But the fact is she just isn't very bright.

As two outsiders in a settled class, they gravitated toward each other quite quickly. They began to dress the same, and to mirror each other's behaviour and dysfunctions. In the space of about four weeks, I witnessed Grace ruthlessly dumb herself down; she made herself *stupid* in fact, in order to become friends with Amerie. Her initially good work suffered, her grades went off the scale, she began arriving late for every lesson. Amerie, whose grades were abysmal anyway, and whose behaviour was never good, somehow, and with a huge effort, made herself a teeny little bit brighter. Now, my lessons with this class are regularly punctuated with the two of them arriving late, both wearing fake smiles and apologising; or they'll get all giggly and embarrassed and claim to have women's problems; demanding to be allowed to go to the toilet. Together.

And if I don't let them sit together, they become super-moody and disruptive. Not in a defiant or truculent way, more of a distressed, can't-control-themselves, motherless-child sort of fashion.

Grace's ability to learn has evaporated in the heat of an intense girly friendship. Weirdly, Amerie is doing slightly better than usual.

This thought was in my mind as I wrote a comment on Grace's report the other day: 'Appears to be welded to her best friend's side,' I wrote, 'and this is to the detriment of both students' education.'

Grace immediately went to show the report to Amerie, and they read it together, giggling loudly. Then Amerie approached me with *her* report, still giggling. She asked me, 'Will you write *exactly* the same thing on my report, please?'

1.12pm – School Cafeteria

They tell me that since the school installed the new Fast Food system in our cafeteria (ironically, about two weeks before Jamie began his *School Dinners* programme), the seagulls have become a huge pest. Well, I don't know what they were like before but now, it's after lunch and I'm watching from the staffroom as they scour the yard in packs, or flocks, shrieking, swooping, pecking at waste food, staff and children alike.

The end of lunchtime sees the yard decorated with waste food, blown polystyrene cups and those beige/brown, flip-lid burger boxes that are used once, and then sit in a hole in the ground for the next eleven thousand years.

But the gulls love fast food.

They're all sugared-up.

They're Sugar-Gulls.

These Sugar-Gulls are mimicking the students in becoming obese, truculent, quarrelsome and aggressive. If the gulls keep eating our fast-food leftovers I've no doubt they're going to start wearing cheap jewellery and baseball caps; they'll be listening to chav music on knocked-off iPods, and receiving anti-social behaviour orders. They'll stop flying; instead they'll drive around the yard in souped-up Vauxhall Novas, with huge exhaust systems. Their chicks will be taking Ritalin for behavioural disorders.

Then they'll start claiming invalidity benefits.

Eventually the gulls made their escape, leaving the yard in its original snow-patched, polystyrene-decorated state and I went back into the staffroom. I scanned the notice-board to see if anything interesting was happening.

Nothing.

To the left of the notice-board was our rogues gallery – a pictorial record of our most *challenging* students, pinned up on the wall so that new teachers and supply staff could finger miscreants whose names they might not otherwise know. Most of the pictures appeared to be two or three years out of date and it was hard to reconcile the cherubic images of fresh-faced eleven-year-olds with the snarling reality of their fifteen-year-old selves.

To the right of the notice-board was another gallery – of those students with particular disabilities or vulnerabilities that we should know about. Helen Shields smiled down from her wheelchair. Junior Donkin stared, blurred and wary, at the camera. One young man smiled toothily at someone standing off-stage. The caption told me his name was James Carr and that he was autistic; I'd never actually seen James around school but the caption told me he was in year eight. Harriet Deacon was peering out from her picture.

There was something disarming and utterly vulnerable about these and other images that wouldn't allow me to look away. Junior rarely attended school, Harriet was currently in hospital undergoing more treatment. Helen had elected to be transferred to a special unit just before Christmas.

Friday 2.34pm – Room 101

At the beginning of the citizenship lesson, as Carl gave out the latest worksheets, I was showing 11*Fick* pictures of Joe. 'In ten years a lot of you will have children,' I said.

'*Sir*, some of us have got one already.'

'I know.' Then I said, 'Put your chewing gum in the bin.' I looked at the other students, 'But a lot of the rest of you will have one too, in the next ten or fifteen years.'

'I'll bring mine in to show you.'

'I look forward to it.'

'Not for a few years though. I want to have a good time first.'

I smiled, stood up. 'Oi!' I said, addressing the whole class. 'Carl, give everyone a sheet of lined paper.' I handed him a sheet of paper. 'We're going to write a poem.'

The class broke out in mass groans.

'But you can collect back in those worksheets, Carl, we're not doing citizenship today.'

A cheer, of sorts.

'We're going to write a poem to our future children,' I announced. 'We're going to tell them what our lives are like, what we think *they'll* be like. What our hopes and dreams are.'

I wrote on the whiteboard:

A Poem to my future children

'Put your names on the back of your sheets,' I said. 'Mikey, give out some rulers and coloured pencils. We're going to make these poems look nice.'

It was as if they'd been waiting all year to be told to do this. The chance to engage in a task that meant something to them.

They got stuck in.

With barely a word of explanation or encouragement from me they began scribbling down poems, haikus and odes to their kids, as yet unborn. I walked around the class, offering the odd comment or word of praise.

Mikey wrote a haiku:

> *Be a pimp, like dad*
> *Earn dollars, sweet, and ladees*
> *Dress to p-impress, boy*

'What if it's a girl?' I asked him.

He looked thoughtful for a moment then wrote an alternative end line:

> *Dress like a Primp-cess*

'Primpcess?'

'It's a cross between pimp and princess.'

'I sort of guessed.'

Beth Kendall wrote a short poem, cut it out and glued it onto a sheet of coloured paper, then she spent the rest of the lesson doing her nails.

'Give me a look,' I said.

She held up her hand, nails outward.

'The poem,' I clarified.

'Oh,' and she handed me the poem.

> *I'm sixteen years old*
> *I don't want babies*

I don't know if
They'd ruin me,
or save me

'I'll keep this,' I told her.

'What for?'

'You can come back in ten years and let me know the answer.'

'Alright. I will.'

I had no doubt she would.

Terri had spent the whole lesson writing her poem. Like Beth she'd cut out the verses and stuck them onto a piece of coloured card. She also coloured in the edges and drew cherubim flying at each corner. She wrote:

Dear future children I know I'll be proud
But please don't cry all night or too loud
I'll feed you and love you and bring you up right
And cuddle you if you have bad dreams in the night

Dear future children you know I'll be happy
But I'm not looking forward to changing your nappies
You can sleep in a cot and cuddle your teddy
But wait a few years longer, 'cos I'm not quite ready

As the lesson ended, I collected in the poems feeling quite good about the lesson, all things considered. But as the students left the room, I heard one of them comment, 'Well that was just *bollocks!*'

Nevertheless, I gathered up their poems, dropped them into a plastic folder and filed them away.

I glanced at one short poem:

I do not want brats
They stink and poo and cost money

True, I thought.

8.43pm – Bainbridge Avenue

'She sounds nice.'

'Don't you know that it's rude to read over someone's shoulder?' I replied.

Joe had pushed a chair next to mine and was sitting reading my emails along with me. I think he's trying to fix me up. He reads all of my emails. Vets them, in fact. Scans them carefully for any sign of availability, or suspected keenness on me. Or we'll be sitting having a cup of tea in Sainsbury's and he'll start pointing out suitable life partners for me. 'Go and talk to her, Dad. She'll like you.'

'No. Eat your lunch.'

He'll mutter something. And then he'll eat, but he keeps looking around. He has absolute faith in my ability to attract a mate.

At seven, almost eight, years old, he's developed a specific taste in women; small, curvy and dark-haired. Kind of like Miss Hall, his teacher. I suspect Joe has a crush on Miss Hall. As I reply to an email I add the phrase JOE LOVES MISS HALL to the end of the message.

'*Dad*! Don't say that!' he tells me, embarrassed, and we grapple over the keyboard while he tries to censor me. We end up having a fun fight and I complete my emails later.

I'm applying for jobs.

Dozens of jobs.

Every day, the post brings another application. And every time I complete one, when it comes to the bit where it asks why I left my previous job, I struggle to find a euphemism for 'because my boss was shagging my wife'.

13

Thursday, 12.32pm – Room 101

Peel and Mountford are always fighting.

Sadly for them, but most entertaining for the rest of the class, they're both rubbish at scrapping. So far I've been fortunate that they haven't had a punch-up in tutor time, because that would mean spending a couple of hours filling in a lot of forms and getting all the witnesses to write statements. But they're always niggling at each other. I have to suppress a smile when I see an argument brewing between them.

Apparently, when it comes to blows, Peel always wins. Mountford is even more rubbish at scrapping than Peel.

Today though, toward the end of the lesson, I could see that it was really brewing up between them. They were exchanging muttered insults, generally based around repeated use of the words *your momma*, as they left my room.

As they steppped into the corridor, and without warning, Peel landed an almighty punch onto Mountford's face.

'Hey man,' said Mountford, staggering back, eyes wide in mighty indignation. 'You're supposed to give me a head start!'

12.48pm Staffroom

'See that?' Judy pointed to a double-page spread in the local daily:

St Cuthbert's to receive a £3m grant.

'The bastards are at it again,' she said. The article explained that, due to their academic success, St Cuthbert's was in line for extra funding.

'They get extra money for succeeding,' she told me. 'Whereas we get extra money for failing.'

It pains Judy that St Cuthbert's even exists; I don't know if she's against selection *per se*, I doubt it, she's a grammar-school girl herself, but it pisses her off that the only way we ever get any decent government funding is when we do worse than we did before.

Also, I don't think she approves of the criteria used by St Cuthbert's to select its students.

In the old days you only went to grammar school if you passed an examination; the eleven-plus. If you passed, you went to a grammar school, and you received a good education. If you failed, you went to a secondary school and your education was not as good. But in many ways, the eleven-plus was fair and democratic, measuring you only on your native intelligence. Plus, it gave a bright student from any background the chance to go to a grammar school and receive a good education. So long as you were smart enough to pass, it mattered not what creed, colour or class you were.

Except, of course, that it did.

While middle-class students were trained and prepped for the eleven-plus months beforehand, some inner-city schools didn't even both entering their eleven-year-olds. And girls, whose pass rate was twice that of the boys, were massively discriminated against to ensure that the male/female ratio at grammar schools was roughly 50/50.

Despite all this, middle-class voters recognised instinctively that the problem with the eleven-plus was not that it discriminated, but that it used the wrong criteria to discriminate. Instead of choosing the 'nice' kids, like theirs, it chose the smart ones. These middle-class parents could not accept a system whereby working-class kids, even smart ones, might receive a better education than their own. It was anathema that gymkhana-loving Poppy was not naturally more gifted and intelligent than Bethany, who lived with her unempoyed mum on the nearby estate.

So the Government, under pressure from these voters, and with collusion from the other political parties, who had their own reasons for hating the eleven-plus, brought in the comprehensive school system, whereby all students went to the same school (which would then give them a 'comprehensive' education). But, forty years later, grammar schools are still with us. Their numbers are growing. Only now, they're called 'Faith Schools.'

Ahem.

To the great relief of yummy-mummies throughout the land, what has happened, instead of a truly comprehensive system of education, is that academic rigour has been replaced by social selection. Via postcode and interview, the New Grammar Schools get the middle-class kids they always wanted. No more diamonds in the rough, no more rent-payers with gifted children. No accent-awkwardness or social embarrassment. Just pliant mums 'n' dads with 2.4 children, a Labrador and a mortgage.

Now, the bright working class no longer dream of being scientists; instead they work in call centres, they don't become politicians or cultural leaders, because they don't go to Oxbridge.

The simple fact is, a bright eighteen-year-old from a council estate has less chance of going to Oxford or Cambridge than did their grandparents. But a middle-class student has more. So while there were good reasons for getting rid of grammar schools – the sexism, the stigma of failure, elitism – what we have now is worse. For the majority of young people, 'little chance' of a quality education has been replaced with 'no chance'. Merit has been replaced with money and suitability for a place at one of these high-flying religious grammar schools is often decided by how well you fit a profile drawn up by the wealthy millionaires who fund them. The rest of us, sadly but inevitably, have been lumbered with a comprehensive system in which no one fails and no one really succeeds.

Which sucks, and blows, at the same time.

I looked across at Judy as she re-read the newspaper article. She's taught for over thirty years; she's extremely good at her job and, without her, what remains of the department would fall to pieces.

Teaching is her vocation.

But everything has changed; we are no longer teachers; instead we've become a combination of social worker and data collection programme. The system has betrayed Judy's students and it's betraying her too.

I could see her beginning to wither.

Monday 3.42pm – Room 101

Choosing your kid's name can be high risk; there's a girl in year seven called Summer; Mum should have called her *Drama*, because she cries all the time and she's as miserable as sin.

There's a kid in year eight called, and I'm not joking, *Macho*. He's a wimp.

So calling your son Jet is high risk for a number of reasons. He might have delta-wing ears. He might have a huge and pointy, Concorde-like nose. He might be scared of heights.

But above all, it's a stupid name.

We have a boy in year nine called Jet and, cruelly, he *does* have bat-like ears and an aquiline nose that swoops from just below his Draculine brow to a point slightly below his top lip. His opinion of heights I can't comment on, as there's no way I'd ever do anything as litigiously brave as go on an outdoor activities trip with students.

Jet is also a pain in the arse; he's badly behaved, a lardy liar, a taunter, winder-up and vociferous victim, all rolled into one wheezy, red-faced mummy's-boy. Twice last term Jet called home mid-lesson to complain about being reprimanded by me for misbehaving, or to make accusations of ill-treatment at my hands, that saw his mother, accompanied by Big Cyril, the Deputy Head, standing at my door before the end of the lesson. He smirks at me as I explain to Mum why I made the mistake of attempting to enforce learning on his sensitive brain.

'He was premature, you know,' his mum always manages to explain at some point.

Oh, did I mention that he's as camp as a sugar-coated pink biscuit? The current euphemism thrown about the staffroom is 'has lots of female friends', but that's nowhere near as funny as sugar-coated pink biscuit, is it?

Yesterday, Jet was picking an argument with Stewie Laws. Stewie, unencumbered by notions of political correctness, told him straight: 'Jet, you're fat, you're gay and you've got a stupid name.'

'Sir!' Jet moaned, turning to me, a combination of angst and whinge smeared across his weaselly face, expecting me to intervene on his behalf.

As I paused to consider my reply, I recalled the dozens of lessons that Jet has stalled, disrupted and overturned in the months I've been at the school. I recalled his defiance, his lies, his tell-tale phone calls, his threats and accusations.

At this particular moment I can't be bothered to engage the *doublespeak* function that sits between my brain and my mouth. 'Well, what part of that statement *wasn't* true?' I asked him.

Big Cyril is at my door within seventeen minutes – asking me to fill in one of our yellow statement forms, explaining my comments.

Statement completed, I glanced at my watch, went back into my classroom to get my phone and called Joe's teacher. 'Hello, Jane Hall,' a crisp voice informed me.

'Hi Jane, it's Daniel, Joe's dad. Is he OK?'

'He's fine Dan,' she said, her voice softening, and I pictured her smile and dark hair and her heart-shaped face as I listened.

'I had to stay back anyway,' she said.

'Well, thanks. You've saved my neck. Had to write a statement and get it finished.'

'Fight?'

'No. If I'd only had to wait until the Police Community Support Officers (PCSOs) arrived, I'd have been on time.' Again, I said, 'I'm sorry about keeping you back.'

'We primary school teachers don't get away early like you secondary teachers do.'

'But what about your baby?' I asked, remembering too late that she had her own commitments.

'Millie? Oh, Stuart's got her tonight.'

'Well, thanks for your help. I really don't have a problem with teenage boys insulting each other, but when I get dragged into it the paperwork takes hours to complete. I'll come over for Joe in about twenty minutes,' I said. 'And thanks again.'

'Stop saying thanks,' she said, and then hung up.

The streets were beginning to darken when I got to Joe's school.

I hoped that I'd have to go into Joe's class to fetch him and, maybe, have another chat with the curvy Miss Hall, but he was already running toward the gate when I got there.

He leaped into my arms. 'Hey,' I said, unpeeling his grip and setting him back down. Then I ruffled his hair and asked him how the homework club had been. 'It wasn't the homework club,' he corrected me. 'Just me and Miss Hall. Colouring pictures.'

'Well, come on then,' I said, 'let's get a Big Mac for tea,' and as we walked toward the car I noticed that he was pulling *gangsta* poses; walking with arms folded threateningly, shoulders dipping, frowning. I asked him, 'What are you doing?'

'I AIN'T GETTIN' IN NO PLANE!' A voice that sounded like Mr T told me, and Joe burst into giggles.

'Who said that?' I said loudly, looking around theatrically.

'Me!' Joe told me.

Then Mr T's voice instructed me to 'SHUDDUP FOOL!'

Joe began laughing, and held out his hand, which contained a yellow gizmo that played the various and celebrated aphorisms of Mr T.

Very loud.

I said, 'So, is that a Big Mac or chips, Mr T?'

'I AIN'T GOIN IN NO PLANE!'

'We'll take the car.'

'SHUDDUP FOOL!'

'Hey Joe, calm down!'

'SHUSHUSHUSHUDDUPFOOFOOFOOSHUSHUDDUP FOOL!' Joe countered, repeatedly pressing the button, scratching like a pro DJ.

'Give me that,' I said, and put Mr T into my pocket and asked him, 'Where'd you get it?'

'From Big Joe.'

'Big Joe?'

'Yeah, he's in my class at school.'

We got in the car and Joe sat quietly as I fastened up his seatbelt. He told me, 'I'm Little Joe.'

Cool, I thought. A nickname. A non-threatening nickname too. I mean, who's going to pick on someone called Little Joe?

Especially when his friend is Big Joe.

A car drove by and pipped the horn; Miss Hall gave us a wave. Joe waved back and I did too.

'Well, you'll have to give Big Joe his toy back,' I told him.

'He said I can keep it. I'm in Big Joe's crew,' he informed me with pride.

6.41pm – Bainbridge Avenue

I started working here because my relationship with Joe's mum had fallen apart. Well, in the sense she'd left me for someone else, it had fallen apart.

Left *us* for someone else.

So I took a job away from where his mum's new feller and I both worked.

Along with this new job, Joe and I got a new home too; a two-bedroom garden flat that came complete with period features such as a purple bathroom suite, 1980s stone fireplace, rising damp and a condemned central heating system. Plus, an old man who paints the bench that sits near the bus stop at the end of our street. Every weekend.

There's also a nice couple who live upstairs. And a woman who lives on the top floor but never comes out.

But we've done OK. So far.

I'm writing this because I think I come across as being pretty content with my lot, a bit bemused at times maybe, but mainly OK. But I know, I see every day, that kids from single-parent families struggle to succeed, and I see that kids thrive when they have both parents to support them. Yet, I'm a single parent myself. There's absolutely nothing wrong with being a single parent. I'm a reasonably good dad.

Joe's a great kid.

My folks help out a lot and so does my sister.

But being a child from a broken home isn't easy; I worry about Joe not having his mother's love when he needs it.

14

Scott Reid came into my classroom; he slapped an essay onto my desk. 'That's an A,' he said confidently.

'OK,' I said.

'Make sure you give it an A,' he said.

I looked at it: Basketball – by Scott Reid. This was Scott's GCSE English 'original writing' essay, long overdue, and worth one fifth of his overall coursework mark.

'I'll mark it tonight,' I told him.

As it was, I glanced through it as I ate my lunch, and it looked good enough that I wanted to mark straight away. It looked too good. Too good. After reading the first three or four sentences, and being impressed by how well it was written, I became suspicious, so I Googled a random phrase from the essay. I quickly found its original source; a sports review from an American magazine. I checked the original article against Scott's coursework essay and it was the same, word for word. In large letters I wrote **Plagiarised – U** across the front of his essay.

The thing is, and I've come across this a few times already this term, Scott won't be failed for his blatant attempt at cheating. He won't even be given a U for that particular module.

Instead, I will have to ask him to hand in another essay. He'll get another chance.

The school is obsessed with statistics. No one can be allowed to fail.

Not even cheats.

1.41pm – Library – Free Period

I looked again at the marking criteria: '...*explain and comment on writers' use of language, including grammatical and literary features at word and sentence level...*'

Grimly, I searched in vain for something that made sense; something that was written in clear English. Marking criteria, I decided, is written by civil servants, who are in league with the devil.

'...*evidence for identifying main purpose precisely located at word/sentence level or traced through a text ...*'

In the words of Sherlock Holmes, give me the most abstruse cryptogram, I thought. It couldn't be any less clear than this. Marking criteria, I decided, is written by *paranoid* civil servants, who are in league with Beelzebub. I suspect that *they* suspect that teachers may attempt to use their own *judgement*. They are determined that this should not happen.

The people who run education want English to be like maths, where $1+1 = 2$.

Grey areas where things like opinion, argument, disagreement or, *God forbid*, persuasion, might leap out and bite the unsuspecting number-crunching civil servant or junior education minister on the arse, are anathema. They are a threat to the smooth-running offices of those suits in Government who decide what we can and cannot teach.

Shakespeare himself, if he were alive today, couldn't get a job as an English teacher.

Not with his spelling, his habit of inventing new words, and re-writing history. That just wouldn't be allowed.

I put down the SATs practice papers and drew a deep breath.

'Trouble?' a voice asked.

I looked up to see Merlene.

I've been avoiding the library due to the fact that, well, I quite fancy the librarian. Which is awkward, because she is uber-cool. I'm not.

'These bloody marking criteria,' I told her. 'They don't make sense.'

She said, 'I don't think they're *supposed* to. Are they?'

'Ah, a wise-woman,' and I nodded agreement, 'to be honest, I was coming to the same conclusion.'

'Are you reading that?' she asked, pointing at a copy of *The Tattooed Mum* lying on the table.

I shook my head. Jacqueline Wilson wasn't my first choice. Not my last choice either, mind. 'Just looking for a quiet place to read this stuff, and try and make sense of it. The staffroom is too loud.'

Merlene nodded, picked up the book, piled it on top of the other books she held in the crook of her left arm and said, 'Well, feel free. It's usually quiet until lunchtime.'

At lunchtimes, the library suddenly becomes packed with students who don't want to hang around in the yard. The school is located less than a hundred yards from low rolling cliffs that look over onto the North Sea.

The wind is bitter. The library is warm.

'Is that Jet Mercier's mock paper?' Merlene asked.

I nodded.

'He was *premature* you know,' she said with a slow smile, then she drifted off to slot the books into their rightful places. I watched her for a few moments, until I thought my gaze might be bordering on, I dunno, stalking or something, and then I forced myself to turn back to the marking criteria:

'*...including summary and synthesis of information from different sources or different places in the same text ...*'

I sort of understood that bit if, mentally, I squinted hard enough. But I wasn't too sure how I'd recognise it in the essay of a typical Bog Standard fourteen-year-old.

Ten minutes later and I was still struggling to decipher the 'grade indicators' that tell me how well a child can read or write. Merlene appeared again, put two mugs of coffee on the table and sat down on the table opposite me. 'Here, have a break.'

'Thanks.' I picked up the coffee, had a mouthful. 'Mmm. Just right.'

Merlene nodded. 'I can do three things "just right" – coffee is one of them.' She gave me one of her mysterious smiles then looked down at my grade-criteria book: 'Why don't you just ignore the criteria and mark the kids' papers at the level you think they're at?'

'What. Use my own judgment?'

She laughed, quietly, 'Well, it's always an option. If you're desperate. You are, I suppose, a *teacher*.' Then she changed the subject and said, 'Here, I got a new tat, look.' She peeled back the sleeve of her t-shirt to reveal a bare shoulder now stained a pink-edged, deep-indigo tattoo. 'It's an Omega,' she told me.

'I can see.'

'To remind me that life is finite.'

'That's a bit gloomy,' I said, and picked up the mug, 'But the coffee is nice.'

'It is not gloomy,' she told me, taking a sip. 'It's just a reminder; a spur; telling me "Merlene, don't waste time".'

Oh-oh, I thought, 'don't waste time'. That could be a sign. A hint. A signal.

'It's good,' I said, 'I like it.' Then I said, 'Well, in the interests of not wasting time, any *more* time, that is, do you want to go for a drink with me? Some time.'

She wrinkled her eyes into a smile, took a sip of coffee.

There was a pause that seemed to last a long, long time.

'No,' she said, eventually, quietly, but she kept smiling at me anyway.

'Hmm,' I said. 'Shot down in flames.' My hand mimicked a plane crashing in flames into the table and I made a sort of 'whee' sound followed by an explosion noise to go with it.

'Do all boys come with sound effects?' she asked.

'Uh, yeah.'

She shook her head, bemused.

'Not your type, huh,' I said.

She shook her head more vigorously, 'You *are* my type. You're just not ready.'

'For what?'

'For *us*.'

I drank the last of my coffee. 'Does that mean there's an "us"?'

She took the mug from my hand. 'I'll come to your room sometime...you can make *me* a coffee.'

'Right,' and I was wondering what the two other things she did that were 'just right' when Alice the office secretary came into the library. 'This came for you this morning,' she said, handing me a letter.

'Thanks.' I gave Alice a big smile; a lot of people didn't know my current address but knew where I was working, so mail kept coming to the school office. And Alice made sure I got them, asap.

It was a buff envelope. Hand-written address. Second-class stamp. I opened it.

It was from a solicitor.

Jenny wanted to re-establish contact with Joe.

On my return to room 101 I found Iwan Wenkel in my class-room, rummaging through my desk, looking, I assumed, for some valuable and, crucially, portable educational trinket that might be worth stealing from my room.

Now, I can't accuse Iwan, without proof, neither can I search him for the evidence that will provide proof. He's in my room and his hands are in my desk drawers and he looks as guilty as a boxer dog caught with its head in the fridge and a string of sausages in its mouth. But anything he has in his pockets is now his.

Theft being nine tenths of the law.

I can't be alone in a room with Iwan or he just might make an accusation of assault or abuse (despite looking to be about 24 and having the build of a professional wrestler, with a beard to match). I would immediately be suspended and, to all intents and purposes, my career would be over. His family would receive compensation from the LEA to boot.

So I hold the door open, 'Out you go, Iwan,' ushering him away in a firm but friendly voice.

'I'm not a thief,' he tells me, indignantly, even though I haven't actually accused him of anything.

He's smirking.

'Yes, you are,' I reply, and I realise that I need to do some work on my Doublespeak skills if I wish to have any sort of long-term career plan. But I'm too tired to keep the pretence going and lie.

A spasm of fury passes across his face. 'You can't call me a thief!'

'Well empty your pockets then. Prove to me your innocence.'

He mutters something in Czech, or Esperanto, no doubt insulting my family or my good looks, and I look him in the eye and say 'ditto'.

He just smirks a bit wider and saunters past me, saying, 'Later,' as a sort of admission cum warning.

Friday 3.34pm – Room 101

The latest craze in school is for those kids who have been diagnosed with ADHD to sell their medication to friends. The going rate is a couple of pounds, or ten fags. You can spot this in action; the ADHD child will be twitchy and prone to bouts of shouting and disruption where normally they'd be semi-comatose and more malleable than warm Blu-tak.

Meanwhile, little Dwayne Pipe, who usually sits at the back left-hand corner flicking chewed-up bits of paper, shouting out rude words and generally pulling the threads out of the fabric of my lesson plan, is now leaning against the wall, head lolling and smiling benificently into the middle distance.

Hey, you lose some – you win some.

But as the ADHD kids have legal, Ofsted-able protection, this problem has been officially noticed amongst the senior management, and we've been asked to keep an eye out for, and report, any abnormal behaviour in class. This is difficult when the behaviour of 40 per cent of the class is already far, far beyond what ordinary people might consider normal. And most of the other 60 per cent are just very naughty.

But, ironically, we've also been asked not to make any outright accusations against a student, not to even suggest a possible causal link, or hint at *any* sort of reason for their unusual behaviour. Not unless we have somehow, magically, managed to get a signed confession, witnessed by three priests, an elder and a mullah.

Captured on videotape.

In the presence of their mum.

Any unproven allegation made by a teacher, even a well-meaning error, even if it is manifestly true, can be used in evidence against the school, should the parent decides, via an 0898 phone-call to 'Lawsuits-4-U' that young Connor has been the victim of a campaign of bullying from staff. So, we simply have to mention 'abnormal behaviour'.

This is also why, when my year tens arrive in class, stinking of dope, giggling, falling asleep, *on the classroom floor*, munching through chocolate digestives, cheese sandwiches, Yorkie bars, I can't even suggest that they've been coughing down lungs of home-grown marijuana at lunch-time. The other kids can. And do. They all call the year tens 'Smokies'. For some reason, dope-smoking is endemic amongst year ten kids. More than any other year group, it's their *thing*.

So, at the end of lesson five, I watch the kids traipse out and then I jot down the names of those students whose abnormal behaviour is differently abnormal to their normally abnormal behaviour. Three of them, this lesson. My guess is that Carl, ADHD-certified, has sold two tablets. One to Liam. One to Chelsey. I write their names and simply jot down their behaviour that lesson. Let the social workers join the dots. I fold the note about the possible Ritalin-retail incident (Retailins as they are called in the staffroom) and then pick up the letter I've drafted to Jenny's solicitor too, thinking that I'd pop it into the outgoing-mail box in the office.

Leaving my room, and walking along the corridor past the Science block, I come across three girls sitting in a huddle on the stairs at the top of one of the stairwells. My first reaction is to ask them if they haven't got a home to go to; have a little joke. But I don't. They're crying. Consoling each other.

I pause.

'Oh sir,' one of them, Becca, says, and she gets up and comes over to me, buries her head in my chest, sobbing inconsolably, 'It's Harriet.'

My heart sinks. Somehow, I know what she is going to tell me and I want to avoid the words that I know Becca is about to say.

I try not to hear them.

'She's died, sir,' and her tears are soaking into my shirt. 'In hospital.' Slowly, in a dream, my arms wrap themselves around her shoulders as she cries. 'She was having another operation and she died.'

And tears well in my eyes too as I hold Becca and think of Harriet.

And Joe.

And me.

And what a shit-awful year we've had.

I think of Harriet's frail body as she walked down the stairs, the last time I saw her, and I hear her telling me, 'It's alright sir, I can manage.' Biting back my tears, I picture her, round-faced because of the steroids she takes; her stilted walk; her stout, *loveable* little person. I see the project she did for me that I've got stapled onto my classroom wall.

Becca is shaking, rattling almost, as she sobs against my chest, thin shoulders shaking beneath my arms. Then all three girls are hugging me, and each other; they're crying, and I'm just barely holding it together. We stand there, in stunned grief, for what seems like an hour.

'Here, Dan, I'll look after the girls.' I look around and it's Cyril, his eyes are shining, which means he's heard, and that means it's true. I nod and he spreads his big arms out. 'Come here girls, we'll go and sit in the staffroom together.'

His voice is kindly, paternal; 'We'll call your mums, eh?'

They unpeel themselves from me and go off down the stairs with Cyril, still sobbing.

I'm standing alone in the corridor.

Harriet isn't coming back.

And my heart is breaking.

I go back to room 101, lock the door and sit down at my

desk, rest my head in my hands. My face is hot, my eyes are sore, but I'm not crying. I think of Jenny, Joe. Me. And how our lives have exploded. And then I think about Harriet and her family.

I've kept it together this far. If I let myself cry now, I might not stop.

Friday 1.34pm – Room 101

The end of the half-term came subdued and rain-swept. Mr Sweet had arranged for the conference room to be set aside for Harriet's friends to use if they were too upset to remain in class, and there was some talk of inviting in 'counsellors' but, thankfully, this was abandoned in favour of just asking some of the teaching staff to be in the area, should the students wish to talk.

Harriet had gone into hospital for treatment and had picked up an infection while she was in there. Her vital organs, already struggling to cope with her condition, had quickly begun shutting down.

She died in her sleep, surrounded by family.

Four students accompanied Miriam Hopwood to Harriet's funeral, which was yesterday, Thursday, the day before we break for half term. They behaved in an exemplary fashion, Miriam told us this morning, in a specially convened staff meeting.

Becca laid a wreath, paid for with money raised by student donations, on Harriet's grave. Then she stood back, sombre.

Friday came, still raining. The school had planned to break for the holidays early in the day, maybe just after the beginning of lesson five, sometime after 2pm. As it was, we'd barely finished lunch when a runner came round. The year sevens were let away early. Then the eight's and so on. Those kids who had to wait for the bus were allowed to sit in the library or the canteen but most chose to brave the rain rather than wait.

The day finally over, I carried a bag of books to my car, planning to mark them over the holidays. When we returned to school again it'd be March, I thought, and, to me at least, spring would have arrived.

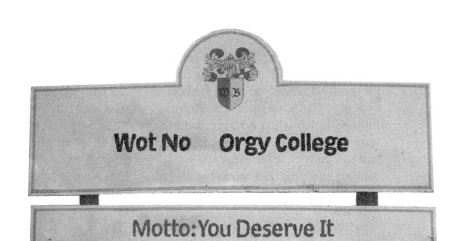

15

Half Term – Bainbridge Avenue

I've spent the first couple of days of the half-term holidays marking coursework. It makes depressing reading but, thankfully, most of the coursework folders are short. But it's still not easy, spending your holidays ploughing through dross, especially when you've got a seven-year-old demanding to be read stories or taken to the park. Or fed, or something.

And who is now scooting around the front street on his bike, pulling skids.

Marking is made a little more difficult because I keep stopping to go and check he's alright. Even when I'm sitting here I keep an ear open for the sound of him having fun or crashing. But it's mainly not easy because the standard of the coursework is dire.

The easiest way to gauge this year's GCSE cohort's lack of commitment to their studies is not by observing their severely depleted levels of energy and motivation in class. Nor is it the absence of anything that resembles focus. No, the easiest way to gauge the dire level of their subscription to their education is to count how many of them come to lesson with any sort of equipment.

Pens.

A single pen.

Or maybe just a pencil.

I've stopped allowing my GCSE students to take their textbooks home. I don't allow them to take their copy of the set text home either. *Of Mice and Men*, if you're interested; chosen because it's short. I don't allow them to take their completed essays home, even if they promise to 'redraft it over the weekend' because, I've discovered, none of it ever comes back.

The attrition rate on books taken home is nudging 100 per cent. They don't so much steal them as lose them through neglect. They just don't care enough about any book or essay to keep an eye on it long enough to be able to find them again on Monday morning. One or two of the girls do have a pencil case. About a third of the rest of the class regularly bring in some sort of writing implement, but the rest don't. Every couple of weeks I have to drive over to Ikea or Argos to nick fifty of those short pencils they have in racks for customers' use.

Before they arrive in class the kids will have spent an hour gelling their hair or laying down a thick layer of pancake foundation, and they'll be wearing a good seven pounds, in weight *and* value, of jewellery. Bling that's taken them a good hour to hang from their neck, wrist, lip, ears, navel, eyebrow and anywhere else that's considered rebellious.

But equipment? Nah.

'Get out your homework,' I said once.

No one moved.

'Put your hand up *if* you've done your homework.'

Slowly, Zarah raised a hand.

Michael Ly raised a finger.

I looked around at the class. Then I said, 'Put your hand up if you have a shopping bag under your desk.'

Eleven of the girls raised their hands – I counted – plus three of the boys.

I said, 'Put up your hand if you've got an iPod in your pocket.'

More than half the class raised their hands. I didn't bother to ask who had brought their phones.

Sure, they'll top up their phone and they charge their iPod, the earpiece of which is now stuffed permanently into their ear during lessons. I mused; CS Lewis got it the wrong way round. These kids have more material wealth than any generation that ever lived – and if you combined that with the effects of global warming, you could argue that it never snowed, and it was always Christmas.

But setting aside my cute attempts at inverting phrases to find new meanings, the problem remained; they won't do homework, or pick up a pen on the way to school. And I can't make them.

So I've stopped attempting to give them work to do at home as it simply doesn't get done, and seeing as the worst homework and no-pen offenders are also those who never turn up for detention, that avenue is closed too.

All coursework is done in class. Nothing is attempted outside of the classroom door. When a kid suddenly reappears after missing eight or nine weeks of lessons, I simply park them outside with a list of essay titles and some 'scaffolding'.

Scaffolding is, basically, a detailed essay plan. If it's done properly, if it's detailed enough, all the student has to do is add water and it'll write itself.

So they'll either sit outside with scaffolded essays, catching up, or they'll disappear again.

I add some comments to Rosie Purvis' *Original Writing* essay. This is where the kids get a chance to write their own story. Rosie has written about looking after her baby sister and it's quite a sweet story, very readable, very chatty in tone. But there are no paragraphs.

A couple of weeks ago I remember telling the class, 'Think of a pizza. A lovely, juicy pizza, with a thick, soft, doughy base. Now imagine trying to eat that pizza without slicing it. Try to imagine stuffing a full pizza into your mouth.'

Some of the girls, wedded to the concept, if not the practical application, of starvation as a lifestyle option, make *yeuch* noises at the mere mention of food.

I continued with my analogy: 'Now, the same applies to me when I try to read your essays… and you haven't put in any paragraphs. Your essay sticks at the back of my mind. I get mental indigestion.' I look around, trying to make it clear.

'Paragraphs, ladies and gentlemen, are like the slices in a pizza; they make writing easier to digest; they divide it into easily understood slices; they actually make it more *enjoyable*.'

I tot up Rosie's marks. D.

But I'm nearly done and I have to admit, the cool thing about marking the underclass's GCSE coursework is that it's really easy to do. I'm beginning to see why working in a sink-school can be an addictive occupation; compared to the tectonic layers of paperwork and marking I used to plough through every single evening at Thatcham Grange, a full day's marking from West Bognor can be polished off in under an hour. Sometimes in under less than ten minutes.

And GCSE coursework marking, which used to take up the whole of half-term and Easter, now takes a couple of days maximum.

Looking at the bigger picture though, I'm not sure if this dilatory approach to education is doing the country any good; I wouldn't like to stake the future of our place as a world centre for industry, finance, IT or whatever, on the work-rate and achievement of my year eleven's.

To be honest, they're a third-world class. Worse actually, because in the third world, kids subscribe to the idea of school, of education, of getting on, and they simply don't here. We are post-first-world now; we've moved beyond the third world. We're a fourth-world school.

I go and make myself a coffee. I can hear Joe out in the street, still skidding around. There's only one parked car, mine, and the skip. He's safe.

While I'm filling the kettle I think about getting him to 'do a job' for me. He'll get bored with cycling soon and anyway, I think, kids love to do jobs, and his could be to clear up the small patch of evil-smelling weeds, ivy and dirt that surround the steps to our front door. The four square feet of wilderness that we call our front garden.

After the heartbreaking events of last week I want to ensure that Joe and I enjoy every moment, and that I enjoy being around him while he's having fun. He's got homework to do too, because even seven-year-olds have education targets now, but we'll do that together.

And I've begun making sure that I don't just tuck him in bed at night; we talk, I read to him, we sing daft songs. We make up stories.

I'll mark until he comes in. Then we'll do the garden together.

Monday, 2.11pm – Room 101

It's Monday and I'm back in school, trying to teach English to a year seven class. It's fourth lesson, straight after a lunch of high-sugar, high-caffeine drinks and chips. Here's what is *supposed* to happen.

After the obligatory *starter* activity, some brief and interesting worksheet lifted from one of the many educational websites, I'm supposed to... wait for silence... then share the lesson's learning objectives with the class; at the start of every lesson I'm supposed to write down a bespoke set of lesson objectives on a specially designated whiteboard. Then I'm supposed to explain these objectives to the class, then scaffold, or structure or *spell out* exactly how we are going to reach these objectives.

Then, forty-five minutes later, after an eventful, entertaining and invigorating lesson, I'm supposed to do a plenary, where I tell the class what we have achieved, how we have achieved it, and what we are going to do the following lesson.

Then, via a short question and answer session, I *check for learning*.

But here's what *actually* happens.

I sit them down, using whatever threats work to quieten them down, and read out the register; then we talk about the book we are reading and what happened in the last lesson. Then we read another chapter. Then we write about the chapter – describe a character or summarise the events or something. Sometimes we just talk about it.

Then I give them merits.

But sometimes even this simple plan can go awry.

Today, having read with the class for fifteen minutes, I told them to 'read up to the second paragraph of page twenty', then I said, 'When you have done that, you can continue with the worksheet.'

I wrote this on the board.

They appeared to start well but, within perhaps ninety seconds, hands had started to go up.

'Do we put the date?'

Yes.

'Do we read *up to* page twenty, or *just* page twenty?'

Up to.

'I haven't got a pen.'

Borrow one.

'Neither have I.'

Borrow one.

'Sir, I can hear music.'

I raised an eyebrow, as though to say *so*? Instead I say, 'Get on with your work.'

'Can I go to the toilet?'

No.

'What's the date?'

I point at the board.

I deal with about twenty pointless questions in less than five minutes. And hands are still going up.

'Put down your books!' I say loudly.

And nothing, absolutely nothing, is guaranteed to make kids begin working more than being told to stop. They all begin reading intently.

'Everyone! Books down! Now!'

Reluctantly, they put down their books.

I glare at them. 'I have given you *clear* instructions. They are *written* on the board.' I point at the board and read them out – 'One. Read up to the second paragraph of page 20. Two. Continue with your worksheet.' I give them the hard stare. 'Today's *date* is written on the board,' I point to the date, 'There.'

I walk slowly around the room, 'Does anyone *not* understand what they have to do?'

They stay quiet. They know, and I know, that their constant questions are a stalling device. Today, for some reason, they just can't be arsed.

I struggle on anyway, 'Right. Get on with it.' And even as I turn to walk back to the front of the class a hand shoots up.

I turn slowly.

'Mr McKenzie,' I say, very slowly, 'this had better be a really interesting question. It had better not be a question to which you *already know the answer.*'

Kyle McKenzie looked a little worried for a moment, then his hand went down. 'Nothing,' he said.

'Good. Now get on with it.' But I hadn't reached my desk when, out of my peripheral vision, I saw a hand shoot up; Kyle again, no doubt having mentally rephrased his original question.

'Yes?' I say this quietly, and with some attempt at venom.

'Where do we read to?' Kyle asks brightly.

I look at him evenly. '*You* read to Outside That Door.' I point. 'Go on.'

He shrugs, slumps to a standing position, picks up his book, pencil, coat and bag and goes to sit at the desk outside of the classroom door.

Checking the class is now on-task I follow him out and hand him a sheet of paper. 'You're going to write lines. Two sides of lines,' I tell him. 'You are going to write this sentence: **I must listen to teacher's instructions.**'

I look at him: 'Two sides. Understand?'

He nods.

'And, Kyle, *do not* come back into the classroom unless I tell you to.'

I go back inside, and the class, having stopped working and begun to chat in my absence, fall quiet again and pretend to be interested.

I sit down.

A minute passes, then the door opens, Kyle pops his head in the door and asks, 'Sir, *what* do I have to do?'

Tuesday, 3.32pm – School Hall

'Tidy your outfits away!' I bellowed. 'Put all the clothes back into the box. Or we aren't going to go home!'

I was in the hall with my year eights, winding up a drama lesson and attempting to leave the hall in some sort of reasonably tidy state. Kids were dashing about, pushing, shoving, shrieking. Some, well one, was putting away the panto outfits, stuffing them into the large chest we kept below the stage.

'Who're they?' Michaela asked me.

I looked in the direction she was pointing to see Mr Sweet, Jane, the school secretary, and four people in smart suits. 'It must be interviews,' I told Michaela.

'Who for?'

I shrugged.

'It's for the new head teacher's job,' Paul Gilberts, one of my chipper year eights, told us. I didn't dismiss this out of hand; the kids were more likely to hear stuff than the staff. But the one person who would know for certain was Jen, the cleaner. I decided to check it out later. Having the drop on fresh gossip was a good way to earn brownie points in the staffroom. I waved at Mr Sweet and the suits.

They left.

I continued to try and get the kids to tidy the hall until the bell went. Then I stood by the door and refused to let them leave until they cleared away the mess. This worked, eventually. I let the kids go and gave the hall the once over.

One thing I kind of accepted at Bog Standard was the fact that the school didn't have a Head Teacher. We had Mr Sweet, the Deputy Head who shouted at the kids, and lately we've got a new Deputy Head who is nice to the kids. And there are a few other vaguely senior management types who occasionally, and furtively, dash from office to office when the kids are safely locked into their classrooms. There's Cyril, of course, who is, maybe, not the Shrek I first thought he was.

But there's no actual Head Teacher. Because the Head had been off work with stress for about a year before I arrived. And so long as she didn't actually resign, or retire, they couldn't replace her. This presented a real problem, one that I had inadvertently come to believe was simply part of the day-to-day fabric of the school – lack of leadership.

It turned out that none of the twenty-five or so Deputy Heads, Assistant Heads, Senior Teachers, Heads of Year and Heads of Department, were actually *in charge*. Some, like Mr Sweet, had assumed a sort of temporary authority, while others, like Cyril, had attempted to fill the void by trying to be around whenever the shit hit the fan, or shortly thereafter.

The cleaners office is a large cupboard adjacent to the back of the school hall; I popped my head in. Jimmy was sitting with a cup of tea in his hand, eyes closed, murmuring along to the music in his headphones.

'She's in the staffroom,' he told me, without opening his eyes or turning down his music.

'Thanks, Jimmy,' I said, and headed for the hall. Jen was polishing the glass case of the fish tank when I found her and she filled me in on the details; 'There are four candidates for the Head's job,' she said, 'Three men and one woman.'

'Who do you think will get it?'

'The most stupid,' Jen told me.

'Sure?'

She nodded, and said, 'Well, we'll find out soon enough,' and then got back to her vigorous polishing.

Jen isn't just the school oracle; she's a professional cleaner. Monday to Friday she works split shifts at the school, but she also has a half-dozen 'customers' who she cleans for, twice weekly. Rumour has it she earns more than a classroom teacher. And if Jen pronounces on something, she's more often right than not.

Wednesday, 8.31am - Room 101

Walking up to room 101 the next morning I was still mulling over the implications of getting a new Head, of just *having* a Head, stupid or otherwise, all of which, I surmised, were positive but, for a supply teacher like myself, could spell trouble, when I noticed a group of year eleven's, most from my own tutor class, 11*Fick*, standing outside of my room.

I've started locking 101 because if I don't, everything inside tends to get stolen. This means my tutor group can't use it unless I'm in, which is a shame. I'd prefer it if they could use it to study, or just hang out. But they can't. They'd use it to smoke, or fight or indulge in heavy petting sessions.

'Hey Mr Ken,'

'Hello,' I replied, guarded; I could sense a request approaching. And this usually meant more work, for me.

Becca was there, as was Marnie, along with Little Beth, Dicka, Terry, Marty and, er, Carl.

Becca smiled her big smile and announced, 'We've got a plan.'

I unlocked the door. 'Tell me,' I said, intrigued.

'We're going to set up a memorial for Hattie,' Becca told me.

I ushered them into my room. 'That's an excellent idea.'

'Will you help us?'

I nodded, still a touch guarded; after all, I didn't want to sign up to some madcap scheme: 'If I can help.' Then I said, 'Tell me about your plan.'

They crowded around my desk, Becca took out a file from her bag, and unrolled an A3 sheet of paper with a design on it. 'This is the design for the memorial,' she said, and pointed out the salient features of the design.

'And we only need a thousand pounds to get it made!' Carl piped up.

12.14pm

I was still thinking about the students' plans for a memorial as I summed up at the end of my lesson with my bottom-set year eights. 'These essays are the result of your hard work.' I held up the sheaf of papers – essays completed by my bottom-set year eights – and waved them in the direction of the class. 'You've written them. You've redrafted them. You've Copied Them Out. Neatly.'

I waved the papers about a bit more. 'And some of you,' I gave them a big smile, 'have drawn *pictures* on them. To make them look even nicer.'

Inwardly, I didn't try and fool myself; I knew that the essays were, in the main, only just legible, barely literate. But I also knew that they'd worked very hard. They'd *sustained* their effort, something they found very tough.

'These essays are like honey!' I told them.

'Sir, you're a crackerjack,' Tommy told me.

'I'm a *very pleased* crackerjack.'

I looked to the class. 'I feel like a beekeeper who has opened up his hive and found a jar full of the best honey that he has ever tasted.'

'You don't get jars in beehives,' Chris muttered.

I nodded, 'I know, but I'm using a metaphor.' I looked around. 'A metaphor is …?'

'A naming word!!'

I shook my head. 'Good try but no, it's when you say one thing is …?'

'A plural!!!'

'Hmm. Not really. I'll tell you. It's when you say one thing *is* another.'

'That's stupid.'

'OK. Well, I am telling you that your brains are the Beehive and these essays are the Honey.'

Blank looks.

'As a reward, I've bought you all a mini bag of buttons.'

Sudden comprehension. I'm pleased. They're going to get chocolate.

Twenty kids rush the desk.

Tommy, who is sitting opposite me and doesn't need to move, looks at me with an enlightened smile and says, 'Sir, you've been surrounded by a swarm of hungry bees.'

'That's a *metaphor*, Tommy. Well done.'

'Thank you,' he replied, with a smile.

16

Wednesday, 11.20am – Staffroom

Judy, our Head of Department, is due to retire in three years. Her ferocious intellect and her cut-glass accent betray a grammar-school education from the days when only the top 3 per cent of girls were allowed to pass their eleven-plus. She is quite simply an awesome teacher; her subject knowledge is unsurpassed. She can silence a rowdy class with a glance. She can silence me, too.

Today, sitting in the staffroom, she was talking about her teenage years, living in Cheltenham, and I asked her why she'd moved here.

'For love, darling. Affairs of the heart.'

'What happened?' I asked.

She looked me in the eye, smiled and said, 'That's none of your business.'

A couple of weeks ago we'd been discussing music and I was reminiscing fondly about the time I saw the Happy Mondays. I saw that Judy was listening and asked her if she'd ever seen any good acts. She thought for a moment and then said, 'Well, I suppose, *yes,* I have.' And I was waiting to hear her Tony Bennett story or the time she took part in an amateur production of *Madame Butterfly* when she said, 'Hendrix. Twice. Cream, of course. Captain Beefheart, now there was a *really* good live band...'

Judy scares the Senior Management Team, who only communicate with her when they really have to, and then by memo, or by sending Big Cyril with a message.

If she is impatient with the 'Leadership', then her patience with lesser mortals, me included, is equally legendary and her professional support always welcome. But she gets away with being a near-perfect teacher because she has a foul mouth and, if legend has it, puts away a half bottle of Gordon's every night.

Just before half-term, Judy got a memo telling her that her new job title was 'Head of Learning and Achievement'. Sitting in her chair in the staffroom, she read out the memo to me, and snorted. 'It says here that neither my pension nor my increment will be affected.'

She gave me *that* look, the classic over-the-top-of-the-glasses look. 'What that means is *they aren't going to pay me any extra.*'

Last year she was Head of Learning. The year before she was Learning and Achievement Co-ordinator. Before that Subject Learning Co-ordinator.

'I've had seven different job titles in the last seven years,' she told me. 'But whatever they call it, it's the same old shit.' She looked up from the memo, and in her cut-glass tones told me, 'And however hard you rub, you simply *cannot* polish shit.'

Smiling at the memory of this I opened a fresh page in my journal and wrote a title: **Things that unsettle a class**.

Then I compiled a list.

Wasps

Inclement weather e.g. snow, thunderstorms, heavy rain

Moving the desks

Love notes being passed around

Tired teacher

Supply teacher

A fight in the previous lesson

The return to class of a bad kid

Watching a film or DVD

The teacher having a mishap

Someone feeling sick

The wind
Silence
Someone *being* sick

Satisfied with this, admittedly incomplete list, I wrote another heading beneath it: **Things that *settle* a class.**
I wrote:
Routine & predictability
Examinations
Watching a film or DVD
A teacher who is:
Alert
Authoritative but not shouting
Listening
Smiling
Students seeing that they are progressing

Looking back on the list I thought that from a purely practical, day-to-day, perspective, the thing that settled a class best was routine. The thing that most unsettled a class was changing their routine.

Thursday, 11.20am – Staffroom

Terry sat down opposite me, and the mere fact that a Deputy Head was in the staffroom should have alerted me, but I was engrossed in a comparative study of derailleur gears on the latest full-suspension mountain bikes, as discussed in *Cycling Today*.

He cleared his throat. I looked up. 'Daniel,' he said, 'I was just wondering what your strategy was for raising the achievement of your most underperforming students.'

'Wha?' I put down my magazine, thinking, *teach them?*

'I've got a print-out of 11F's mock examination performance and, to be honest, it doesn't make good reading.'

He handed me a candy-striped sheet that had a list of names at one side. 'The names coloured green are those students who are on target, the names coloured amber are those who are just below their predicted grade and, well,' he smiled at this point, 'you can guess the rest.'

The sheet had twenty-seven names.

Four were green.

Seven were amber.

Sixteen were red.

And yes, I sort of guessed what the red stood for.

'So,' Terry said, 'I need to know what your strategy is.'

'What strategy?'

Terry clarified:'For boosting their grades.'

I looked down the list: 'Well, Junior never attends,' I pointed at another name, 'She had a baby last year.' I stroked a finger down the rest of the red-highlighted names. 'These are mostly non-attenders, or regular excludees,' my finger paused, 'Bethany is functionally illiterate. Carl is on medication to modify his behaviour...'

Terry interrupted, his voice soft but insistent, 'So what are *you* doing about it, Daniel?'

Then he got up and patted me on the shoulder, gave me one of his 'heartfelt and genuine' smiles; 'I know it's not easy, but will you let me know when you've devised a stratagem for improving their grades?'

I nodded, glumly.

Short of sitting their exams for them, I couldn't think of what I could do that would improve their academic performance. That would make them arrive, on time, and do their work well.

Nothing.

I picked up my magazine and returned to my gear systems.

'So you're doing the fund-raiser?'

I looked up from *Cycling Today*, this time to see Keith Keill; Keith is a science teacher, one of the old guard, a good bloke too. 'It seems so.' I pointed at my magazine. 'I'm looking for tips.'

'Don't get a sore arse. There's a tip,' he told me, filling the staffroom kettle.

I opened the magazine to a particular page, 'It's all written down here: Top Tips for the Novice Distance Rider. See.'

Keith took the magazine from me, scanned it for information. Then he gave me it back. 'Want a coffee, Dan?'

'No thanks.'

'Well, do you want a support car, for your trip?'

Becca and crew, when they're not getting me into trouble for refusing to be educated beyond the standard expected of most seven-year-olds, had a fund-raising idea to complete a sponsored cycle ride, in the Lake District and I'd been volunteered as the designated 'responsible adult'. Word was getting around.

'Really? You'd do that?'

He nodded, 'Yeah. I just had a lesson with 11 *Fick.*'

'Everyone's favourite class, at the moment.'

Keith raised an eyebrow as though to say *trouble?*

I smiled, shook my head.

He didn't pursue it. 'Well, favourites or not, they've been talking about this cycle ride. Non-stop. They seem really keen on erecting a memorial for Hattie. And paying for it themselves.' He paused. 'Anyway, if you're definitely going to do it, I know a place in Keswick that will hire out bikes. We could do a round trip from there to Borrowdale or somewhere. Camp out overnight, or find a Youth Hostel.'

'Keith, that would be great,' I told him. 'You are, in fact, a marvel.' Then I said, 'You've done this sort of thing before, haven't you?'

'Haven't *you?*' he asked me in return.

'No. And everyone I know who has, has done it with a boatload of funding, a half dozen teachers and a couple of parents along for the trip. Or the ride.'

Keith sat down. 'Well, we'll need to do a Risk Assessment, and keep the numbers down to about six, if you're the only one riding with them.'

'Do you think anyone else will volunteer to help out?'

'Probably not,' he said.

Then he said, 'But I can borrow my brother's pickup truck, meet up with you every couple of hours with hot sweet tea, haul in the slackers at the back, fix punctures. *And* I'm first-aid trained.'

'That'd be great. Really. You're very kind.'

He smiled; 'I think it'll be a hoot, actually.' Then he said, 'They're not bad, really, 11F. Oh, I know, they're little shits, they kick off, and they don't do any work. And they make your added value statistics look desperate.'

'Added value' is the relationship between a student's target grade and their actual examination performance. In the case of 11*Fick* it was going to be depressingly negative. *Subtracted value*, in fact.

'But they really want to do this, and it's a good thing, isn't it?' he said. I felt that Keith had spotted an opportunity to be involved in something positive and, rather like the prisoner of war who had secretly built an aeroplane in which to escape from Colditz Castle, he was going to do everything possible to help make it work.

'Yeah. It's a good thing,' I agreed.

A few hours later I was sitting having my tea. Joe was sitting on the sofa playing on some sort of hand-held game he'd borrowed from a friend at school. It made noises like Dit Dit Dit Craaaaaaaassshhh Dit Dit Dot Dot Boing Craaaaaaaaaaaashhhhhhh.

I thought of Keith's welcome and generous offer of help. It could help turn the kids' dream into some sort of reality. His practical support meant that I could go to Mr Sweet with the fund-raising plan and, perhaps, get him to agree to it. The school might even offer to underwrite some of the costs too.

Otherwise the expenses of hiring bikes and stuff would come out of the money raised.

It'd mean I'd have to ask my sis to look after Joe too. In

theory it'd be possible to have him sit shotgun in the pickup truck with Keith, but he'd be bored senseless sitting there for eight hours.

Then I looked over at him, engrossed in his Dit Dit Dot Craaaash-ing hand-held computer game.

Or would he? Yeah, I thought. Probably.

I took out my notebook and jotted down a few thoughts; costings, options, numbers involved. Then I took an OS map of the Lakes that I'd borrowed from the school library. I tried to remember routes that I'd walked or cycled in my younger days.

I was feeling excited about this; ignoring for a moment the amount of planning I'd need to do, the forms and reports that would have to be completed, the equipment we'd need to borrow and, crucially, the flaky, lazy and in one particular case, morbidly obese, sixteen-year-olds who were intending to complete this two-day cycle in the Lake District, it seemed like a good plan.

Yeah, it was a good thing. It *might* work.

Friday, 11.44pm – Room 101

It's ironic that amidst a generally chaotic and often turbulent environment I nevertheless feel pretty safe, physically, at West Bognor Technology College.

Then today Connor Small threw a punch at me.

'Did you just throw a punch at me?'

His cuff had grazed my nose, but otherwise I was unhurt.

He'd missed me. From a range of about three feet.

Connor looked threatening and squared up. 'You shouldn't try telling me what to do,' he told me.

'Well, it's my job to teach you. That involves telling you what to do.'

He scowled, uncomprehending. The problem was that Connor was thick, illiterate and also, it appeared, prone to violent outbursts when actually pushed to write stuff down.

'What'd you do if I smacked you again?' he asked me, displaying commendable ability to focus his attention on a given subject, something I hadn't witnessed from him in months previous.

I ignored the chance to tell him that he'd actually missed me the first time round and stayed calm, thinking, if you hit me *I'd fall over*, probably, and instead said, 'I think you'd better go.'

He waited a moment or two then stalked out, all bristling hackles and glares.

The rest of the class were staring, open-mouthed, in silence.

Inside I was shaking. Connor was only a little guy, though very aggressive and a member of a local criminal clan, the Smalls, and I didn't think he was actually capable of beating me up – I could have picked him up in a bear-hug and carried him down to the office if I'd had to.

But I'd have probably been sacked for laying hands on a kid. And Connor's dad, Billy Small, was, by all accounts, a fearsome street fighter. So I didn't really want to go there.

'You alright, sir?' a voice asked me.

I nodded, 'Sure. He missed. Anyhow, let's get on with our coursework, huh?' I gave them a big smile and the class pretended to comply with my instructions, but they were, in reality, just sitting talking about Connor's attempted assault.

A few moments later Beth asked me, 'Should I go and fetch Mr Sweet?'

I said, 'Yeah, that might be a good idea, thanks.'

I sat down at my desk and with a mild case of the tremors I jotted down what had just occurred.

Mr Sweet's arrival was announced with a brisk knock; he glared at the class before asking me, 'Mr Keane, would you mind if we had a word. Outside.'

I nodded, feeling unaccountably guilty.

Perhaps I was at fault somehow.

But Mr Sweet was fine; I explained what had happened, gave

him my written statement. 'Do you want me to take over the lesson, go and get yourself a cup of tea?' he asked me.

'No, I'm fine. Honestly.'

He nodded, 'Well, it's probably best that you get right back on the saddle. *They*,' he nodded toward the door of 101, 'will be watching to see if you fall apart.' He smiled, 'So better not start crying or beating the desk or anything.'

'I won't,' I assured him.

Mr Sweet said, 'Well, I'm going to have the pleasure of ringing Billy Small and telling him his son is going to be excluded.'

'Will that be interesting?'

'A few years ago, the head at St Benet's needed police protection after they excluded Carl Small, Connor's brother, for setting fire to the arts and crafts room.'

'Oh.'

He nodded, gave a grim smile. 'Anyhow, that's not your problem, and I know Billy Small from way back, we have a sort of understanding about these things. And making phone calls to people like Billy is why I get paid a lot more money than you.' His smile softened a bit. 'They're getting a bit restless,' he said, cocking his head at the sound of laughter and desks being thrown around in my classroom.

I took this as a signal that the conversation was over.

17

Monday, 11.31am - Corridor

The school has a ghost. A real live, walking talking ghost. But mostly, people don't notice her as she wanders around the school.

She's called Sharnice McAfee and, when she was in year eight, she punched a teacher.

Twice.

Sharnice wasn't very old, but she was, and still is a big girl. I'm just guessing but I reckon she's on the morbid end of the obese spectrum, and she could probably pack a decent punch for a thirteen-year-old. She'd been in the process of punching another kid when Sally Pierce, a Newly Qualified Teacher (NQT) at the time, had intervened and Sharnice punched her instead, loosening both of Sally's front teeth, though some timely dental work managed to save them.

Sharnice was suspended for the massively punitive term of three days.

It was, apparently, a mild suspension too far for the staff of West Bognor Technology College, who took a vote and decided that they would refuse to teach young Sharnice. But the school had put themselves in an invidious position; they couldn't punish the girl twice for the same offence. They invited in her mother for a chat about how to proceed, but she was on holiday with her boyfriend in Tunisia.

'They should have called in social services,' Vic Hughes told me. 'But they didn't. Instead, they waited for her return.' And, when she did, she threatened the school with legal action should they try to have Sharnice removed from the roll. But there were no teachers to teach her; forcing them to do so would have resulted in a strike, kids sent home and, worse still, bad publicity for the school. So Sharnice was given a tutor or, as the staff call her, a minder, and her job was to be within five paces of Sharnice. All day. Every day.

Staff still have to supply Sharnice with daily work; she isn't a physical threat when she isn't in the room, so worksheets are delivered each morning to Emma, the minder, and together they sit in the library or one of the empty classrooms while she does her work. She's now in her GCSE year, and only weeks away from GCSE examinations. She hasn't enjoyed proper schooling in three years.

But she doesn't attend school much; she's a truant. And the school isn't in any rush to drag her back in. Occasionally she'll be spotted in the library or the corridor, trailed by Emma. Union members are under instructions to leave the room, should she enter.

I feel a bit sorry for Sharnice; she should have been sent to another school, for a fresh start, three years ago. By all accounts she wasn't a bad kid, she just made a mistake. But between the school's dithering and her mum's intransigence she got stuck here for another three years. A ghost.

12.37pm – School Hall – Briefing

'Use of the word "gay" is to be banned in school.' Miriam spoke with the certainty of someone who had enjoyed a liberal-humanist state-funded education. Something our kids were unlikely to enjoy. 'It is being used to *insult* people of *other* sexualities and it joins a list of other words that, if used, will result in instant exclusion.'

She sat down.

'Any other business?' Mr Sweet asked.

No one spoke.

The five minutes bell rang. We left the hall.

It's a truism that there's no one less tolerant than a liberal; 'gay' is a pretty bland word. I know it was appropriated by, well, gay people to mean homosexual, and there are supposed to be gender-political connotations in its use; it's supposed to have a certain resonance. It doesn't just describe sexual orientation, it celebrates independence from, and a rejection of, prejudice.

In many ways, it's become a good word.

But now everyone who fought for the meaning of the word to be changed, who struggled to celebrate difference, who changed the law so that consenting adults could put their genitals wherever they want, they're all incensed. Because the meaning of the word has been changed again, without their permission. Because now the word 'Gay' has been appropriated by teens.

To mean 'stupid'.

But it's always been a pretty flexible word. Apart from its literal meaning of 'Cheerful', and its counter-culture meaning of 'Homosexual', in the nineteenth century 'Gay' also meant prostitute. And a couple of weeks ago I sat with Joe reading a Crufts breed book; we were thinking about getting a dog. In the context of this book, gay means lively, happy, exuberant. It means a fox terrier, an Airedale or something similar.

And now it means instant exclusion.

It's joined the 'N' word as being completely beyond the pale. It's replaced the 'C' word which has been downgraded to DefCon 2. And the 'F' word has become a mere conversational trinket.

But the students invent their own uses for words, just like nineteenth-century whores and 1960s homosexuals did. If they want to insult each other they also use the word 'Special' as in Special Needs, or 'Lexy', as in Dyslexic. Or Kappa. Meaning, well, you can guess. And if they like something, it's 'Pimp', whereas *pimps*, as a corruption of *simple*, means easy.

I'm not sure what some of their phrases mean though; 'Do

Your Rip' is a taunt, a phrase used to signify that someone has just embarassed themselves, fallen over, been two-timed, failed a test, been thrown out of class. Whereas we would have sung *nar nar ne nar nar,* the kids here shout Do Your Rip!

So I reckon Miriam Hopwood is backing a loser. Besides, instinctively, I know that the school doesn't want the local newspaper running headlines along the lines of 'Excluded For Using The Word Gay'. So I'll be employing my intermittent deafness ploy; unless someone actually shouts it in my ear, I won't notice it.

'Gay' doesn't come up that often anyway, much less often than a number of other words, but I don't want my mug on the front page of the *Bognor Chronicle* under a banner headline that identifies me as a member of the thought police.

Especially as I'm still job hunting.

And while I'm on the subject of waiting in hope for the postman to deliver me some good news, Jenny's solicitor still hasn't got back to me.

Monday 25th 1.01 pm – Room 101

Still chewing on the etymology of insults, I open the door of room 101 and the kids pile in; I watch them, psyching myself up for another attempt at getting 11*Fick* to complete their coursework.

'Hey Stevie, can you lick your elbow?' This is Peel, unable to focus on his coursework, determined that the lesson shouldn't be a complete social washout. He gurns as Stevie tries to cram her elbow toward her mouth. 'I can't get it in,' she complains, and I can see exactly where the conversation is leading so I intervene.

'Peel, open your file, we've got coursework to complete.' He mutters something and looks toward his essay. This class has exactly four English lessons left before the Easter break. Four lessons in which to do their GCSE coursework. Peel, along with a number of others, is in my 'amber' group – they've done a bit of work, but not enough to pass. Stevie is one of the half dozen currently in the 'green' group – expected to do reasonably well. She's finishing off her coursework.

Boys hate coursework.

Coursework was designed to help girls do as well as boys in their examinations. In general, boys tend to do better than expected in exams, girls a little bit worse. This was felt to be an unfair situation, as it unduly rewarded boys who really hadn't put the work in. Well, they had. They just put the work in boy-style. Which means eighteen months of mucking around plus a couple of months of focused hard work.

But now, with coursework, the girls don't just equal the boys, they do even better. And the boys, faced with the reality of having to work girl-style, are throwing in the towel. They can't do it. Well, some can. But many who would do reasonably well with final exams, do less well because of the coursework.

One of the cunning plans to re-balance this re-balance, this shift toward girls doing better than boys, is to set exam questions that are deemed more boy-friendly. So we get exam questions about fire-fighting, trips to the Arctic and so on. Boy-friendly questions that need factual answers based on empirical information.

If this works, and pretty soon, when coursework is abolished, there'll almost certainly be a swing back toward boys doing better than girls, we'll have exam questions that are more female-friendly. Questions that require empathy and imagination and description.

And that's only the male/female thing. Add in class, social, geographical and cultural variables, and pretty soon we'll have so many conflicting requirements, so many variables, so many competing ideologies to satisfy from an GCSE exam, that the questions will need to be devised by a super-computer programmed by Gary Kasparov.

Whatever. Back here in 101 there are now three and a half-lesson to go. 'Think of it as the length of two football matches, plus stoppage time,' I tell Peel. 'That's all you have. That's all the time allowed to finish your coursework.'

'I'll score a last-minute winner,' he tells me, running with my analogy.

'I'll settle for a score-draw,' I reply.

'Aah, I'll get an extension,' he tells me, confidently, hoping that I haven't noticed the phone he's been using to text to his classmates, that's he's now holding in his left hand beneath the desk. 'Loads of people did last year.'

'No you won't,' I tell him. 'There's no injury time. The coursework is being sent off over Easter,' and, a little shocked by unexpected news, he promptly starts writing with a degree of vigour.

But I'm lying. The coursework doesn't go for another six weeks; he probably will get an extension. Because, guess what, he can't be allowed to fail.

With the class, Peel included, getting on with their work, I sat down and looked at the maps on my desk; the cycle ride. Keith Keill's brother had loaned us a minibus. Mr Sweet had agreed that the school would pay for petrol...and membership of the YHA for all the students involved.

In just over a week, we'd be heading for the Lakes, we'd be starting at Keswick, riding East through Braithwaite and over the Whinlatter Pass, turning South and then North East past Loweswater, South to Ennerdale and then pretty much West to the Youth Hostel at Gillerthwaite where we'd be spending the night.

The next day involved a few kilometres through a forest followed by another steep climb, more likely a get-off-and-push, over the top and down into Borrowdale and then directly North through Grange and back to Keswick.

Easy.

Dale from the IT Department had set up a website/blog to record all the details of the planning, how much money we'd raised so far, and it already contained a few suggested designs for Hattie's memorial. People were starting to be interested.

I hoped it was going to be alright.

I had a list with everyone's mobile number on it. All students had guaranteed that they had a bike that was sound, roadworthy and had a working set of lights. I'd provided each one with a list of minimum emergency kit that they must carry.

On top of that, Keith and I were first-aid trained. I'd done a First Aid course shortly after Joe was born, purely in case he ever choked or something and I needed to know what to do.

I'm pretty squeamish though, so in many of the lessons I'd had to grit my teeth and not give in to the desire to be sick, or faint away, at the detailed discussions of intestines, blood and so on. However, I was fully qualified, on paper at least, though hopeful I'd never be required to carry out any emergency procedures.

Then Merlene came into room 101 with some books for me and I sort of forgot what I'd been thinking about. Laying down the half-dozen paperbacks I'd asked for she looked over my shoulder and asked, 'You writing lists again?'

'I'm always writing bloody lists,' I tell her, quiet enough so that the students close by don't hear me swear.

But when I close my notebook before she can peek she asks me, 'Am *I* in your journal, Mr Ken?' and she raises an eyebrow as she leaves the room.

Yes, I suppose you are, I write later.

9.35pm – Bainbridge Avenue

There's a rhythm to life in education; the days are punctuated by hourly bells, the same classes arrive at your door at exactly the same time and day, three or four times a week, and the weeks themselves are bundled into six-or seven-week packages – half-terms – punctuated by regular holidays.

The rhythm of life in schools can lull you to sleep, and the more you do it, the easier it becomes; that's why those who are ambitious, those who want to climb the ladder of success, those who want to *stay hungry*, get out of the classroom as quickly as they can.

Because inside the classroom, time passes with barely a murmur, and you don't notice. Then suddenly thirty-five years have passed and you're teaching the grandchildren of those you taught when you were a Newly Qualified Teacher. The rhythm of the clock sucks you in and propels you along and, before you realise, twelve months have gone by.

It's been a year since I split with Jenny.

I thought about this scenario and, for the first time in my career, I wasn't sure if teaching was the job for me. The only other profession that I can think of that bears comparison, in terms of its adherence to the hourly clock, is the Royal Navy with its 'watch' system. Though to be honest I've only experienced that through the novels of Patrick O'Brien. Being an English teacher, and a man, therefore both an avid reader and statistically unusual, I get most of my experience of how extraordinary life is from books, while not actually doing anything extraordinary myself. This vicarious experience can make you feel a bit of a fraud at times. I have to tell myself that while I may not have much life experience beyond the class-room, my experience is no different to that of a typical office worker or bricklayer.

OK, if I was a beat bobbie or a paramedic I could maybe have a store of interesting stuff to talk about, or if I was an Air Sea Rescue Helicopter Pilot.

But what makes my job so satisfying, so interesting, so *more-ish*, is the relationship you have with the students.

When I was a fresh-faced, newly qualified teacher, a wise old Deputy Head advised me that when you strip away all the statistics, the strategies, the league tables, the lesson starters, the plenaries and the other good things that the Government decrees we should have in state classrooms, all you really have left is your relationship with your students. He was right.

The energy they give off is immense, you can feel it coming

at you in waves. Sometimes good energy, sometimes bad. Either way, it's kind of addictive.

The way they tell you stuff about their lives, for instance, the fact that some of my year eight kids have, of their own volition, started stapling photographs of themselves as infant babies on one of my classroom walls. 'No one else must put a picture here,' I was told sternly, 'Only year eights.'

'What about a picture of me?' I asked, and this was met with a hail of laughter.

On a good day you're like a parent on a field trip with one hundred and fifty kids. On a bad day though, you can feel like a lonely Aunt Sally. There are only a matter of days before the end of this, my second full term at the school; on a professional level I've settled in. But I have no permanent contract, no security and the school itself isn't what I'd imagined I'd be working in this far into my career.

Maybe it's a signal.

Maybe I should think about moving on to something else.

On the personal front I'm living with my son in a grotty, leased apartment. I haven't been out for a drink with friends, or a meal with a woman, in months; and I think I'm getting a bit fat. It's all a step back. Maybe this isn't a temporary blip, maybe this is my life.

I attempted to shake myself out of this temporary mood of spiritual disenfranchisement, by making myself busy, so I took out the maps and spread them on the table in front of me, checked the list of things to do, the students' phone numbers, the kit I needed to acquire. Food, drinks, First Aid kits, confirming our booking at the hostel.

In less than a week I'd be struggling up some dirt track on a cold and wet fellside, herding a bunch of truculent teens toward a distant Youth Hostel.

Shit, I thought.

I must be mad.

18

Monday, 7.31am – A Car Park in Keswick

'Time for breakfast,' Carl shouted.

'*Fuck* yeah!' Dicka echoed, 'And a smoke.'

We got out of the minibus, stiff-legged, bleary-eyed, it was barely seven in the morning and we'd been driving for a good few hours. I'd been up at four to get Joe ready and had dropped him off with my sister at precisely 4.45am.

'Do you know what time it is?' she asked me, pyjama-clad, eyes barely open.

'Precisely four forty-five.'

'You owe me for this,' she said, as Joe tottered in, still in his pyjamas and I heard her telling him, 'Come on into my bed young Jofus, you can be my hot water bottle,' as she shut the door.

The last thing I heard was him saying, 'It's *Joe*! Not Jofus!'

'The bike shop doesn't open 'til eight,' Keith told me, 'So let them eat their sandwiches, I'll pour some tea, and we'll sort the gear.'

The girls went to find a public toilet and I pulled out the bags and set them in a row at the side of the bus. Then I took out the emergency kit and checked that everything was there; dressings, sun cream, a list of mobile phone numbers; everyone had a list of everyone else's phone number. Then I did the same for the bike repair kits.

Carl told me, 'We're going to find a sweet shop,' and I guessed 'sweets' was a euphemism for cigarettes but, so long as he and Dicka weren't shoplifting, I wasn't going to chase them around. This wasn't school. This was the holidays. We were doing this for a good reason and, professionally, most bets were off. I was merely a cheerleader, at most a shepherd. Not a teacher, not their mum, and certainly not a social worker.

That left me, Keith and Chris Hawkins, a student I didn't know very well but someone who was reputedly fit, sensible and ambitious to join the armed forces directly after he reached the age of seventeen. Chris was kitted out in sensible clothes; shorts, Berghaus t-shirt, chunky trainers. He had two packs, a large one containing his overnight stuff and 'This is for when I'm biking,' he told me, 'See, it's got an internal water bladder, with a tube that I can drink from while I cycle, and room for my soft-shell, sandwiches, phone and,' he smiled, 'tabs,' and showed me a box of B&H in a side pocket. 'I'm cutting down though; I'll be off these by this time next year, when I join up.'

'What regiment?' I asked him.

'Royal Marines.'

He looked fit enough. Average height but muscular and broad-shouldered for his age. While he checked his kit I went for a walk to take a look around; Keswick is very pretty, even from the car park at the rear of the main street; the hills loom on every side and on a bright, chilly day like this the sky is clear, bright; it's a perfect picture of England.

Wordsworth was right to live around here. But I suspected I'd find it difficult to settle here; I would miss the sea, which I'd gotten used to over the last few months.

At 8pm, kit checked, students properly attired, we went to collect the bikes. Keith arranged to park up at key points every fifteen kilometres or so along the road and wait for the stragglers to pass.

I checked the route with him once more. 'Mount up!' I shouted to the kids; three girls, three boys.

'Remember why we're doing it,' Becca told the group.

We watched Keith drive off in the minibus. 'We cycle along that road to Braithwaite, it's only two or three miles,' I told them, 'then we'll stop, check our kit, make sure nothing has …' but Carl had already took off like a rocket on his fifteen hundred pound full-suspension superbike. Within twenty yards he missed a curve in the road, crashed into a parked van, and fell off. Chris and Dicka sped past him laughing as he picked himself up.

'Come on then,' Becca said to the other girls. I followed, and we were off.

After a leisurely three miles we reached Braithwaite, checked the bikes over for any loose bits and headed up the first of the hills. There was no sign of Chris or Dicka. As I followed the girls up the Whinlatter Pass, followed distantly by a red-faced and puffing Carl, I realised that this wasn't going to be just a physical trial, I was supposed to keep this disparate group together somehow, and already I'd failed. Already we'd separated into two, almost three groups. My heart was sinking. I wouldn't have been at all surprised if the two leaders simply kept pedalling until they reached the Irish Sea.

At the top of the pass Keith and the girls were waiting for Carl and me with tea and biscuits.

'I'd better give the lads a call first,' I said.

Keith shrugged, 'If you can get a signal.'

He was right. I couldn't.

'But you saw them pass, right?'

He smiled, shook his head. 'They know where they're going, and Chris can read a map.' He patted me on the shoulder. 'Don't worry, Danny, your teaching career isn't in tatters yet.'

Yes it bloody is, I thought, and the sheer bottom-of-the-barrel-ness of it all had the effect of cheering me up, in a grim sort of way. I was beginning to understand how soldiers must feel when the battle is lost but they have to keep on fighting.

Then Becca said, 'Thanks for doing this, Mr Keane.'

I wasn't sure if it was the thanks, or the mere fact of someone finally pronouncing my name right, but I felt a bit better. 'I'm wiped out already,' I said ruefully.

'Only another five hours in the saddle,' Keith said.

Thanks Keith, I thought, but asked, 'How long we been going so far?'

'About an hour.'

'Pour me another coffee.'

Keith poured us all another coffee, topped up our water bottles, all except Carl, whose drink of choice was a petrol-coloured energy drink.

'It's downhill for the next few miles anyway, then flattish,' Keith said.

'*Ish*?'

He patted me on the shoulder again, 'Don't stress it. Pain is just weakness leaving the body.' His grin was *way* too broad. 'Either that, or nature's way of telling you you're getting old.' He shook his head, smiling, 'I'm not sure. One of them.'

He got back in the minibus, still smiling. He was OK, he was driving.

The rest of the day followed a pattern; me following the girls, trailed by Carl who, though slow and unfit, didn't seem particularly ready to give up and who, it had to be admitted, showed absolutely no fear going down the various steep and narrow lanes. On a number of occasions he passed me and the girls, feet splayed out to the side, yelling his war cry of 'C'Mon!', sweeping through crossroads and junctions without a sideways glance.

'C'Mon!'

Sheep scuttling in every direction.

'C'MON!'

Hands free.

If he breaks his neck, or hits a tractor, I thought, his mum will kill me. I didn't doubt that she would, or that she knew of some studded biker punk who would beat me to death on her behalf.

Every hour or so we'd find Keith parked up on the way, with sandwiches, tea and, for Carl, a litre bottle of blue pop.

'Where does he put it all?' Keith asked.

We watched him down his latest bottle of blue pop in one long glug.

'And why blue?' I asked.

'I dunno,' Keith conceded, 'It must be a genetic thing; liquid woad maybe.'

And then, finally, at long last, in the late afternoon, I caught up with the girls who were stopped at a wooden gate from which hung a Gillerthwaite YHA sign. 'Is this it?' I asked, and we dismounted, wobble-legged, and pushed our bikes up the short lane to the Youth Hostel where we found Dicka and Chris waiting.

I noticed that Chris was wearing only his shorts and was fast asleep. Dicka was hanging upside down from a tree. My suspicions that they were drunk appeared confirmed when Dicka greeted us with shouts of 'KEANO-OH! KEAN-OH!' and I thought, well, on the bright side, that's twice today they've got my name right.

Then he giggled, hiccoughed loudly and dropped heavily from the tree. He got to his feet unsteadily, leaned over a dry stone wall and vomited what appeared to be a half gallon of clear fluid all over a Wordsworthian splendour of daffodils.

'That was more than five hours,' I muttered to Keith, who pulled in behind us a couple of minutes later. He got out of the minibus and together we watched Dicka do his level best to desecrate an area of Outstanding Natural Beauty before turning to us and announcing, 'Buckfast Wine. Brewed by Monks. Drunk by drunks.' Then he lay down on the grass and fell sound asleep.

'I guess that means more baked beans for us,' Keith said, brightly.

The Youth Hostel at Gillerthwaite is an unmanned cold-water bunkhouse. It has toilets, sinks, an unstocked kitchen and a small stove. It has bunks in two small rooms. The kids all piled into one room, Keith and I took the other.

Tuesday, 7.24am – Gillerthwaite

It's after 7am. I get up, walk stiffly into the cooking area and boil the water for coffee. I take a mugful to Keith' who has also woken. 'Here.' Then I go outside and sit on the step.

The Youth Hostel is idyllic; it sits by a brook, there are plantation trees all around and the sun has risen at the top of the valley. I fish out my phone and dial my sister's house. I want to ask Joe how he's doing. I want to tell him we'll come here ourselves in the summer.

Call failed.

After breakfast we pack our bags ready for the final, winding ascent up and over Green Gable and down into Borrowdale, then North toward Grange and, eventually, Keswick. This is the shorter of the two days.

'How much have we raised?' Carl asks me.

'I don't know.'

'I do,' Becca says. She's taking pictures. 'We've raised over five hundred pounds in sponsorship. We're going to have the full amount by September.'

Satisfied, Carl sits down on a deckchair to watch the rest of us pack. His face is bright red. Redder than his hair.

Chris and Dicka are already ready to go. 'Stay in touch,' I tell them.

'We'll see you back at the car park.'

'Don't get arrested,' Keith warns them, 'And don't lose the bikes. Lock them if you leave them.'

The rest of us saddle up a few minutes later.

This second day is shorter and steeper, more of a 'get off and push' day; we're alone for this bit, no support van, no hot cups of tea. At the top of Green Gable we were able to coast a lot of the way, pausing only to take photographs of a waterfall near Seathwaite. Careering hands-free down a grassy track, Carl swerved to miss a sheep and crashed his bike again.

'Are they *allowed* to be here?' he asked, dismayed.

'Yes,' I told him, 'They're called sheep. This is the countryside.'

He rubbed a bruise on his shin, got back on and took off down the bank again, shouting his war cry, undaunted.

I watched him go. Becca and Marnie watched me.

'You want to try that?' Marnie asked.

I shook my head.

'Go on.'

I shook my head.

Becca looked at Marnie. 'I will,' she said, and she took off Carl-style, down the hill, shrieking with delight, arms and legs splayed as she disappeared around a bend.

Marnie looked at me, shook her head at my cowardice and then sped off in pursuit. Little Beth watched both of them go for a moment, then dashed after them. I watched Marnie disappear around the corner, like Carl, hands and feet-free, steering, it appeared, through sheer force of will.

'Oh bugger,' I thought. I pedalled tentatively, forward, reaching the apex of the hill as Marnie too swerved out of sight.

What have I got to lose, I thought? How hard can it be? Then I went for it, pedalling fast to gain momentum. I tried to remember how to steer using only my bum and bodyweight. As I built up speed I took my feet off the pedals. The wheels whirred beneath me. As I reached the steepest part of the bank I took my hands off the bars, raised them outwards.

'C'Mon!' I shouted. 'Come *On!*'

The countryside fled past me in a shuddering blur.

The tyres hummed.

I couldn't hear myself laughing, but I was.

Worst Leech Boggy College

Motto: You are not a failure

19

'Sir, you could be a Moslem, if you wanted to be. I could tell you about it.'

I look at Umayr 'That's very kind of you. Thank you.' I smile but then shake my head, 'I'm afraid though that I'm faithless, Umayr.'

'You don't believe in God?'

I shrug, 'I'm not sure what I believe in.'

Today, Umayr has kindly brought in his prayer mat and hat; he's going to explain to the class the details and rituals of his daily prayers. Umayr displays all the positive aspects of good Moslem kids; he's kind, honest, he's hard-working. His offer to help me convert is sincere.

He's eleven years old.

The class sits quietly listening as he explains the way he, and all Moslems, pray five times a day, and how they wash and clean themselves first. A lot of his understanding is via the rote learning he does at his Islamic school, an institution he visits for two hours every night after state school, and he pauses to think of how to explain the importance of certain parts of the ritual. On a couple of occasions he confers with Shazim on how to explain in English a concept he really only understands in Arabic.

'Do you mind if I take a picture?' I ask, enthused.

'Sure.'

I capture an image of Umayr kneeling on his mat. Facing east.

The kids listen intently; most of the white kids are even more godless than me. West Bognor has a few Moslem kids, maybe a couple in every class, but the majority of students here are ex-Christian chavs with value systems based around state-funded living, wide-screen TV and Lawsuits-4-U.

Umayr on the other hand is hard-working and quietly devout. He can be quite cheeky at times, but not in an unpleasant way.

'At my Islamic school, if we talk in class, the teacher hits us with a stick,' he says.

Some of the audience of unruly eleven-year-olds get a bit annoyed at this and express their amazement at the idea of being hit by anyone, never mind a teacher. 'No, it's true!' Umayr tells them, 'But it's alright. Because my culture allows it.' Then he looks at me with a smile: 'But, you can't hit me, sir.'

'I've no intention of striking you,' I smile.

He winks. Then he carefully rolls up his mat and, as per my instructions, he asks the class, 'Are there any questions?'

A lot of the kids ask questions and they're mostly positive. They want to know why he prays five times, why he fasts for a month during Ramadan. If *they* will go to heaven too.

They tell me there's racism at this school and I've no reason to doubt that, but it seems to me that the Moslem kids are reasonably well integrated. There's no overt antagonism.

Only one kid in the room seems affronted by Umayr's presentation.

Anil asks, 'You pray *five* times a day?'

'Yes.'

'And you have to face Mecca?'

Umayr nods.

Anil shakes his head in disbelief; 'That's just *stupid!*'

'Anil,' I say, 'We don't insult each other's religious beliefs in my classroom.'

'Well, it's daft.'

'At least we can eat bloody beef,' Umayr responds.

'That's enough, you two.' I turn to the rest of the class, 'Any other questions?'

At the end of the lesson, Umayr asks me if he can store his prayer mat, safely inside a kitbag now, in my cupboard.

'Sure,' I tell him. Then I tell him that I was impressed by his knowledge and his belief.

'It's a good religion sir,' he tells me and this is when he offers to help me convert. I am deeply touched though, unfortunately, not saveable.

'You won't let anyone touch my prayer mat?'

'No way,' I reassure him.

'Not even you,' he warns me.

I nod. 'Not even me.'

Umayr leaves the room, warily eyeing Anil, who has waited until everyone else leaves before speaking to me.

'Mr Ken, can *I* do a presentation next week?'

'Sure.' I enjoy it when my students talk to the rest of the class; having the confidence to talk publicly is a skill that many kids around here never manage to acquire and, like my being completely unable to text more than four words a minute, it's quite a social drawback. I expect that Anil wants to talk about his own religion, as a riposte to Umayr's talk on Islam.

Anil is a Hindu and there's a clear but unspoken antagonism between the two of them. They rarely communicate with each other, except to verbally prod and criticise.

'What do you want to talk about?' I ask him.

'Cricket!'

My look of surprise must have been interpreted as doubt because he continues quickly, 'I can bring my full cricket outfit into class, my pads and gloves and stuff. I can explain the rules, show some of the different bowling techniques; demonstrate the strokes.'

'That sounds really good.'

'And I can tell them about the best player in the world.'

'Who's that?'

He looks at me with disbelief; 'Tendulkar!' he tells me.

'Of course,' I say, reassuring him, and his expression tells me that, so long as everyone knows that the best batsman in the world is Indian, everything is alright with the world. I nod approval of his enthusiasm. 'Good, good. And you can end by asking the class if there…'

'Are there any questions.'

'Right.'

He leaves the room proudly, his mind buzzing with ideas for next week's presentation.

I thought Anil would want to give a talk about his religion. I think that's what he's going to do.

Friday, 11.22am – Room 101

This morning I got a cover lesson with a year ten GNVQ General Studies class. They're currently studying a module on Human Rights.

As everyone knows, NVQ means Not Very Qualified. GNVQ, it follows, means *Generally* Not Very Qualified. But seeing as the Government, in its wisdom, has decreed that a GNVQ is equivalent to four GCSEs and schools, being obsessed with statistics, have quickly cottoned on to the fact that one GNVQ plus a gimme such as Media Studies or Woodwork (FYI now known as Resistant Material Technology) means the kids have, in theory, gained the magic number of five GCSEs. OK, we now have to count English and Maths, so the scam has been diluted a bit, but GNVQs, as useless as they are, still add a fistful of statistics to the school results table.

So today I get to teach GNVQ General Studies to 10C. Known to all as 10*Crap*.

There was something on Radio 4 the other day about lowering the voting age to sixteen. Well, in the light of my lesson with 10C, bring it on.

Kids are natural authoritarians. Especially the badly behaved ones. For a class full of foul-mouthed, violent, sexually predatory, unemployable teenagers, 10*Crap* are remarkably old-fashioned in their values and expectations.

As part of the Human Rights module they'd been studying 'Law & Order' and we were discussing acceptable social behaviour, both in and out of school. They were quite clear in their values; teachers should never swear in front of students (I agree). Teachers should not threaten students (again, I agree). Students should have a voice (true). Then they went further; parents should be allowed to wallop their kids (hmm...). Burglars and thieves should have all their worldly goods confiscated, though not those of their kids, who are not to blame (fair enough).

Car thieves should be run over (!!!).

Mothers of rape victims and parents of abuse victims should be allowed to castrate the offenders (hmm... actually, they have a point).

Foucault would have been proud.

As they warmed to the subject, they became even more authoritarian. '*Three strikes and you're out,*' someone said. 'What', I countered,' if you do two burglaries and then one day you don't pay for a pizza?'

That's three strikes. You're outta here.

Capital punishment?

Bring it back. Now.

Hanging?

Sooner the better.

Flogging in public?

Yes. Immediately.

CCTV? Police brutality? Death by firing squad?

Yes. Yes. Yes.

Judicial torture?

Yes.

Soon.

And publicly.

I gave them the standard anti-death-penalty argument; what about those wrongly convicted?

Bad luck.

No smoke without fire.

Worth it in the long run.

197

There isn't a current political party right-wing enough for 10C GNVQ General Studies. I await the proposed reduction of the voting age with a mixture of awe and alacrity.

Tuesday 12.56pm – Corridor Outside Head Teacher's Office

'Educated off-site?'

Mr Sweet nodded. 'Which means, in practice, that Connor will not be back. He's due in for his examinations in May and June, but I've made it clear that if he steps one inch out of line we'll exclude him from the examinations too.'

'Thanks. How did Connor's dad take it?'

'Billy? He attacked Connor. I had to intervene. Managed to stop him committing actual-bodily-harm against his own son, right there and then, in my office.'

We stopped outside of Mr Sweet's office. 'God help Connor when he gets home.'

'You weren't worried he might attack you instead?' I asked.

Mr Sweet raised an eyebrow, 'It's always a possibility, I suppose. But Billy's family have enough trouble right now. The eldest son, Tom, is on remand for armed robbery. The middle son, whose name I can't remember, we excluded him for theft and assault, way back, when he was in year eight, he's doing time now for a knife attack. And Billy's got a war brewing with the Murdoch clan.'

'The Murdochs?' They were another criminal brood with a smattering of children at West Bognor.

Mr Sweet nodded, 'The last thing he wants is any more trouble right now. The knife attack was on one of the Murdoch boys, John, I think.

'John Murdoch? I don't know him.'

'A complete waste of space. He left here three years ago. The attack was quite nasty. Reconstructive surgery needed. You know the sort of thing. Well, anyway, that particular Small got sentenced a couple of weeks ago.' He smiled grimly 'Rumour has it that Mrs Small, the mum, has warned Billy that if any more of her sons ends up inside, she's leaving him. You teach one of the girls, don't you?'

'Yeah, Alicia Small. Year eight. Nice girl.'

'The Small girls are nice enough,' he said, nodding, 'But the Small boys should be lined up and shot. They're animals.'

He told me, 'The Smalls have a very good marriage by all accounts. Six children. They were childhood sweethearts. Went to this school too. But Susan, the mum, is sick of his criminal ways and the effect that this is having on her children. So, happily for me, Billy isn't in the mood for assaulting anyone at the moment.'

The door to his office opened as we spoke; a couple of workmen were carrying out a desk. We moved aside.

'You getting new furniture?'

'No. We're getting a new Head Teacher.'

'I'd forgotten,' I admitted.

He told me, 'We're getting a guy called Stuart Trucks. A number-cruncher, by all accounts.' He paused as if he was going to say more but all he managed was a wry, '*Perfect.*'

I asked, 'You didn't fancy the job?'

Mr Sweet shook his head. 'I've been teaching for thirty-seven years, Daniel; I've got two more years and then I'm retiring to a cottage in Northumberland.'

We watched one of the workmen unscrew his name-plate from the door. 'Why spoil my last six terms?' he said as the name **Mr J Sweet** came off. Followed by the word **Deputy**, leaving only the title **Head Teacher** still affixed to the door.

'I wouldn't wish that job on anyone,' he told me. Then he patted my arm and said, 'Stay off the greasy pole. Stick with your department. It's a good place for a smart young man.'

He went into the office and the door shut behind him.

He was talking about me, I think.

Hmm…

20

Junior Donkin is fifteen, and if he'd been born a medieval forester, or a stone-age hunter-gatherer, his gifts would have been hugely appropriate. As it is, I have no doubt that if bird-flu or a stray Iranian nuke were to land on our doorstep, Junior would survive.

And thrive.

Junior knows how to fish; he can repair simple machinery; he's comfortable spending the weekend hunting rabbits with his pals; he's quick and lean and strong.

He works part-time in a local butcher's and in six months he's progressed from sweeping up the blood and sawdust to cutting up the fresh carcasses; his ambition is to produce his own line of sausages; choice meats, with herbs and spices; 'No hooves or stuff,' he told me, on one of his rare excursions into school, 'Though there's not much wrong with the odd eyeball, to give a bit of texture.'

But in 21st century Britain, in his final year at Bog Standard Technology College, and about to sit his GCSE examinations, Junior is at a loss. He has no appropriate survival responses.

So most days he simply doesn't attend.

Junior is too honest, and he's unusual. He doesn't know how to fit in. Kids beat him up. He's not stupid, but he's not easily measurable. And that pisses off some teachers.

While Junior excels at distance running and rock climbing, it would be a simplification to use the current euphemism for being thick, and say he's a *kinaesthetic* learner, because he is visually and aurally perceptive too. He's just not designed for life behind a desk. But I like Junior. He's a one-off.

Back in October, in one of the few lessons he attended that term, I watched as he made a presentation for his GCSE coursework entitled 'Riverside Flowers and Vegetation'. He made the point that creatures and plants thrive in suitable environments but that, in a hostile environment, they still grow as best they can. He brought in three riverside plants, in a carrier bag, and he showed them to the class and talked about them at length.

As his tutor, I was proud of him that day. It seemed to me that Junior had expressed a universal truth; we survive best in suitable environments but, in hostile environments, we get on with the business of life as best we can.

How can we ignore stuff like that, I thought, how can we ignore that level of perception from our students? Because, I reminded myself, expressing a universal truth, as simple and unintended as it may have been, is not measurable. So educationally, by which we mean statistically, it doesn't count.

Today I was attempting to complete my year eleven coursework-marking when my classroom door burst open and Helen 'Bunny' Boyle, Head of 'Whatever They Currently Call Cookery', burst in. She was holding Junior Donkin by his collar.

'Mr Ken?' she demanded.

'Yes, Ms Boyle?'

'Is this child one of yours?'

I nodded my head. I didn't know what crime Junior had committed during cookery/domestic science/food technology and, to be honest, I didn't want to know.

Silence followed.

I looked at Bunny, then at Junior and then back at Bunny, hoping one or both would disappear. But they didn't. Ms Boyle knew how to stand her ground; I was implicated somehow, and it didn't matter that I was unaware of my role, or the crime, or my role in the crime.

I put down my pen, cleared my throat and asked, 'Has there been a problem, Ms Boyle?'

There had. It turned out that Junior had been caught with a bumblebee in his pocket, and that the bumblebee could no longer bumble, because it had no wings.

Junior had de-bumbled the bee.

There was no denial. He'd admitted the offence. I sighed; it seemed like such a 1950s crime. A grey-flannel-shorts crime. Pulling the wings off a bee. I wondered if Junior's mum still used a ration book. I pictured his mum cooking stew in a big pot, on a range. Wearing a pinny. And Dad puffing away on a pipe.

I asked, 'Why did you pull the wings off the bee, Junior?'

He looked at the ground, 'Dunno, Mr Ken.'

'See,' Bunny said loudly, 'He doesn't even know why he's a murderer! DID YOU KNOW, Mr Ken,' Bunny continued, louder, 'that serial killers usually start by killing small creatures, in their teens, and progress to larger animals before eventually moving on to the *mass slaughter* of humans?'

Actually, I had read that somewhere, though it was a bit of a leap to pin it on Junior.

She looked at me, suspecting I wasn't taking her seriously enough, and snarled, 'You're supposed to be good with *challenging* students Mr Ken. Apparently they listen to you.'

This sounded suspiciously like an insult; perhaps I'd been displaying some kind of professional weakness.

'Would you like me to talk to him, Ms Boyle?'

She nodded, 'I would,' and she turned to glare at Junior: 'And I'd like you to explain that a murderer like him WILL NEVER KNOW LOVE! NEVER!'

And then she left the room.

I looked at Junior. He was staring at the floor, fifteen years old, tears welling in his eyes. And I thought that, sometimes, teachers can be bullies too.

Back in September, during one of my first lessons, Junior was sitting in my class and he was wearing a huge combat jacket. It was hot in the classroom but he kept it buttoned.

Being a teacher, I have eyes in the back of my head and I

could see that the kids were giggling and nudging and looking furtively at Junior whenever I looked away.

I sort of guessed what was going on and when, eventually, Junior's coat gave a small bark and began wriggling, and the class collapsed into fits of suppressed mirth, I walked quietly to his desk, leaned over and said, 'Perhaps you want to take him out onto the school field.'

'It's a she, Mr Ken,' he told me, 'A bitch.'

I gave him my classroom pass.

I didn't see him for, oh, maybe two months.

'How's the puppy, the, er, bitch doing, Junior?' I asked him.

He looked up, a smile sweeping across his face. 'She's a really good rabbiter Mr Ken. I go out with her every weekend.'

'What breed is she?'

'She's a cross collie and Bedlington terrier.'

'A bit big for rabbitting?'

'She doesn't go down the *burrows*,' he smiled at my ignorance, 'she runs them down for me to shoot.'

I pictured Junior in some midnight forest, with his cross terrier bitch, hunting rabbits. Then I thought about him sitting in the school hall, attempting to focus on his GCSEs – Shakespeare or algebra or chemical equations or something – his feet drumming with pent-up energy, his mind racing across fields with his cross-bred terrier.

> *But to go to school in a summer morn,*
> *O! it drives all joy away;*
> *Under a cruel eye outworn,*
> *The little ones spend the day*
> *In sighing and dismay*

Forget Ofsted and its legion of inspectors, William Blake had education sussed 200 years ago.

'Get yourself away,' I told him, straight-faced. 'If Ms Boyle catches you, tell her I've given you a week's detention.'

His face fell, 'Sir, *a week?*'

'Half term, fool,' It was my turn to smile at his ignorance,

'Now get lost and let me do some marking.'

'Oh, and Junior!' I shouted after him.

'Yes sir,' he paused in the doorway.

'Dispose of the bee.'

Friday, 2.11pm – Room 101

The runner waited at the door while I read and then quickly re-read the note, and then signed to say I'd read it and would attend the emergency meeting after school tonight.

I shut the door, mind racing. Ofsted were coming.

Next week.

With the often appalling behaviour in this school and, if you discounted the GNVQs, the sub-25 per cent GCSE pass rate, we were looking down the barrel of Special Measures. Closure. Unemployment.

Part of me sort of welcomed that idea; retraining might be good. I'd be better paid as a bricklayer or something. At least I wouldn't have to force my bricks onto people who didn't want things built. I wouldn't have to use my trowel while people shouted at me. I wouldn't have to take a load of bricks home at night and build more walls.

No extra work. The idea of life lived without the constant background noise of things that needed to be done. And if it rained I could go home.

Joy.

Then I thought of my dad's response to me retraining: 'a *dilutey*' he'd snort, meaning not a fully time-served tradesman. 'Then what'd you bother studying for?' he'd ask.

I put my escape fantasies on hold for the moment. On Wednesday and Thursday next, we were going to be inspected. And quite possibly, we were going to be found wanting. Deal with that, I told myself.

All I can do is teach, I replied. That'll have to do.

I went back to my desk. 'What were we talking about?' I

asked the class. They must have guessed something was up and they stayed pretty quiet; what had we been doing? Grammar? Punctuation? I couldn't remember and nor could they.

'Let's watch a video,' I told them.

I had things to think about and, with Ofsted on their way, teaching a lesson wasn't one of them.

Monday Evening – Bainbridge Avenue

A sheaf of lesson plans in hand, I opened my front door.

'Hi,' she said. Just standing there, like she'd been at work all day and had forgotten her key.

Jenny.

And my heart skipped a beat.

'Hey,' I replied, and then we stood staring at each other for a moment or two. The silence threatened to become embarassing, so I asked her, 'Do you want to come in?'

'Thank you,' she said, pausing at the threshold to look about, 'Is Joe...?'

I put down the lesson planning sheets on the sideboard, and then the fistful of coloured pens; 'No. He's out with my sister. I was just working …'

She nodded, almost relieved, I think, and stepped inside.

It struck me later, and with some clarity, that Lindsey, who'd offered to baby-sit while I completed the Ofsted lesson plans I needed for the coming inspection, must have known Jenny was coming. That was why she'd volunteered to take Joe out.

I helped Jenny take off her coat and hung it on a hook behind the door.

'This way,' I said and led her into the living room. The apartment felt strange with her in it, like it wasn't my home for the moment, and it felt shabby too; I was aware that I'd be judged on my ability to keep house.

I watched her as she sat down and now it was my turn to judge; lovely, as always, but older-looking, and a little lined.

Thinner maybe. She impressed me; she'd become the person she wanted to be.

I didn't know her.

I wondered how long I hadn't known her. I wondered how long she'd lived with me, and how much of our marriage we'd spent together, with me not knowing her. And I wondered how that made her feel.

We were like two fighters circling each other in a ring, or two grandmasters staring across a chessboard, each sizing up the other. Sitting down, she picked up one of my notebooks that lay on the table, and flicked idly through it. 'You still writing your journals then?' she asked.

'Yes,' I said.

'You once told me they make you feel better, when you write them.'

'Did I? They help me make sense, I suppose,' I said.

'Of what?'

'My life.'

'Oh,' she said, 'And am I in them?'

'Not so often now,' I told her, truthfully. 'You left.'

She put down the notebook, 'You should write a blog;' she said, 'I can see it now, "The life of a single father". They might even publish it.'

'Who might?'

She shrugged. 'I don't know, *publishers*?'

'I don't want to be a writer,' I said, 'I'm a teacher. I like teaching.'

'Still?

'Yeah.'

'I thought you might have got over that by now.'

'Got over it?' I half laughed, 'What, like an illness?'

She frowned, 'Yes. In a way. You should have progressed by now, got on. Got out of the classroom. You should have been promoted.'

I could see where this was leading; 'How is *Freddie* by the way?' I asked.

She looked pained. 'Daniel, there's no need to be unpleasant.'

'It pleases me to insult him,' I told her, flatly. Jenny's boyfriend has a moustache quite like that of Freddie Mercury.

'What do you get out of being sarcastic?' she asked me.

'You're the psychologist. Work it out.'

'Child psychologist,' she corrected.

'Even better,' I said. 'Didn't you always say dog owners grow to be like their dogs and ...'

'Teachers grow to be like their children?' she smiled. 'Yes.'

I stood, felt a year of grief and anger welling inside me, I wanted to punch something, instead I said, 'Coffee all round, I think,' and escaped into the kitchen to boil the kettle. I thought it would give her a moment to settle in, think about whatever it was that she'd come to tell me. And have a surreptitious look around, no doubt.

Five minutes later and I was back in the living room; I handed her a mug of coffee; I felt a little better too, less stunned; my heart rate was slowing. I felt resolved to be a bit, well, tough. Not in the mood for pleasant chats, or a meeting of minds.

'Why're you here, Jen?' I asked, sitting down to face her. She took a sip of her coffee, put it on the table. 'Place looks nice.'

'Yeah. If you like living in a 1980s bedsit.'

'I miss Joe.'

'He misses you too.'

'Does he?' her eyes shone a little.

I didn't feel much sympathy. 'You can see him.' I told her, 'whenever you want.' My voice got a little harder. 'You've had a whole year to make some arrangements. So when'll it be? Saturday in McDonalds? A Sunday in the park? Maybe you want a whole weekend away at Alton Towers.' I looked evenly at her, 'That's if *Freddie* lets you out of bed long enough to visit your son.'

'Please don't,' she asked. 'Don't be cruel.'

I felt like a shit, but I couldn't stop myself. 'Come on,' I said, 'We'll make the arrangements now.' I picked up my notepad and pencil. 'I'll write it down,' I said, my anger growing, 'in my journal. I could even set up a website!' I said, hotly, 'so you could log on and confirm the details. So you don't forget. And be late. Like a *year* late.'

I made her cry.

Quietly.

It didn't make me feel any better, to be honest.

After a couple of minutes she composed herself; dried her eyes. 'How is he?' she asked.

I stopped trying to be cruel, and turned my thoughts to him; Joe. I thought about his face, his expression, the warmth of his body as he lay asleep in my lap while we watched TV.

'*How is he?*'

'He's our son,' I told her.

'How are you?' she asked, dabbing her eyes, turning her attention back to me.

I took a very deep breath; be a *good* man Daniel, I instructed myself, and decided to fall back on some humour, 'They say the first eighteen months are the hardest, and after that it's pretty much, er, shit,' and I gave her a wry smile, and she giggled.

'Sorry,' she said.

'I'm sorry too,' I told her.

We almost hugged but instead I said, 'Drink your coffee and talk to me, Jenny Keane. All this touchy-feely stuff is a bit random... and I'm not good at righteous fury, so come out with it. Tell me what you want from me.'

I thought she'd come here for a divorce, and I was ready for that. Or maybe she wanted regular access to Joe. I was ready for that too. She straightened her face, looking downwards a little as she stroked the coffee mug, thinking to herself. Rehearsing her next words. Then she took a deep breath, looked at me and sighed.

'I want Joe,' she said. 'I want full custody.'

And I wasn't ready for that.

21

Tuesday, 3.57pm - Room 101

Room tidy.

Lessons planned and linked directly and recognisably to Government-approved schemes of work taken directly from one of the many state-approved teaching resources. Wall displays rearranged into something less random. Book-cases orderly.

Books marked up to date. Not just ticks and comments but *constructive* comments focused on particular areas of concern, along with short, medium and long-term targets for word and sentence level, reading level, writing level, vocabulary and more. All of this good, to one degree or another, but it seemed that we spend more time recording evidence of progress than we do actually progressing. To the point where the students' basic ability to read and write functionally is impaired by all the measurements we impose on them.

But it's OK. I'm up to date.

-ish.

No matter that I have no secure future because the school is so afraid of being put on Special Measures they won't commit to employing any new staff on a permanent basis.

No matter that a large percentage of my students see absolutely no need for education. In a way they're right – they're certainly smarter than we give them credit for – whatever happens, however irresponsible they are and no matter how little effort they put into learning, they're guaranteed the three basic necessities of life: fast-food, benefits and iPods.

The only people that Ofsted scares, the only people it's *supposed* to scare, are the teachers. But so long as I'm not observed attempting to teach my bottom set year eights, who are just too mercurial a bunch of jokers to want to bet my future career on, I've got a chance. So long as I'm not observed attempting to turn 11*Fick* into politically correct, multi-cultural, non-gender-specific model citizens via another hastily photocopied 'Citizenship' worksheet on 'How to Recognise Bullying' or the latest good news via *Cultural Studies IIIB – Welcoming Change & Migrant Culture* there's an evens bet that I'll still be allowed to teach come September.

At a pinch, I could get away with being observed with one of my year seven classes. They're still more *pre* than pubescent.

I turned back to the latest pre-Ofsted missive 'How To Be Outstanding!' with no real enthusiasm, flicking dutifully through this, the latest publication from the school office that explained how we were going to ace, absolutely *nail*, the due-any-minute-now Ofsted visit.

Thank goodness for Ofsted, I thought.

We're all teachers now.

We inspire, excite and educate.

Every lesson.

Every all-singing, all-dancing, planned, targeted, assessed and value-added, learning-down-the-throat lesson.

The problem is, life isn't like that. It's mainly dull, and a bit boring. There's lot of work to be done that doesn't result in any kind of reward. Lots of stuff where no one rewards, applauds, or lets you do it again if you screw up.

But thankfully, I'm immune to boredom. I sail blithely across the seas of dull and uninteresting; I crash manfully through walls of dirge; I scale the peaks of delayed gratification. And do you know why? Because I had some really *crap* teachers when I was at school.

But they were a brilliant preparation for life.

Three in particular: Mr Fairhurst was one of them. Funtime

Fairhurst we called him. The technology teacher who never spoke.

He spent his days, his terms, whole academic years, doing whatever you call the opposite of communicating. His classroom was a black hole of learning. It sucked dry any enthusiasm you might have.

We'd enter his room, in hushed awe at the prolonged silence that emanated from Fairhurst; his room vibrated silence. He'd barely look up; an uncomfortable hush filling the air as we read the lesson plan, and all necessary instructions, that had been written on the whiteboard some five or six years previously.

He sat at his desk reading comics, while we laboured away, using tools, craft knives, drills, hammers and the like.

One day, Michael Dobson broke three of his fingers in a 'tyre-lever incident'. He yelped loudly and then staggered down the class, cradling his arm and weeping quietly, quickly supported by two classmates, Tom Heron and Billy Young. In hushed, and ever-so-slightly guilty, tones they delivered a hastily concocted version of what had occurred, indicating the injury.

Dobson's rapidly swelling hand was turning an impressive shade of purple. Mr Fairhurst listened impassively.

They waited for a reply.

He stared at them. Blankly.

After a minute or so, Billy Young looked at Tom Heron. They both looked at Mr Fairhurst, who was still staring at them. They looked at Michael Dobson, whose agony was such that by now he was barely able to stand upright.

Mr Fairhurst still stared at them.

Tom murmured, 'We'll, er take him to…'

'…the nurse.' Billy completed the sentence, and they half-carried Dobson out of the class.

Mr Fairhurst stared after them for a moment or two, and then went back to his comic.

Mr Fairhurst kept an airgun too. His classroom faced the school playing fields. At one time the fields were plagued by dogs who wandered around barking, growling and defecating. So, Mr Fairhurst began shooting pellets at them. In complete silence, I'm sure. Like an ace sniper.

We'd be kicking a ball around on the school field, we'd hear a brief thrumming noise in the air, and twenty yards away a snuffling dog would suddenly howl, leap sideways and then run away. And we'd see a brief flicker of reflected sunlight as Mr Fairhurst closed his window.

The dogs stopped coming onto the field.

One day, shortly before his retirement, I saw him carrying a brace of pheasants into the staffroom. I was sixteen by then, so I ventured a comment, 'Been hunting, sir?'

'Bagged these beauties out on the moors,' he replied. 'On the way in.'

Which was the first and only time he ever spoke directly to me. And left me wondering about this teacher, who lived a life of austere, monastic silence and, apparently, kept a loaded shotgun in the boot of his car.

I realised that, as unusual as he was, Mr Fairhurst was a person. A real person, who had a life outside of school. As weird as that life might be. Now, I don't think I'll ever want to shoot pheasants, or dogs, but Mr Fairhurst taught me something.

Since that day, I've always considered that teachers should be human, whenever possible.

Even if that means, simply, flawed.

Whiskey Watson, the music teacher, had a tenuous grasp on reality. Or perhaps he just wasn't bothered. His lessons though, were a preparation for life; an object lesson in the futility of the vast majority of our dreams and aspirations. We'd enter his class and, for an hour, three times a week, we'd sit and watch him as he sat, eyes closed, listening to music on his headphones, while waving a baton in the air. At the crescendo, he'd rise and gesticulate wildly, his arms flailing.

The hour would pass; occasionally he'd open his eyes to give the Look of Death to some pupil or other, then close them again and return to his Gregorian chant, or symphony, or rock opera or whatever music teachers listen to for pleasure.

And then we'd leave his room and go on to the next lesson.

All I ever learned about music was what was written on the posters that decorated his classroom. But sitting in Whiskey Watson's class, just waiting for it all to end while some higher being completely ignored you, is a bit like how you feel when you unwisely enter a trendy clothes shop, or wait interminably on the line while some automated call centre connects you with a computer graduate in Delhi.

In an earlier age, it would have been preparation for purgatory.

Miss Primrose, my third worse teacher I can remember, was a spinster who only owned three dresses. One was pink. One was blue. One was grey. She wore pearls.

And real shoes.

I think she taught biology but, to be honest, I'm not quite sure. It might have been Food Technology. Or Badminton. She alternated the dresses – two days per dress – in a six-day cycle. You knew when it was near the end of term, because she'd be wearing the pink/grey dress on a Monday again. These dresses were made of the sort of stuff you expect bandsman's uniforms to be constructed of. I would not have been surprised if she had three matching busbies in her wardrobe.

What I admired about Miss Primrose wasn't her brogues, or her dresses, or her complete absence of inspirational teaching. Or any sort of teaching. And it wasn't her pearls.

It was the seventh-level-of-hell, demonic venom in her quietly rasping voice when she addressed us, each and every one of us, throughout the academic year.

She *hated* us. I think she hated all pupils.

But I have to believe though, that she only came to school for the money, and that outside of school she was a key player in some wonderful, exciting, exotic, quite possibly risqué, social scene. And her three dresses were a kind of extended practical joke, played daily on us, her pupils.

I have to believe that, behind the pearls, the brocade and the frown, she was a coke-snorting, wild-child, party-monster. Because the alternative, that her fussy, dour and acrid classroom demeanour was really her, and that it presented an accurate reflection of her life, was too tragic to contemplate.

So I'm glad we have Ofsted.

Because, with their supportive, guiding hand, we can educate and entertain, scaffold, model and teach and do all those other good things we do, every lesson, every day, every minute, from our starters to our plenary. As Charles Clarke famously said, while minister for education, 'education for its own sake is a bit dodgy'.

No longer, Mr Clarke.

Now, we teach for targets. We teach for purpose. We teach for league tables.

It's all good.

Of course, this is linked to a pervasive idea that, somehow, education is a vast marketplace where the conscientious parent can *choose* the flavour and quality of their child's education, as defined in the annual league tables. Learning is perceived as some sort of consumer paradise, where market forces will prevail to ensure children get the highest-quality education. This view of education is kind of like thinking, if you don't like the underwear range in M&S you can buy them from Debenham's instead.

In a society where shopping is the defining lifestyle activity, viewing education as the learning equivalent of a row of shiny, exclusive, glass-fronted High Street emporiums is quite logical. But while the aspiration is all farmers' markets and fresh, home-grown, quality produce, the reality is more Iceland. Or Lidl.

So, on reflection, I'm pleased I was forced to endure Funtime Fairhurst, Evening Primrose and Whiskey Watson, despite the fact that what I learned from them wasn't course-work, value-added, or even faintly academic. Nor was it even remotely *assessable*, in that gladiatorial way we currently have of measuring schools now.

But I learned to look after myself, to change what I could, and accept what I couldn't. I learned that people belong to themselves, and crucially, I learned that life isn't a monologue, nor yet a dialogue – it's one huge bloody conversation. People often say stuff we don't want to hear, or they ignore us because we are of no use or interest to them. And we learn to get over it. Because the world *doesn't* revolve around us.

Now there's a lesson for life.

It's almost four: I've got a bag of marking to finish tonight. On top of that, I've got official lesson plans to complete. Lesson plans that take an experienced teacher three-quarters of an hour each to complete.

I turn; take a look at room 101. I'm getting used to her. I switch off the lights, close the door and walk along the corridor, hoping vaguely that my car starts first time.

Ofsted are coming.

22

Tuesday, 8.47am – Corridor

Kelly Watson, one of this year's Newly Qualified Teachers, approached me in the corridor and asked if I had any ideas on how to persuade a group of year ten boys not to hang around outside her class during break and lunchtime; they'd been sitting on the radiator box that stands beneath the stairs, barracking passers-by and causing a general commotion. The radiator box is warm, with a flat surface at exactly teenage-boy seat height; its location puts it out of sight of most teachers, except Kelly, whose classroom door is exactly opposite.

The boys are cosy, hidden, very noisy and disruptive. Their targets for insults apparently include Kelly who, it must be acknowledged, is a teenage boy's dream; she's in her early twenties, with a pretty face and nice figure, and she's yet to discover her Inner Bitch, one of the unspoken, but iron-clad prerequisites of long-term survival as a teacher.

'Ask them to move,' I suggest.

'They just refuse, and give me abuse.'

She looked embarrassed but didn't elaborate; I could imagine the comments.

I almost suggested that she have a word with Big Cyril, but I got the feeling that, as a probationer, Kelly didn't want to be seen running to management every time she had a small behavioural issue to deal with.

Just at that moment, Vic Hughes walked by. Vic has been teaching longer than I've been alive; he's a short, wiry Irishman with a PhD in pragmatism and a Professorship in classroom management.

He also has a sharp nose for poking in wherever there is a spot of bother and he could see Kelly's glum expression. 'Problem?' he asked.

Kelly related the situation to Vic, who nodded thoughtfully and, after a moment or two said, 'I think I have the very solution. Wait here.'

We waited for his return but, about five minutes later, Jimmy the caretaker turned up instead. He was pushing one of those wheelie mop/bucket things he normally uses to clean away sick.

Jimmy announced, as though he was reading words from a page, 'That radiator cover is dirty,' and he began to swill down the radiator box, using copious amounts of dirty, sudded water. After a minute or two he paused; the top of the radiator box was now swimming in a half-inch layer of grey, grimy liquid.

'There,' he announced with some satisfaction. 'Much better.'

'Are you finished?' I asked.

He nodded and slid the greasy mop-head back into the bucket. Then he said, 'I've been informed that this radiator cover gets dirty every day, and that I should make an effort to keep it in *pristine* condition.'

'Really?' I asked.

'So I thought,' he continued, still speaking as if from a script, 'that I would Swill It Down. Twice a day. Just before the morning and lunch breaks.'

With that he left, pushing his bucket, his silver techno-stigmata glinting from between swaying dreadlocks.

'Twice a day,' I commented, as understanding began to dawn.

'Just before break and lunch,' Kelly replied.

Genius.

Wednesday, 8.34am – Staffroom

'Hey Danny, we're just discussing alternative ways to set the kids. You know, instead of using SAT's scores.'

It was Liz from PE, sitting with Mick and the guy from music whose name I could never remember.

'Postcode lottery,' Mick said. 'The closer they live to North Avenue, the lower the set we put them in. 'Want a coffee?'

'Coffee sounds fine,' I told him. 'But I'd be bottom set.'

'Well you've got 8Z4 already.'

'Hows about setting by race?' Liz asked, provocatively.

I pulled a slight frown, 'Culture.'

'OK,' she said.

The staffroom was madly, defiantly buoyant; a sort of devil-may-care attitude seemed to have struck what remained of the permanent teaching staff in the face of what could be the final Ofsted inspection – if it was as bad as it potentially could be, the school would certainly sack all of the teaching staff, close and then re-open with a new Head and a new name.

And the current new 'new Head' might never make it to his desk in September. As a long-term supply teacher I almost had a right to join in with the madness.

So I did; 'Top set: Chinese kids,' I said.

'That's race, not culture, you cheat,' Liz told me, but then quickly responded with, 'Set two – Goths.'

'*And* Moslem girls, seeing as we don't actually have any Goths,' the music teacher said.

'Bottom set, chavs,' Mick said.

'Well, of course,' Liz said.

'Wouldn't work,' I told her, 'we'd have one huge bottom set.'

The music teacher, whose name I remembered now as Tim, and who taught the kids to play steel drums every lunchtime, ignored me and ploughed on, 'Remedial class, *ginger* chavs.'

'Middle sets, bright chav girls and Moslem boys,' Liz added, 'but only with a male teacher, 'cos those boys don't respect women teachers as much.'

I smiled ruefully at them. 'We are *beyond the pale*, you know that? If Ofsted could record this conversation, we'd all get the sack straight away.'

'Oh, who gives a *fuck*,' Liz said, with a grin.

Mick said, 'Daniel, sit down, have this coffee.' I sat beside him; the cup said, World's Greatest Teacher. 'We're all due for the sack in the next forty-eight hours anyway,' he said. 'A bit of levity ...'

'Professional reflection,' Interjected.

Mick raised an eyebrow, '... that too. It won't cause any more harm.'

At that moment, three strangers in suits and carrying laptop cases entered the staffroom accompanied by Mr Sweet and a tall thin man who I recognised as one of the candidates for the head's job who'd come into my drama lesson a few weeks earlier.

'The New Head,' Liz told me in a stage whisper. He was wearing a mustard shirt and grey pants.

'Getting his feet under the table,' Mick said, softly.

'They're big enough,' Liz said.

They were. Huge. And sandalled. And he wore mustard socks that matched his shirt.

'Do you think he can't get shoes to fit,' the music teacher asked quietly.

Liz giggled.

Friday, 2.02pm – Room 101

Lightning doesn't strike twice, I prayed; lightning doesn't strike twice. Lightning doesn't ...

Friday afternoon, last lesson, 8Z4.

Ofsted.

Lightning doesn't strike twice.

The door burst open and 8Z4 piled in; they'd been pretty well drilled by me and, God bless them, they tried, but last lesson on a Friday they were never calm or in the mood for study.

'We've just been observed,' Tommy told me cheerfully.

'Were you good?'

He shook his head. 'We were terrible! Shouting out and everything; Miss Smith started crying.'

I shuffled my lesson plans.

'Why'd you do that?' I asked him.

He shrugged, 'I dunno.'

I'd written three minutely detailed lesson plans for this class and, depending on how they presented themselves, I'd give the Ofsted inspector the appropriate one: Lesson Plan A involved reading from their novel, which we'd almost finished, and then discussion, writing and *real* work. Plan B was group work, with worksheets. Plan C was working from a text-book.

And there was Plan X, which involved my walking out of the room, in tears.

'Are we getting observed again?' Nathalie shouted from the back of the room.

'I don't think so,' I replied, wishing that I'd simply said no. An equivocal reply provoked debate.

'But we *might*,' she said in a tone of rising expectation.

'Julian, give out the reading books please,' I said. I went through the register as Julian, MC Joolz to his pals, gave out the novel; almost ten minutes in and still no Ofsted.

'Right,' I told them. 'We have five pages left.'

I opened my book.

'Page 151. I'll start reading and if anyone …' fourteen hands went up.

Then the door opened and an inspector walked in.

Fourteen hands went back down.

Undeterred, I handed the inspector Lesson Plan A, and began reading. After a couple of minutes, I paused to ask a question of the class: 'How do you think Stanley feels about this?'

Nothing.

This is 8Z4, I told myself. I started reading again. After another five minutes I paused again to ask another question. 'This is a very exciting bit,' I told them, 'Why do you think the writer is using short sentences?'

Nothing.

'If anyone wants to read, they can put up their hand,' I said, keeping the growing panic out of my voice.

Nothing.

I read on. But without their input, the lesson would fall flat. An awkward silence engulfed us all.

Way back, when I was a student and on placement to one of the schools near the university, I had a class that was very vocal, very challenging, but confident, and fairly well behaved. It was an interesting mix, a good mix, very much what a new teacher likes to cut their teeth on. And we'd end every lesson with a debate on the meaning of what we'd just read, or some item on the news. So when my tutor, Gill, came to observe me, I was confident of a good lesson. The class started as always, working hard, asking questions, querying my professional abilities, and continued as per plan and when, fifteen minutes before the end, I paused as I had always done, to introduce the day's topic for discussion, the class remained silent.

Not a word. I cajoled, provoked, prodded. But they stayed quiet. So I just talked. Extemporary conversation. For fifteen minutes. To a class of mutes, while my post-graduate tutor observed me.

At the end of the lesson, during my debrief, Gill never mentioned the silence. Instead, she ended with a comment, 'Never assume you know how they're going to react.'

She didn't advise me on what I should have done.

And history was about to repeat itself.

So, as I watched the Ofsted inspector sitting at the rear of the class and taking notes, I wasn't sure what to do with this, my loudest, most volatile class, who'd suddenly taken a vow of silence. 8Z4, it appeared, had become novitiates in some local Carmelite sect.

My mind raced. Could I switch lesson plans, twenty minutes in? Would it be seen as flexibility, or panic? Would I be seen to be pragmatic, or confused?

In reality, teachers switch lessons all the time. Something will start badly, or veer off course, and I might go with it, or change tack or, as happened sometimes, *abandon* something. My year ten class, for instance, 10*Smokey* as they're known, just didn't get *Of Mice and Men*. They couldn't grasp that level of poverty. Not in America.

Their knowledge of the USA was all 'bling' and rappers in white furs and fast cars; their knowledge of the Depression was nonexistent. I showed them a version of the movie and, as we watched Lennie baling hay, someone asked, 'Where's the Indians?' which eloquently summed up their ignorance.

But switching lessons in the middle of an Ofsted observation was more risky.

We were reading *Holes*, an excellent novel about a boy who is sent to prison for a crime he didn't commit. It has everything; wrongly accused teenagers, a family curse, an interracial love story. But for possibly the first time in their lives, the students of 8Z4 had nothing to say. Like a drowning man, I read on desperately, my mood sinking lower with each word that echoed around the silent room.

'Mr Ken?'

I looked up; Alicia Small had raised her hand. 'Yes?' I asked, trying to keep the desperation out of my voice.

'My brother is in jail,' she told me.

Open question, I told myself. Open question. ASK HER AN OPEN QUESTION, I told myself. DO NOT ask her a Yes or No question.

'Is he?' I blurted out.

'Yes.'

Then she went back to her book.

Appalled at my error, I asked her, 'How do you feel about that?'

She looked up, 'Alright.'

A few minutes more passed as I read. Then Tommy said loudly, 'This is *boring*, this is.'

'Why is that?' I asked.

'Well, the class is too quiet.'

I waited for him to say more: 'We're never *this* quiet. It's usually fun.'

Alicia shushed him.

'You don't have to be quiet,' I said to both of them. Tommy nodded toward the inspector, as though to say, *we do.*

'No, really. The inspector wants to see what you can do.'

'Really?' Tommy asked.

'Yes. He's very interested.' Nevertheless, the class were determined to stay quiet.

I have a habit of walking around the class as I read, just looking the kids over, keeping them on task, and as I completed a full circuit of the classroom once more I glanced into my old briefcase, sitting by the side of my desk. I saw the bright yellow colour of Joe's Mr T gizmo and, on a desperate impulse, I picked it out, still reading to the class.

I paused, asked Tommy, 'What do you think you would feel like, digging a five foot hole every day, in the *burning* hot sun?'

Tommy remained silent, staring more intently at his book than I'd seen him do in seven months. He glanced quizzically at the gizmo in my hand, and at that moment, Mr T told Tommy to *Shuddup Fool.* Tommy giggled and went to say something but Mr T interjected, *Don't Give Me No Back-talk Sucker!*

As though a dam had burst, my year eight's came to life. 'What's that Mr Ken?' 'Play it again.' 'Is that Mr T?' and so on.

They had reverted to their loud, argumentative selves. *This* I can handle, I thought, and though they were less malleable, more reluctant to work and suddenly unable to remain quiet, and a whole lot more fidgety, they were at least free of the self-imposed vow of silence, and what followed wasn't great teaching, but for at least half of the lesson it *was* teaching. And maybe a little bit of learning too.

3.15pm

When the class emptied, the inspector, a model of efficiency, gave me a copy of his report. As I took it from him he held onto it for a moment and said, 'They were protecting you, you know.'

I nodded, 'I sort of guessed.'

'They were behaving themselves.'

As he let go his hold of the sheet he said, 'The lesson was well planned, the students feel safe, they work hard, within their abilities. Once they actually *began*.'

He checked my lesson plan; 'Seventeen students in the class have learning issues. Out of …'

'Twenty-two.'

'But only thirteen turned up.'

'That's normal.'

'It was a good lesson.'

I looked at the sheet: 2. Good. Not just satisfactory. And certainly not failing. As he went to leave my room, he turned and asked me, 'And was that really…?'

I nodded.

'Where did you get it?'

'From Big Joe. My son's friend. Little Joe, that's my son, he's in Big Joe's crew.'

The inspector looked a little confused at the surfeit of random information that was pouring from my lips, but the only comment he made was, 'Interesting.'

Back in the staffroom I did a little celebratory jig; James Turner, sitting at a table packing his bag, looked up. 'It went well?'

I nodded, 'Yeah. It was a bit mad though.'

'Do you know what grade you got?'

'I got a Good. Which is weird. The lesson was shit.'

James nodded, folded the last of his magazines into his briefcase; 'Well, it's Friday. I'm off.'

He stood.

'Didn't you get observed?' I asked him. He hadn't mentioned it.

He nodded. 'I did. Got a Satisfactory.'

'Thought you'd be an Outstanding.'

He shook his head. 'No. Not enough interaction. Too teacher-focused. Not touchy-feely enough.'

I've read the grades; James Turner gets the best scores in the school.

He smiled, 'I can live with a Satisfactory,' he told me, smiling. 'Because I've got a life. Anyway,' he added, 'I've just heard that the school scraped through, somehow. We've been judged as Satisfactory, so we're not going on Special Measures.'

'That's good,' I said, but I thought, if this school is Satisfactory...

I heard James says, 'Night,' as he left the staffroom.

'See you next week,' I replied to the closing door.

23

Thursday, 8.47am – North Avenue

Coming out of the mini-market, on my way to work today, I spotted my old rugby teacher, Mr Jamerson. Worse, he spotted me.

I cringed, smiled weakly and muttered, 'Hullo, sir.'
Hullo sir!!!
The embarrassment.

He nodded, or rather, glowered, acknowledgement. I walked stiffly, self-consciously, to the Toyota, wrenching open the door with some effort. I wondered what he was doing round here. Did he live nearby? Even though I'm a teacher, I still have this vague idea that teachers, especially those who taught me, don't actually *live* anywhere, but are stored in cupboards in school basements.

When I was fifteen years old Mr Jamerson was the embodiment of all things tough and manly.

He was old-school.

A big guy, tall, heavy-set and bearded, he's probably retired now, I can't think of any reason why he'd be hanging round West Bognor than he has *a lot* of spare time on his hands, but he still looked like the fearsome rugby coach he was in his, and my, prime.

Turning up for Mr Jamerson's lesson without your kit would result in a huge, distended knuckle being rapped sharply on your forehead; wimping out of a tackle or complaining of a heavy cold saw you running laps after school, usually, as I seem to recall, in the rain.

'Exercise is good for you!' he'd roar, and if anyone dared

complain of being soaked-through, he'd yell, 'All that moisture will clear your tubes!'

And then he'd make us run some more.

Despite this, the lads loved him. Feared him too, but not in an unpleasant way, more a 'he's madder than us' sort of way.

I was never any good at rugby or cross-country running, but I liked Mr Jamerson; he was honest. Straight up. And I don't think he minded you not being good at sport either; what he valued was determination and bravery. There was no 'restorative justice' with Mr Jamerson, neither did he 'negotiate a way forward' with his most challenging pupils; if you stepped out of line he would simply clap his huge hand across the back of your head.

Hard.

But if you tried hard, if you gave it your all, he'd pat you on the back and say, 'Good game.'

That was praise enough. And the 'challenging' kids loved him most.

It's probably as well he's retired; nowadays, being so old-school would probably get him fired. Or arrested. I think that even then, he was probably too old-school.

But seeing my hulking, beetle-browed former PE teacher outside the mini-market was quite a shock, I can tell you; it brought back a flood of memories and reduced me in an instant to my fifteen-year-old self.

I truly expected him to point a gnarled finger in my direction and roar, 'Daniel Keane! 5B! You're A WASTER! You always were and you ALWAYS WILL BE!' And then rap a knuckle against my forehead.

But his glower turned into a smile of recognition, he paused briefly, said, 'Good morning, Daniel,' and then went into the shop.

No knuckle.

No roar.

No running laps of the nearest field.

I was sort of disappointed.

Relieved.

But disappointed.

Saturday Morning – Bainbridge Avenue

'It's easy, Dan.'

'How easy?'

'Well we, the company that is, get anything from £120 upwards for every essay we write. You take 75 per cent of whatever the fee is. That's a minimum of £90 an essay.'

'Aren't the exam boards getting rid of coursework in the next few years?' I asked him.

'Yes. Which is why we're moving into 'A' levels, undergraduate stuff too. And we can charge *more* for those.'

The deal was, I could make a thousand pounds a week, as opposed to my current less-than-£500. And for that I'd write ten to twelve English GCSE essays for students who wished to pay us. And possibly sell my soul.

'It's immoral,' I said.

'But it's totally legal,' he told me, sounding almost surprised himself. 'We don't say we're writing the essays *for* the students; we're just giving them a model of a decent essay.'

'And if they choose to cut and paste the whole thing …'

'…that would be their problem.' He went on, 'Once you've got a bank of essays written, you can start cutting and pasting yourself. It ends up, after a couple of terms, you're earning fifteen hundred pounds a week and you're not writing more than a half dozen essays a month.'

'And you get 25 per cent?'

'Yes.'

'I don't know.'

But it wasn't Lee's percentage that bothered me. It wasn't the unsound financial future of such a move. And it wasn't the work, which would be fun.

It was the cheating.

Lee was rich. He'd grow richer. I wasn't growing anywhere. 'I have to give this serious thought,' I told him.

'Look, I'd really like you to do this,' Lee told me, 'You don't have to, but someone will. And we're old friends. Might as well be you.'

Lee told me there were literally thousands of students, tens of thousands of foreign students, who would pay us a lot of money for writing their coursework. It was morally dubious but so long as we pretended to just supply essay 'models' it was totally legal.

'Hey,' he said. 'No worries either way. Tell you what. I've got tickets for the Foo Fighters gig on Tuesday. Come along. I'll pick you up about eight.'

'OK. Thanks.'

I put down the phone; looked around at the apartment.

Then I picked up the letter from Jenny's solicitor advising me of the date of the hearing; I re-read it. Two months hence. I was surprised she hadn't asked for an earlier date; when Jenny decided to act it was usually well-planned and swift. Hence the split. But still no divorce, I thought.

Thursday, 8.47am – Room 101

Merlene caught me in room 101 and dropped a file on my desk; 'Can you do me a favour?'

'Sure.'

'That's my thesis,' she says, 'I was wondering if you could give it the once over.'

'Thesis?'

'Yes.'

I look at the file. On the cover it says *The Applicability of Code Compatible Prime Numbers*. 'It's about using prime numbers as internet security.'

'I won't understand it,' I said, explaining, 'Too right-brained, see? English teacher. All arty-farty nonsense. Maths doesn't make sense to me.'

She pulled a bit of a face.

'I could teach you how to Be A Tree,' I said, waving my arms. 'Drama, I can do. But not maths.'

'Well, do you think you could try and use your right-brain to see if this is set out clearly, check it for typos and stuff like that.'

'OK.' I said, as my waving branch returned to their normal, arm-like state.

'Thank you.'

'So you're some kind of mathematician?' I asked her, 'You're not a librarian?'

'I'm both. My degree is in IT, which you have to do now to become a librarian, and this is just the result of being interested in the field of program security.'

I must have looked blank because she explained: 'Basically, you write computer programs, code them with a prime number formula and then no one can do stuff with your programs that you don't want them to.'

This I understood. 'Big business will love that.'

'They do,' she nodded, seriously, 'I've got a couple of offers already, look.' She shows me the inside cover of the file. 'I've registered my theories as patents.'

I'm impressed; 'You're going to be rich.'

'Possibly.'

'Then what?'

'Oh, I don't know. A life of travelling, possibly. Reading. The odd passionate affair with my favourite English teacher. Maybe more research. Take up ...'

'Whoa!' I said, 'Back up! The odd *what*?'

'Well, one of these days, maybe. If I find a decent one.'

I paused, 'And what if you don't get rich?'

'Oh, pretty much the same. Probably.'

She went to leave my room, paused and said, 'Thanks, I owe you.'

'I already owe you coffee,' I reply.

'Then we should get together sometime and honour our debts.' Then she was gone.

I smile to myself, open the file. 'See you later,' I tell no one in particular, but as a sort of promise to myself.

Tuesday, 9.51pm – The Venue

I think I'm getting old.

Yet it started off so well; on arrival we got the beers in, mingled, had fun, enjoyed the opening act and awaited the first set.

I felt almost human. But after twenty minutes, the noise coming from the Marshall stacks was turning my stomach; I felt like I was standing on a mountainside during an earthquake or an eruption. Unlike the horde of teenagers bouncing around in the mosh pit and who seemed to be surfing on the waves of sound, it was just making me feel queasy.

I left Lee and the others and went out into the foyer to get a breath of fresh air and to call in. I dialled my sister's number; 'Hey Lindsey.'

'He's fine,' she told me, anticipating my next question. 'Watching telly. Want to speak to him?'

'No. Text me when he goes to bed.'

'OK,' she said. I closed my phone and turned as someone shouted out my name.

I spotted a woman of about my age, tattooed, studded at lip and eye, peroxide crop, singlet top and combat pants.

She was smiling at me.

'Oh God,' I muttered to myself. I've met Carl's mum, Marie, a couple of times, once at a school parents' evening, and the other time when she picked him up on the day we arrived back from the Lakes cycle ride.

She's a formidable woman. I smiled back as she approached, 'Hi, it's Mr Ken isn't it?'

'Keane,' I said. 'Daniel.' Someone opened the door and for a moment the noise drowned out her reply but I heard her murmur, 'Marie,' and then she was standing very close, plastic beer glass in hand, smiling up at me. She hooked her arm into mine as she chatted. *Oh bugger,* I thought, desperately looking for an escape route. This surely can't get worse.

But it did.

I spotted Merlene by the main entrance and she looked stunning; slender and dark, and she was talking to a man. I tried to look away but, too late, I caught her eye and she looked at me, then gave Marie the once over. Her expression was quizzical and, I suspected, slightly mocking.

Merlene turned to leave, accompanied by the man, and as she did she winked at me. I smiled bravely then I said to Marie, 'I need a drink,' and headed for the bar.

'Me too!' she answered, with too much enthusiasm.

'Have you thought it over?' Lee asked me, as we walked back to his car.

I shrugged, admitted, 'I can't argue with the money.'

'You could put Joe through school. A good school,' he told me.

'It's tempting. Very tempting.'

At that moment I heard a shout coming from the mob of teenagers who were walking just behind us. A tall hoodied youth ran out of the group, toward me. As he got closer I could make out what he was saying to me.

'Mr Ken! Sir! Hold on a minute.'

I recognised Graham Wilson, one of 10*Smokie* and, relieved that I wasn't about to be happy-slapped, I waited for him to catch up.

'Hey Graham,' I said.

'Hey sir. Good gig, huh? Didn't expect to see you here.'

'It's a surprise to me too.'

'Were you in the mosh pit, Mr Ken?' he asked, a twinkle in his eye.

'No,' I smiled, 'My knees won't take it.'

Then he said, 'The thing is, I was wondering, could you give me an extension on my homework?'

'When is it due in?' I asked him.

'Tomorrow,' he told me, adding sheepishly, 'I would have done it but I was, erm, *here.*'

I thought it over, only for a second. Any student of mine

that liked the Foos was worth cutting a bit of slack. 'Get it in by the end of the week,' I told him and he went back to his friends with '*thanks*' and a smile.

I turned back to Lee, who was standing by his car, wearing a rueful expression. An expression that recognised what I didn't.

He shook his head. 'Jenny was right. You'll never leave teaching.'

'You spoke to Jenny?' I asked.

We got in the car. It was a Porsche.

The following Monday, just before the bell for first lesson, I found Graham's coursework sitting on my desk. A few moments later, I unlocked my desk drawer to get out my class register and found a memory stick had been placed on top of it.

A post-it note was wrapped around it. I unpeeled the note to read the message, 'Foo Fighters live at The Venue.'

I pushed the memory stick into my laptop and opened the file. A few bars of the opening song confirmed that it was unmistakeably a bootleg of the gig that I'd attended. And not some recording taken from a mobile phone; it was studio quality, downloaded at source from the mixing desk, I guessed.

Setting aside the question of how it had gotten into a locked drawer, I sort of guessed who it might be from, but couldn't be sure until a couple of hours later when I saw Graham in the corridor.

He gave me a big wink and said, 'Morning, Mr Ken. Listened to any good music lately?'

Sunday, 11.00am – The Park Cafe

This felt suspiciously like a pay-off.

I opened the envelope. 'You know, I've been so busy, just working, being with Joe, setting up the new apartment, I forgot about this.'

Jenny nodded, watching me, having handed over a cheque that amounted to the median figure of three property surveyors' estimates of half the value of our town house. I looked at the amount written on the cheque; enough to buy an apartment outright, and not one on North Avenue either, and then I looked at her. 'This a sweetener?' I asked, dubiously.

'No. It's yours, whether or not we reach an agreement over this.'

This being Joe.

I nod.

'What are you eating?' I ask her.

Then I go to the counter and order us a couple of sandwiches and more coffee. Then afterwards, we go for a walk in the park, sit on a bench and talk some more.

It's all very civilised; there's even a string quartet playing on the bandstand and people sitting in chairs listening. And at the end we haven't agreed on anything except that Jenny wants custody and I can't face that.

'You won't lose him,' she reassures me.

After that we part ways and I go to pick up Joe from his gran's and take him home and make tea; beans on toast. I tell him about his mum wanting to see him.

'I know,' he says. 'I heard you talking to Gran about it.'

'Would you like to see her?' I ask.

He nods, between bites of toast, 'Yeah.'

'Would you like to live with her?'

He shrugs. 'I'm not bothered.'

I wipe tomato juice from his mouth and ask him, 'Do you like living here? Just us two?'

He gets off his chair, pulls out his yellow plastic Mr T gizmo and presses a button and Mr T tells me SHUDDUP FOOL! SHUDDUP FOOL! on Joe's behalf.

Then he stares at me angrily, tears in his eyes, before going to his room.

24

'Will you sign my book Mr Ken?'

Silently, and probably for the last time with this class, I correct my name: *Keane*. 'Sure,' I nod and write, 'Best wishes for the future, D. Keane'.

'Sign my book too.'

'OK.'

'And mine.'

Today is the final day. The day the year eleven's leave school. They've been warned; any drunkenness, sex, verbal abuse, violence or other forms of bad behaviour will lead to being banned from the Prom. No threat is greater, no big stick is wielded to greater effect, than that of being banned from the Prom.

They return for their exams, starting next week, some of them, but that's all they'll come back for.

11Fick wandered into registration wearing even less uniform than normal; the boys in sportswear and baseball caps, the girls ladled with pancake and shock mascara. They're nearly all wearing their blazers though, because these are ritually torn up at the end of the day. Some of the kids have books and they're getting their school-friends and teachers to sign them as a keepsake. Others have allowed their friends to sign their shirts and the magic marker daubs on Carl's shirt are already smearing into a sweaty blur.

This is where I came in, I thought.

Arriving at the car park, I performed a quick Goth count.
Forget 'percentage of free school meals' or the school's
behaviour policy, the best way to gauge behaviour is to do
a Goth count. The number of moody teenagers dressed in
black and wearing studded bracelets is in inverse
proportion to the amount of bad behaviour in a school.

In this case, there were none. All the boys had skin-
heads. Or were obese. Or both. And the girls dressed like
Vicky Pollard's interpretation of Colleen McLoughlin
attending a Heat Awards Night.

'Listen up!' I shouted. iPods were turned down and
conversation slowed as twenty-two sixteen-year-olds turned to
listen to me for probably the last time. 'In ten minutes we're
going downstairs to the hall where awards and presentations
will be given out. In less than two hours you will be leaving
school.'

A small cheer murmured around the room. I looked over
them; loud, painted, overgrown children. 'Don't get drunk!
Don't throw things about! *Behave* yourself today.'

Then, just as they were about to turn back to their
conversations, I added, 'And have a good life.'

They went back to their conversations.

Someone said, 'You too sir.'

A couple of the lads approached, shook my hand. I signed a
couple of more books, posed for a couple of pictures.

It was over.

I gave my name to the receptionist who sat behind a
toughened glass screen. A loud buzzer indicated that I
should enter. 'Mrs Price will be with you in a minute.'

I sat down opposite a woman in a dark suit who I
assumed was one of the opposition.

I smiled; she blanked me.

I took a deep breath. Relax. It's just an interview.

Down in the hall the students sat in the class rows, facing the Management team, who were sitting on the stage.

I stood at the rear of the hall, next to Mick. He nodded at the throng, 'What a sack of shit.'

'Students. Or management?'

He laughed, 'I'm really not sure, to be honest.'

Mrs Price, Judy, Head of English, guided us through a tour of the school, picking up litter, interrogating students and closing windows as she went. 'The Head is off sick at the moment so the acting Head asked me to show you round,' she said, deftly bending to pick an empty Coke bottle and drop it in a bin as we swept along the corridor.

There were three candidates: Power Suit from reception, an ambitious NQT.

And me.

The Library; 'Temporarily closed I'm afraid,' Mrs Price explained, 'the librarian retired due to ill-health and her replacement has since gone on the sick. We're hoping for a new one in September.

The Science Corridor; 'Mrs Hills is Head of Science,' she told us, stopping to interrogate a group of boys, 'Are you supposed to be out here listening to music boys? Shouldn't you be out on the streets terrorising pensioners and immigrants? Or at least be sitting disrupting a classroom somewhere?'

They moved on, grumbling.

'Mrs Hills is poorly at the moment,' Judy informed us, 'and her job is being filled by supply.'

We followed her up a staircase.

At the end of speeches, awards were given and I applauded loudly those kids who I knew or had taught, exchanging brief smiles with a few. Probably embarrassing them. Then, in tutor groups, we walked out of the hall, out of school and to the gates.

They ran about, shrieking, a couple of eggs were thrown,

jackets torn. One girl was drunk, or pretending to be. Her friends led her up the road.

But the energy quickly dissipated; some of the kids waited at the bus-stop, others meandered down toward the beach, others still were picked up in cars and taxis.

Year eleven tutors, management team and senior teachers stood at the gate like guard dogs.

Torn blazers littered the ground.

> *Sitting in a small semi-circle we introduced ourselves in turn: first off was Power Suit, a born-again divorcee with ambitions to run her own department. Ambitious NQT followed and he too was, well, ambitious.*
>
> *And me? Well, the honest truth was, the school was close to home. I could drop my son Joe at primary school on the way.*
>
> *But how did I phrase that in my application? How did I explain that I was new to the area because my wife had walked out on my son and me, that I'd moved here because I could no longer afford to pay the mortgage on the lovely town house that we, my family as was, had lived in for six years. That I'd just this week moved into a grotty basement flat that came complete with overgrown garden, rising damp, the smell of cat pee and joss sticks, a nasty 1980s stone fireplace and a purple bathroom suite.*
>
> *I desperately tried to recall what I'd written about the school's proposed multi-million new-build scheme and the opportunities it offered to an ambitious classroom teacher.*

I walked back to my classroom feeling a little flat. I opened the windows in room 101, tidied up the desks, slotted books back into their cases. 11*Fick*'s 'Citizenship' books sat in a blue plastic crate; I took them out and dropped them into a bin. They were of no use any more, if they ever had been. At the bottom I found a plastic envelope with the poems they'd written to their future children.

These I'd keep and protect.

Mrs Price showed us some of the department's schemes of work, chatted to us about our life experiences; she seemed interested in me being a single parent, how I might empathise with the chaotic home life of some students.

Just then the classroom door crashed open and a small, angry-faced man strode in, leading a thoroughly depressed -looking teenage boy. 'We're just going to use the room next door,' he announced, disappearing into an adjoining class. 'That's Mr Sweet,' Mrs Price explained, 'the Acting Head.'

'Tell me, Mr Keane,' she continued, 'where do you see …'

BANG!

CLATTER!

Our conversation was interrupted by the unmistakable sounds of chairs and tables being thrown across the room next door.

Mrs Price continued gamely, 'It says on your application that …'

'YOU FOOL! YOU STUPID BOY!' came bellowing through the walls.

'…that you…'

'DON'T DARE CHALLENGE ME BOY! '

'…are interested in …'

'I'LL THROW YOU OUT OF SCHOOL TODAY! '

'…nineteenth century…'

No one was actually listening to Mrs Price now, though all three of us made attempts to nod sagely and frame our replies.

'YOU WILL FAIL ALL YOUR EXAMINATIONS!!! '

BANG!

CLATTER!

Mrs Price gave a weary smile. 'Would anyone like a cup of tea?' she ventured.

I sat down at my desk, listening to the noise of nearby classes. Opening my desk I found a card and paper bag containing a quarter pound of sweets.

Fruit pastilles.

Inside the card, picturing a cartoon teacher wearing a mortar board and gown and holding a cane, was a folded note: *Thanks.*

Signed, with assorted comments, by every member of 11F.

'Hello, Mr Keane. Daniel. This is Judy. Judy Price. From West Bognor School? We met this afternoon.'

'Oh, right.' Joe was hugging me as I spoke; I hugged him back. *'Hello Judy. How are you?'*

'Totally stuffed, to be blunt. The other two candidates weren't what we were looking for at all.' I nodded which, on the phone, is the same as silence.

Judy continued, *I'm sad that you withdrew.'* She paused. *'The thing is, I'd really like it if you'd reconsider filling the post.'*

I weighed this up for a moment, *'The other two both withdrew as well?'*

Judy snorted with suppressed laughter, *'Bugger! I'm not a very good liar am I?'* Then she said, *'But I was disappointed when you withdrew.'*

I paused, trying to think of a good reason not to agree to take up the offer of gainful employment.

Even if it was only for a half term.

Judy must have taken my silence as a sign of weakness because she ploughed straight in. *'The thing is Daniel, your references are excellent, we need a good teacher and, to be perfectly blunt, you need a job.'*

It was true.

And that's why I ended up here.

I popped a fruit pastille into my mouth, pushed my chair back, put my feet up on the desk and closed my eyes.

Room 101 was quiet.

25

Monday, 12.32pm – Sports Hall

'Leave your bags outside the hall!'

Dumping their bags, the students trudge into the examination hall; a few make their way to the 'Higher Paper' section but most of them find their seats in the 'Foundation Paper' section.

'Make sure your phones are switched off and left in your bags. Not in your pocket!'

The sports hall is kitted out with rows of desks. A few minutes later Judy asks, 'Does anyone need a pen?' and about thirty hands go up. This isn't as bad as the Literature paper where only eleven out of ninety-eight students (*ninety-eight!*) had remembered to bring in the novel we'd supplied them with.

We distribute the pens then give out the question papers, instruct them how to fill in the details on the front of their answer paper.

Mr Sweet stalks into the hall as Judy looks over at the clock: 'You have two hours,' she tells them. 'Open your papers.'

She writes the examination Start and Finish times on a whiteboard as ninety-six papers examination papers are opened. Only two kids are absent; one with appendicitis. The other is Junior Donkin.

Tuesday, 9.22pm – The Monarch Hotel and Ballroom

A white stretch limo pulls up outside of the Monarch Hotel

and Ballroom and half a dozen West Bognor students climb out, the boys resplendent in tuxedos, the girls shimmering and glorious in silk and satin tiaras and glittering shoes that wouldn't be out of place at the wedding of Cinderella and Prince Charming.

This is the third stretch limo in the past ten minutes.

The Monarch Hotel and Ballroom sits at the end of a half-mile gravel path and every year it hosts West Bognor's Leavers' Ball. The kids do it in style; more effort is put into Leavers' Ball outfits than ever goes into exam revision and, unlike at school, we're pretty much guaranteed 100 per cent attendance. What's really nice is how smart they all look; even the most chav-ish of boys manages to kit himself out, James Bond-style, in a suitable penguin suit and bow-tie.

The uniform black of the tuxedos is broken by one or two students who arrive wearing white tuxes, and quite a number who are wearing brightly coloured cummerbunds.

Carl outdoes them all, emerging alone from the back of a Bentley in a splendid gold tuxedo complete with royal-blue satin shirt waistcoat.

'How do they afford all this?' I ask Vic.

'The black economy,' he replies.

A minute later, two girls materialise like gilt-angels from the back of a pastel-pink Hummer.

'Good evening Simone, Ashleigh,' I say.

'I like your kilt,' Simone tells me and they pass into the hall, giggling. The music is winding up and the lights are clearly flashing through the doors. Others arrive, wonderfully glamorous in their tuxes and their multi-layered frocks; Vic and I are doing the greeting.

'Can you hear that?' I ask him when there is a lull. In the distance I can make out a rumbling noise. 'Thunder?'

Vic frowns, 'No, V-Twin. Look.' He points at a girl arriving side-saddle on the back of a huge, low-slung Harley Davidson. She is wearing a black, skin-tight rubber dress that barely covers her pneumatic, low-cut décolletage.

'Sweet Jesus,' Vic says quietly. 'I taught her when she was eleven! When did she turn out like that?'

I raise an eyebrow; being responsible males, we try not to stare as she totters past in six-inch heels. The Harley rider, a big bearded guy, raises a salute to us, grins, revs the engine and disappears back down the drive in a hail of gravel.

'Magnificent,' is all I say. It's Prom Night at West Bognor and, while the students may struggle with learning and with behaviour, they know how to put on a show.

Wednesday, 10.44am – Room 10

The warm afterglow of the Prom lasted until the moment Big Cyril hauled me into his office this morning and gave me a thorough dressing-down for not wearing a tie in class.

I am, apparently, 'Far too casual' in my mode of dress. It sets a bad example.

Guilty as charged.

Stretching a full inch, from my Adam's apple to the top button of my teacher-issue checked shirt, my throat was as naked as the day I was born.

But it's hot. It's in the 90s. Or is that the 30s? Whatever, as Shakespeare once wrote, 'For now, these hot days, is the mad blood stirring.'

Or, as the *Sun* replied, 'Phew! What a Scorcher!'

We've had six fights this week. On Monday, one of the Wenkels was arrested and escorted off-site, handcuffed to a police officer; school was the only place they could be sure to find him.

Attendance is hovering around 65 per cent, though many absentees can be spotted on the beach.

I've got 28 references to write by the end of the month. It's so hot that I'm drinking an extra three litres of water a day. To be honest, neck attire, casual or otherwise, has been low on my list of priorities, until now.

As I walked back to my classroom after our 'meeting', I was feeling as wronged and embarrassed as Kevin or Perry on being discovered hiding beneath the duvet with a well-thumbed copy of *Nuts*, and as morally outraged as a career criminal accused of doing the one crime for which he wasn't actually responsible.

Feeling a tad browned-off, I locked into full self-righteous mode. So I performed a 'skimp' count. That is, I counted the number of female teachers wearing skimpy tops, flip-flops, hipster-style combat trousers, shorts and so on.

And apart from outer-wear, I also sighted countless bare shoulders, a few bare midriffs, a couple of tattoos (tramp-stamps, in current student parlance) and at least one whale-tail.

Which is not a good look on anyone over eighteen stone. Then I did a quick calculation and came up with the figure of about 80 per cent of female staff who were wearing what could generously be called 'casual' attire. Alternatively, you could call it 'Appropriate' attire, this being a heat-wave and all. Or if you were shopping for souvenirs on the main street of Playa Den Bossa.

And the male staff?

Shirts.

Ties.

Trousers.

Socks and shoes.

And are we better teachers for it? Or are the female staff worse teachers for wearing flip-flops and vest tops? The truth is, I don't know. And I don't know if the students would take me less seriously if I wore a polo shirt in class, although, they probably would if I wore Gola. Or Kappa.

Besides, do students learn any better for wearing a tie in class? I understand the general argument about uniform, and to a large degree I agree with it, but the truth is, the students subvert whatever uniform we impose anyway, to the point that it looks like theirs, not something the school thought up (and you can argue about whether that's a good or a bad thing in your own time).

And they fasten their ties in such a way as to not look like a tie anyway. They sort of invert the whole thing inside their shirt, so that all you can see is a thin crust of blue and gold edging at their throat.

Or they fasten their ties using the skinny end to make the knot, so that the bit you see is a centimetre wide and an inch long. A sort of 'wiener' tie.

To be honest though, setting aside the gender inequalities of school dress codes, I agree with the students on this one; ties are rubbish. Along with those other nineteenth-century inventions, the bustle and the stove-pipe hat, the neck tie has no obvious function. And it doesn't actually tie anything.

Back in my classroom I had a free lesson: non-contact time, it's now called.

So, with three fans blasting humid air across my perspiring face, both of my windows open wide, my door wedged with a volume of Wainwright's guide to Hadrian's Wall, and a bottle of ice-water on my desk, I attempted to catch up on my marking.

Tie-clad. As per instructions.

Thursday, 9.22pm – Louis Restaurant

'Every time I see you, you're with a different woman.'

'Me? I haven't been on a date in years.'

'I saw you at the Foo Fighters gig with a punky little woman,' she says.

'That was Carl's mum, a lad in my tutor group. Total coincidence; I was out with my friends that night.'

'Carl? Oh,' she pauses, 'He did the bike ride with you? That Carl?'

I nod confirmation.

She takes a sip of her wine. 'Yeah, I saw the pictures in the newspaper.' Then she says, 'Well, I saw you in the park a few weeks ago, with a woman.'

'In the park? I never go to the park.'

'See,' her eyes glittered triumphantly, 'You liar!! I was listening to a string quartet and you walked past with this woman in a power suit.'

'Oh, right! I remember now.'

She downed her drink, went to the bar and returned with another two glasses of wine. 'See, you come across like Mr Mellow, and you're out in the park with power-dressed women in heels.'

'That's just stupid,' I reply. 'Anyway, you were at the Foo's gig with a guy, too.'

She slumps back a bit. 'True. What an *arse*.'

I wasn't sure if she was talking about me, him or passing comment on herself.

'That woman in the park; that's my ex-wife,' I told her. 'We met to discuss custody for Joe, my son.'

'Oh,' she slumps back further.

'Are you *drunk*, Merlene?'

'Yeah,' she admits, telling me, 'I was nervous, so I had a few stiffeners before we met.'

'Nervous? Of me?'

She nods.

'What time do you have to be back?' she asks.

'Eleven-ish.'

We both look at the clock; it's half-nine. Merlene looks miserable. 'Aah,' she says out loud, 'I've done it all *wrong*. I'm drunk and I picked a fight with you. Our date's a washout.'

'Let's order,' I say.

I look at her as she scans the menu; she's done the unexpected again. I was looking forward to Merlene dressed, I sort of guessed, in a cool, elegant outfit and prepared for a night of wry humour, dry wine and verbal fencing. Instead she's wearing a denim mini, too much make-up.

And she's drunk.

It's our first date, and I'm utterly charmed, to be honest.

Monday, 8.22pm– Staffroom

'I've got an interview,' I told Judy, holding the A4 envelope in my hand.

She smiled. 'I know. I've already written your reference. Want to read it?'

'No thanks.'

'You should. I might have mentioned strengths that you can play to. Or weaknesses you need to avoid.'

'Not weaknesses, areas of development,' I chided, as I poured hot water into my mug and stirred in a spoonful of coffee. 'Anyway, I prefer to remain in blissful ignorance of any major character defects or professional weaknesses.'

'You didn't write that on your application, did you?'

I shake my head.

'Well make sure you wear a tie,' she tells me, with a faint smile on her face.

I sat down beside her, popped open a tube of chocolate digestives, offered one to Judy, and took three for myself.

Judy was thinking to herself, staring forward, eating her biscuit. 'You'll be missed,' she said, finally.

'You think I'll get it?'

She nodded, slowly, as though she was confirming something to herself.

26

Thursday, 9.22pm – St Cuthbert's Faith School

St Cuthbert's is a new build. State of the art. Sweeping roofline, tan block walling, lots of glass; I imagined the Microsoft campus looking something like this. The glossy booklet that was attached to my interview letter detailed the excellent GCSE scores, the IT links in every room, the on-line lesson-planning, the classroom video cameras via which the head teacher could observe any lesson at any time.

I was struck by the absolute lack of hubbub as students walked in through the gates, ties fastened correctly, hemlines exactly as per legend – two inches below the knee. The students didn't stare at me in the way that they would have done at West Bognor, but just moved quietly out of the way of my Toyota.

After grounding out the exhaust on a speed-bump, I pulled into one of the visitor's parking bays and turned off the engine, leaving it in gear because of the failing handbrake. I got out, straightened my tie, tugged at my suit jacket and approached the wide double entrance doors. They opened with a swish and I entered.

There were five candidates.

'St Cuthbert's is the best school in the region,' Mr Parks the head, told us. 'Our GCSE A–C score is unbeaten outside of a half dozen grammar schools in major cities at least fifty miles away.' He paused to smile. 'If schools were cars, we'd be a

Bentley.' Then he looked at me. 'Other schools in the area are, at best, pre-owned *Fords.*'

His gaze shifted to what appeared to be a mother and child leaving one of the offices, saying to us, 'May I introduce Mrs Watt and...'

'Jen,' Mrs Watt supplied.

'Jennifer, yes,' Mr Parks corrected. He turned to us and explained, 'We have a waiting list for places in St Cuthbert's. Jennifer is currently attending a local secondary school and has been offered a place at St Cuthbert's, subject to passing some basic skills tests of course, which, I'm guessing,' he glanced at his watch, 'she has just completed.'

He gave Jen Watt a lugubrious smile. I almost thought he was going to pat her on the head but instead he spoke to Mrs Watt. 'We'll process the test results and call you on Monday.'

Mrs Watt looked a little overawed by the whole process. Jen, on the other hand, appeared quietly confident.

Inwardly I frowned, because I know that basic skills tests can be marked in fifteen minutes, and I knew that making Mrs Watt wait from Friday morning until Monday to find out if Jen had passed the test was simply a way of exerting authority and control.

The whole charade was about making Mrs Watt more pliable.

I looked at Mrs Watt's expression, almost expecting her to curtsey as she shook hands gratefully, and a little fearfully, with Mr Parks. 'Come on mum,' Jen told her, taking her hand and leading her out the door.

'Right,' he said, turning his attention back to us. 'Down to business.' He clapped his hands together. 'Coffee, interviews and home, I'd guess.' He smiled again, his bared teeth an expression of quiet, immeasurable power, 'We don't waste time at St Cuthbert's,' and again he smiled at me as he said this, then he looked out at Jen and Mrs Watt as they crossed the car park, his smile fading: 'And we don't make mistakes.'

Friday, 2.22pm – Staffroom

Friday afternoon is usually a bit of a wind down, and with the school hurtling toward the summer holidays there's a real end-of-term feeling beginning to swell in the school.

So I was a bit surprised when, during lunch duty, I got an emergency call over the radio, telling me to go to the yard behind the PE block.

'Chav corner', we call it.

Arriving there I found that a sizeable proportion of the student body were being reluctantly dispersed by staff, as Big Cyril and a couple of other senior teachers stood in a ring around one of the larger, mature trees we have at the rear of the school.

'Are they Morris Dancing?' I asked Vic.

'Billy Bingham is up a tree again,' he replied.

Oh. Well that makes sense.

Our school is plagued by *runners*; kids who, when faced with any difficult situation – whether it be a detention, a class or teacher they don't like, a coursework deadline they can't meet – will simply *leg it* out of school until whatever furore they're avoiding dies down to a manageable level.

But Billy Bingham doesn't run; he climbs up the nearest tree.

And then he waits.

Senior staff are then faced with an impossible choice; they can leave him up there, but if he falls and injures himself, the school will no doubt be sued for negligence, or they can attempt to bring him down, but of course, if he falls, the school can... well you can guess the rest.

So what usually happens is that Big Cyril, and some other senior members of staff, including the Inclusion Team (*motto*: 'It's not your fault') simply stand around the tree, wringing their hands and pleading with him to come down.

By the 1pm bell he's still up there and I guess he'll remain there until the school day ends and he loses his audience; no one wants to go to lessons, of course. Professionally, I have to go and teach now, but on a human level, I'm having so much fun watching highly qualified members of senior staff being taunted by a crazed twelve-year-old.

'There's a quarter of a million pounds worth of professionals, trying to bring that kid down from a tree,' Vic says, observing wryly, 'I could do it for a fiver, using a hose.'

'Come down, Billy,' Tara, our welfare officer pleads.

'*Fuggingerrofyefugginwangersyafugginbasta's,*' Billy replies eloquently from his treetop kingdom, and follows this tirade by lobbing a burst of crab apples, picked from the branches.

Everyone leaps back.

Billy shouts, '*nomyfoltyafuggntozzersfuggnateme.*'

'Come on Billy, we don't hate you,' Big Cyril argues, and by way of reply, a crab apple glances off his shiny pate. He ducks, but *way* too late.

Vic, still standing next to me, whispers, 'We *do* hate him. He's a lunatic.'

'But a lunatic with a good aim,' I say, when Billy catches Tara on the back of her wrist with a crab apple. She steps back in quiet, do-good fury, wiping juice from her skirt and blouse.

'I have to go and make a couple of calls,' I say, and reluctantly leave Vic to make my way back to room 101, winding through the throng of teenage spectators.

I don't attempt to make them go to their lessons; the kids at Bog Standard Technology College have an instinctive understanding of the concept of Plausible Deniability.

They know that, though you *know* they heard the bell, you can't prove they heard it, over the din of the shouts of 'jump!' and 'chuck more apples' and 'Come down Billy!'

And I'm not prepared to waste ten minutes losing an argument with two hundred teenagers.

As I walk along the corridor to my classroom I'm sure there'll be at least one or two kids waiting patiently at my door.

I'm late.

I'll tell them I didn't hear the bell.

Wednesday 7.02pm – Bainbridge Avenue

'You sound unsure,' Merlene said.

'It's nothing I can really put my finger on, just a general feeling of, well, I don't know.' I racked my brains, trying to think of a valid reason; 'It's like a pie.'

'A pie?'

'Yeah, you know if you bought a pie from an expensive shop, and it was well wrapped and looked nice but it didn't *smell* right.'

'You are too right-brained,' she told me, 'but I know what you're saying and no, I wouldn't want to eat it.'

I nodded. Then I poured her another glass of wine.

'But, to follow your analogy,' she said, 'there's nothing else on the plate. So you'd better make up your mind. And soon.'

I nodded again, a little glum. Then I said, 'And what's your news?'

She smiles, 'Say my name.'

'Merlene.'

'My full name.'

'Merlene Stewart.'

She shakes her head, 'Na *ah!*' and laughs. 'You missed a bit. My title.'

I say, 'Merlene Stewart. School librarian.'

She mouths a word, and I work it out in my head before saying, 'No, you got it? *Doctor*?' and she nods slowly, smiling hugely, eyes glittering and happy.

We do a jig around my room. 'Time to open another bottle of wine,' I tell her.

'Cool,' she says, her facing glowing with pleasure. 'Let me tell you my plans.'

And then, fifteen minutes later, though I'm happy for her, and am falling for her quite a bit, I'm not feeling quite so happy. Things aren't working out how I'd like them too. Not at all.

But we kiss for a bit, and that takes the sting out of it for a while.

I can sense a tsunami of change approaching my life, and I don't know whether I'm going to swim, surf or drown. A happy notion occurs to me at that moment – whatever I do, however I face the coming days, whatever response I choose, it's up to me. I'm in charge of me and even if all I decide to do is go under gracefully, then it's my choice. Not Jenny's, not West Bognor's, not my parents' or even Merlene's.

No one else's, just mine.

I pause from kissing Merlene to let out a small chuckle.

'What?' she asks me.

'Nothing,' I reply, still smiling.

She wrinkles her eyes 'You can be very cryptic, *Mr Ken,*' she tells me, but I don't want to discuss it. I kiss her again, because it's fun, but mainly just to shut her up.

27

Friday, 7.19am – Bainbridge Avenue

I check my phone. There are three messages from St Cuthbert's. It's time to make a decision, or two.

Of course, decisions are easy to make. For example, it's easy to tell your pals, 'I'm going to the cinema instead of the pub,' or say to the barista, 'I'll have the fair-trade skinny latte, not the full-fat exploitation one, please.'

Sometimes, of course, you can go to the cinema, *then* go to the pub after, or you can buy the fair-trade latte *and* have it with full-fat milk. Or you can decide to just stay at home with instant and a DVD.

And sometimes you can go out and find a girl. And you can get a good job. And keep your seven-year-old son safe at home.

But then things get complicated. What if getting the girl isn't really getting much at all? What if all you get is a trace element of a girl. Because she's planning to go off and do other stuff for 99 per cent of the time?

And what if you realise that the job you've been offered amounts to gilded slavery? And whatever you earn will be bartered with pieces of your soul. And what if you know that your son would be better off living, for at least some of the time, with his mother?

And just because a woman doesn't love you any more, doesn't mean that you should punish her by taking away her child. And though you can fight to have him live without his mum, and maybe even win, it would be a bad thing, an unforgivable thing, to do.

And what if getting on, progressing, means *diminishing*, somehow? What if the Hollywood movie of my life suddenly got a big budget, became glossier and filled with stars… but my own role was reduced to a bit-part.

A walk-on.

Maybe I should tell Merlene, 'Thanks but no thanks,' and leap headlong into my well-paid new job, fight my way up the greasy ladder of success, leave the classroom, demand sole legal responsibility for my son. Maybe I should accept my reward.

And then it hits me, if I did that, if I was that sort of man, a career-driven, M3-driving alpha-male, Jenny would never have left me.

But I'm not, and she did.

If my life was a story it wouldn't be a Hollywood block-buster, it'd never make it onto TV, never mind the big screen. It'd be a Tuesday night comedy-drama on Radio 4. And I like it that way.

And realising that, I know what I have to do.

I get out of bed, having made a tectonic, life-changing decision before breakfast. I switch on the radio then go into the kitchen, fill the kettle, pour cornflakes and milk into a bowl for Joe. Then I go into his room. 'Hey sleepy head, are you awake?'

He mumbles something, turns over. I sit on the bed beside him, and I can feel that something is slipping away from us, but I have to let it go.

'Last day at school today,' I tell him, 'Then the summer holidays begin.'

His eyes flick open, instantly fully awake; he turns over, gives me a big smile, jumps out of bed and goes to his wardrobe. 'We're allowed to take toys into school today,' he tells me, excited.

I think for a moment that maybe being a primary teacher would be a good job, and then I imagine Judy muttering 'ankle biters' and it makes me smile, *no thanks*.

'Well, decide what you want to take to school, and then come for your breakfast when you're ready.'

I switch off my phone; I want to be the one making calls, when I'm ready. When I've built up the nerve.

8.54am – School yard

School takes on a different identity when students aren't in uniform. At West Bognor they don't usually wear full or correct uniform but they usually pay lip service. Today though, the kids are kitted out in their street wear; iPods drape unashamedly from gold-ringed ear to Adidas pocket, knuckles weighted with keeper rings, teenage throats resemble Mr T in their glittering and bejewelled glory.

Everyone is in sportswear, baseball caps and expensive trainers. Teachers are in civvies; I'm pretty splendid too, in my chino shorts, desert boots and Curt Cobain t-shirt, my only badge of office the battered leather briefcase in which I intend to carry away all my worldly goods from Room 101.

Today, the final day of the academic year, is activity day. We're all dressed down and ready for the off. And my 'off' is a bit more final than most.

9.02am

11*Fick*, my tutor group, has left school, so while most teachers are in registration, I'm free to help in the preparations. I go out onto the field and begin to fill the gunge pools with an admixture of liquid jelly, white flower, vegetable dye and buckets of water.

Terry Calhoun, master of the statistic, and usually to be found poring over an Excel program, organising cover staff for absent colleagues or attempting to redraft the school timetable, is standing near me pouring an even thicker version of this gunge into... I look puzzled. 'Jelly-wellies', he tells me with a grin.

Jimmy the caretaker is laying out a huge sheet of plastic on the grassy slope of 'the mound' to use as a water slide. The kitchen staff are setting up what at first looks like a picnic area; tables are set with rows of cream cakes, but then I notice the stocks opposite and realise that these cream pies have a slightly sillier purpose.

There are inflatable sumo suits.

Pogo sticks.

The 200-metre running track is set out for a fancy-dress relay-race.

Terry pauses, straightens up from the wellies that are now filled to brimming with brightly coloured, geliferous gunk, looks over at me and grins again. 'Hey Dan,' he says, 'We get *paid* to do this, can you believe it?'

I smile, shake my head.

He says, 'It doesn't get better than this, does it?'

'No,' I tell him, 'It doesn't,' though my reasons for today's quiet exhilaration are probably different to his.

'Are you in the relay?' he asks me.

'No. You?'

He nods.

The management are dressing up like punk rockers, he tells me, while the kitchen staff have hired 'Fat Elvis' suits and, along with two other fancy-dressed teams, are going to do a relay race, through various obstacles while being pelted with cream pies by students.

This happens every year, apparently. 'We all have to do something,' he tells me. 'It's tradition.' Then when he sees the look of fright on my face he says, 'Look on the bright side; it'll only happen to you once. This time next year you'll be up the road with the God-botherers. They don't do fun.'

'I have to go and make a couple of phone calls,' I tell him, taking my phone out and switching it on. It bleeps to tell me there are two more messages.

'Coward,' he calls after me as I hurry back to the staffroom. Once there I take out my phone, listen to the messages, and dial the number for St Cuthbert's School.

I need to tell them my decision.

Then I call Jenny.

Ditto.

Then, twenty minutes later, I'm sitting on the only comfortable chair in the staffroom, asking myself what the bloody hell have I just done? Decisions are easy to make.

Take what you want, the saying goes.

Then pay for it.

10.11am

On the last day of the school year, we go through the motions; classrooms are filled with students watching DVDs while teachers tidy up their rooms and pack their bags ready for the holidays. Then the bell goes and the kids traipse to the next lesson, where they watch the first fifty minutes of yet another movie; usually it's something lightweight like *Shrek*, or *Cats and Dogs* – twelve-year-olds who sit up all night watching *Cannibal Ninja III* are forced to watch *Bring it On, Again.*

Again.

They don't mind too much; as the saying goes, better 'view' than do. But even then there are students who cannot behave, who cannot sit and watch a film without being naughty. In fact, watching a film makes their behaviour even worse. They take 'watch a film' as code for 'do whatever you want'. For girls, that's hair-plaiting, putting on make-up and gossiping, and for boys, that's mischief.

Halfway through *A Cinderella Story* I spot Jordan throwing midget gems at Danny, again, so I send him outside.

'Aw, please, sir,' he begs.

I point at the door.

'Give me one more chance.'

I've given him four chances already; the floor is littered with multi-coloured sweets. I point at the door.

'Give me another chance.'

Instead, I give him a wordsearch and make him sit outside.

12.32pm – School field

Lunch is an hour earlier and, at 12.30, what would be normal lunchtime, the kids are already sitting on the school field, waiting for the fun to begin. Someone has rigged up a sound system and gangster rappers are recounting tales of murdering their foes and beating on their ho's, as the fun begins.

I've managed to avoid any gunge-related activities and am sitting on a grassy slope next to a bunch of 10*Smokie*, watching teams of relay runners in fancy dress being pelted with cream pies.

Then the heads of year are made to race while wearing wellies filled with jelly. Then a lull, during which I learn that Snoop Dog is gonna bitch-slap the Five-O.

The sun is shining on us. I lie back in the grass, close my eyes, and relax.

By two o'clock, I'll be unemployed and, next weekend, I've decided, I'm going to agree to let my son live with his mum. But for the first time in over a year I'm not feeling stressed, or wired, and I don't have anything to learn, or cope with, or endure.

It's all over. My career has flatlined. My love life has stalled. My son is going. The whole West Bognor adventure is over.

I'm having the summer off, I decide. I'm going to sit on one of those prettified benches on the reclaimed railway line behind my flat, reading lots of cheap bestsellers and drinking wine all day.

I might even start keeping my journal on-line: Bog Standard – Diary of an ex-teacher.

The sun burns through my eyelids, music is banging away in

the background, I can smell the faint evidence of dubious substances; some of 10F are probably ensconced down by the dip in the ground next to the fence, smoking something illegal, but I don't care. In an hour, I'm off.

Something nudges my arm, I open an eye; Judy is sitting next to me, watching the next phase of activities on the field.

'You not getting gunged?' I ask her.

She looks at me over her glasses. 'You didn't take the job,' she says.

'Word gets round fast.'

'Not many people turn down the Head Teacher of St Cuthbert's.'

'So I'm told,' I said, 'But I did.'

She smiles; I raise myself up on my elbows. 'I did too,' she tells me, 'once upon a time,' and when I'm sitting comfortably, her voice merry, she tells me, 'A few years ago, when St Cuthbert's first opened, he asked me to be head of English. I turned it down, of course. Horrible man. Horrible school.'

Then she looks at me. 'We are such fools, Daniel,' she says. 'Bloody idealists, that's us.'

I nod, and having had her chat, she gets up to go. I wonder if she is going to say a formal goodbye or something. After all, we've worked together for a year now, and I haven't let her down.

She doesn't.

Instead she says, 'Mr Sweet wants to see you, before you go.' Then she goes back to the throng.

I lie there in the sun for a while longer, enjoying the sun, then the wind switches to an off-shore breeeze, making it too cool to relax; I sit up reluctantly, check my watch. Half an hour to go; I decide to go and check my mailbox, pick up my bag and drop off the keys for 101 at the office.

On the way back in I see Terry Calhoun, who smiles, another merry soul. 'Seen Mr Sweet yet?'

'No.'

I wonder if he's got some summer-school work for me. If he

has, I'll say no. And I don't want another term's supply work, so if he offers, I'll turn that down too. I've got enough money to survive for a few months; I'll take my chances somewhere else.

Doing something else.

Mr Sweet is in the Head's office, packing boxes. 'Hey there,' he says to me as I pop my head in, still stuffing files into a blue plastic box.

'Hi. You want to see me?'

'You turned down the St Cuthbert's job?'

I nod. 'Word gets around.'

He pauses from packing, 'This is all my stuff,' he explains, 'The new Head won't want it.' Then he asks, 'Why did you turn down St Cuthbert's?'

I try to think of what made me turn it down, and all I can think of to say is, 'Too nasty.' Then I say, 'It's not a place of learning; it's more like a religious cult, where they worship statistics. And hierarchy.'

'Nothing wrong with a bit of hierarchy,' he says. 'But I know what you mean. It's a bit of a meat grinder up there.' He sits down, opens a desk, and tells me, 'The New Head takes over in September and, between you and me, he's a bit of an arse, bit of a Mr Logic, so it's up to me to get the place sorted to the point where he can't destroy it within six months of taking over.'

I nod, diplomatically.

'Well,' he says, pulling a chair up behind his desk, 'I'm supposed to do this officially, adverts and all, interviews and stuff but, well, what're they going to do to me?'

I'm not sure if he's talking to me or to himself; I must look a bit puzzled.

'Do you want it?'

I frown. 'Want it?'

'A job. Here. A permanent job. You could be my last decent decision before the new fella takes over.'

'A permanent job? Here?'

'Repeating my words and simply adding a question mark at

the end of them isn't the same as giving me an answer,' he tells me.

'Oh,' I say. 'Right.'

He looks at me, waiting.

'Yes,' I say.

Seeing that I'm sitting there in stunned silence he tells me in a conspiratorial voice, 'This is a sink-school, Dan. People are so relieved that we don't have riots here, every day, that they let me get away with murder. Like hiring people on the spot, without interviews.'

He nods, to indicate that this particular interview is over. 'Right then, see you in September.'

And with that he turns back to his packing.

In something of a daze I go back up to room 101 and pick up my battered leather briefcase. I open it. I turn it upside down and empty the contents back onto the desk. Then I fasten it, shoulder it and leave the room, locking the door behind me.

1.44pm

By the time I get back out to the school field events are reaching a climax; Mr Sweet arrives moments later, dressed as one of the Village People; he indicates that someone turn down the music, comes to the microphone and makes a short speech before giving out a few prizes.

Then the final act: students vote to choose a teacher to receive a whole-school gunging. Usually, I'm told, they choose the strictest or angriest member of staff, who is then forced to sit in a chair, in the middle of the gunge pool and get drenched by about two hundred kids.

Rumour has it, Judy got gunged one year. I'm wondering who's going to be the chosen one.

Mr Sweet reads out the names of the staff, and some receive cheers, some are subject to a huge amount of booing. Mr Sweet marks down those people who get the strongest response and these will go through to the next round of cheering/booing.

My name is read out, and I receive a middle-order mix of boos and cheers. Eventually, Mr Sweet reads out the names of those six teachers who got the biggest verbal response. I'm surprised to find myself on the list. As Mr Sweet goes through the list again I can hear a murmuring chant coming from the kids closest to the fence; no doubt 10*Smokie* are ensconced in the middle, rousing the rabble. I can hear a vague *here we go-oh here we go-oh* rising and falling on the wind.

Mr Sweet pauses from his list as the noise rises. They're chanting louder now, as more kids catch on, only I got it wrong, they're not shouting here we go, they're shouting something else.

Keano-oh

Keano-oh.

Oh *bugger*. I'm going to get gunged.

And then five minutes later I'm sitting on a plastic chair, in the middle of a paddling pool, up to my desert boots in gunge. Little Nathalie shows her broken-toothed smile, picks up a bucket and walks toward me. The kids crowd around me, watching intently.

I start to laugh madly and a big cheer goes up as the contents of Nathalie's bucket land on my head.

Epilogue

The general rule is, the worse the school, the more support you get from fellow members of staff.

It's the Blitz spirit.

On the other hand, as I knew from experience, the better the school, the more hours you have to work, the more stressed you get and the more chance you have of being shafted, or having your wife stolen, by an ambitious fellow teacher. Alternatively, there is an iron rule which says that anyone who professes to be a humanist, liberal, pacifist, feminist, vegan or in any other way a 'right-on' human being will, absolutely and without exception, be a heinous bastard to work with. Impossible to work *for*.

And also, no matter how charming, plausible or qualified, anyone who wears a sharply pressed suit but doesn't actually *work* in the classroom is the devil and must be avoided at all cost.

But there's this other rule that I was vaguely aware of, but didn't fully understand until today; it's this: if you work in a place where you are forced to run a race in jellie-wellies while being pelted with cream cake and then you get gunged by a tiny, gap-toothed girl called Nathalie.

And if you work in a place where eleven-year-olds offer you religious conversion, where the librarian writes a PhD thesis in her spare time, where the bad people are mainly loud and feckless and where kindness is never 'ironic' or measured, where everyone has a common purpose, no matter how scant or blunt are the tools available to fulfil that purpose.

If you work in a place like that.

Stay there.